Startling details on the riches c

TONY BUSHBY

THE
PAPAL
BILLION$

Unknown facts about the Vatican's accumulation of wealth

Joshua Books
JoshuaBooks.com

Joshua Books
JoshuaBooks.com

All correspondence to the publisher
Joshua Books
PO Box 1668
Buddina 4575
Queensland Australia

Copyright © Tony Bushby 2007

The rights of Tony Bushby to be identified as the moral rights Author of this work has been asserted by him in accordance with the *Copyright Amendment (Moral Rights) Act 2000* (Cth)

Without Prejudice

First Printed 2008

Publisher's Disclaimer

All rights reserved. No part of this book may be reproduced, transmitted or utilized in any form or by any means, electronic or mechanical, including photocopying, recording, or by any information storage and retrieval system without permission in writing from the Publisher. Whilst every care has been taken to ensure the accuracy of the material contained herein, neither the author nor the publisher or its agents will bear responsibility or liability for any action taken by any person, persons or organisations claimed to be based in whole or in part upon the information contained herein.

Category: Author: Religious & Theology: History: Ancient Mysteries

ISBN 978 0 9804101 1 2

Master Distribution world wide through Joshua Books
www.joshuabooks.com

ABOUT THE AUTHOR

Tony Bushby was born in Australia in 1948 and is the author of six international books, all of which are regarded as classics of their genre. In 1985 he began research into the origins of Christianity and has since revealed incontrovertible evidence from Church sources of fraudulent papal activities, forged Gospel narratives, and priestly cover-ups. Tony's books on this subject have received worldwide acclaim and are curricular reading in American universities and Enlightenment centres. Tony is also held in high regard for his book and documentary articles on Near-Death Experiences and has personally interviewed over 600 people worldwide who have experienced the phenomenon. Tony lives in Cairo, Egypt, and researches constantly in the Middle East and Europe, seeking further evidence of Truth, gathering information that challenges the basis of our core beliefs. He has access to ancient papyri in the Rare Manuscripts Room in Egypt's Alexandrian Library and has been privileged to explore subterranean temples under the sands of Giza. He is regularly commissioned to write articles for Australian and American magazine publishers, some recent ones being, 'Ancient Cities under the Sands of Giza', 'The Criminal History of the Papacy', and the 'Forged Origins of Christianity'.

In general, Tony has developed a specialism in a non-orthodox approach to Christianity and Egyptology, and adopts the attitude that 'regardless of how many people may be disturbed, there is no religion superior to Truth'.

CONTENTS

A few words to the reader   8
Introduction ... the half has not yet been told   9

PART ONE

1. **Early presbyters and Church laws**   13
   Payment for soapbox operas   14

2. **The first ecclesiastical council and missing records**   21
   The secret history of the New Testament   25
   Bishops, worldliness, and gain   27

3. **Powers of acquisition given to the Church**   33
   Amplifications to Christian texts   37
   A major economic interest   38

4. **Pope St. Peter establishes a money-making precedent**   43
   The attempt to stem priesthood wealth   45
   No money worries   46
   The coffers of the rich   47

5. **The cult of the Blessed St. Peter**   51
   Increasing revenue   53
   Worldly ambition   54
   The first Catholic Balance Sheet   55

6. **The offensive that yielded the papacy 1800 square miles of land**   59

7. **A celestial letter from St. Peter**   63
   The true nature of the Holy Fathers   65

8. **The great papal forgery**   69
   Birth of the Papal States   70
   The pope claims the Americas   72
   The fraudulent takeover of the former Roman Empire   73
   Pope paid in pure gold   75

9.	**New tombs of St. Peter**	77
	Blatant priesthood embezzlement	79
	Misappropriation of the truth	83
	The 'Church Hoax' published in newspapers	86
	The most cherished female saint	88
10.	**The bishop and the platter of gold**	91
	The battle for control of Vatican wealth	92
	French gold in the Church of Rome	95
	Prostitutional income from the nunneries	97
11.	**Paying for the release of a soul**	99
	The pope's urgent call for funds	100
	The bridge to purgatory is down!	103
	The toll-gate of the Church	104
12.	**Protecting Church revenues**	107
	The pontiff who could fill the Sistine Chapel with sacks of gold	108
	How a pope replenished his treasury	110
	The pontiff on a white elephant	111
	Dollars and sense (or nonsense)	113
13.	**The Vatican's marketing machine**	117
	An extra US$20,000 for the Holy Mother Church	119
14.	**'The Bishop's Oath of Allegiance' and its effect**	125
	Enriching the Church from the confessional	127
15.	**Maintaining priesthood profits**	129

PART TWO

16.	**The Church suffers a set-back**	133
	The Vatican joins the Billionaire Club of America	135
	Birth of a new Vatican financial empire	137
17.	**The man with the Midas touch**	143
18.	**Church invests in War Industries**	149
	Untaxed profits	150

	The rapid development of Vatican wealth	151
19.	Land speculations in Rome and elsewhere	157
20.	The fabulous wealth of the Church in Spain	161
	Hitler and the Church tax	165
21.	The failed attempt to bomb Vatican City	167

PART THREE

22.	The pope's new bank	173
23.	'Insider trading' in Vatican gold	179
24.	Catholic Church investments in America	181
25.	Scandal in the popes' Bank	187
26.	Cardinals into stockbrokers	193
	Economic factors behind the mysterious death of Pope John Paul I?	196
	The Palace swimming pool	198
27.	Imponderable sources of income	203
	A pope sells Ireland to England	205
28.	Intangible billions	207
	A billion dollar art collection	209
	The value of suppressed artworks	212
	The value of rare Bibles	214
29.	What is the Roman Catholic Church worth today?	221
	Devoutness a false front	224
	Is a financial crisis looming for the Church?	226
	Pope verifies the claims in this book	226

Bibliography		**229**
	The Library of the Fathers	244
	The writings of Dr. Constantin Von Tischendorf	244
	Encyclopedias and dictionaries consulted	244
	Bibles used as comparative references	247

'Truth is such a rare quality, a stranger so seldom met in this civilization of fraud, that it is never received freely, but must fight its way into the world'.

Professor Hilton Hotema

A FEW WORDS TO THE READER

This book reveals extraordinary new information about early Christian development and the source of that material needs to be clarified. Some revelations are drawn from a 70,000-word manuscript written by a former Vatican archivist shortly before his death in Paris in 1988. He was a close friend of several cardinals, one of who later became Pope John Paul I (Albino Luciani, d. 1978), and spent time with Luciani when he was Bishop of Vittorio Veneto. He called his document, *The Church Verses True History* and it was sent to me by his elderly sister after she had read one of my books. This is what she said:

> You would have gotten on well with my brother. He worked for the Church in the Castel Sant' Angelo [The Secret Vatican Archives] and learnt things that left him disturbed. He had read a book called *Peter the Sinner* written by Angelo Mercati [1870-1955], Prefect of the Archives of the Vatican [later Cardinal], and it disturbed him. After he retired, he moved to live with me and it wasn't until that time that I really got to know him ... sometimes he would sit alone in the darkness ... at other times he would open his heart to me ... he was a good man, a good Catholic, but he was immensely sad; he wanted to believe, but was troubled. Something was wrong.

His manuscript was occasioned by the discovery of hitherto unknown documents in the Vatican vaults and is to be published *verbatim* in a new book called, *Confessions of a Vatican Archivist*. He reveals the true origins of Christianity and his findings are supported in ancient historical records.

INTRODUCTION ...
THE HALF HAS NOT YET BEEN TOLD

Just what is the Roman Catholic Church? Externally, it appears to be preoccupied with the riches of heaven, but internally it is the most formidable accumulator of riches in the World, indeed, the wealthiest institution on Earth. Hidden behind high-sounding papal pontificating in St. Peter's Square lies a beating economic heart that is stunning in its enormity. The startling contradiction of Vatican wealth with the preaching of the Gospel Jesus Christ is too glaring to be ignored, and its existence initiated this investigation into the extent of the Church's fortune.

What does the Holy Mother Church own ... what are her tangible and intangible assets ... what is the extent of her real estate holdings ... how much is invested in stocks, trusts and bonds ... is it true that she has vast deposits of gold in Swiss, American and other banks ... what are the rumours about off-shore bank accounts? These are difficult questions to answer because the Vatican employs suppressive measures to conceal the value and extent of its empire. However, it is possible to gather together snippets of information and present a digested view of the affluence of the Catholic Church today.

Stretching from St. Peter to the 21st Century, this book is a unique disclosure of the most formidable financial empire the world has ever seen. How did it all begin ... the answer to that question is recorded in ancient Church records, and reveals that Christianity was founded purely on financial principles.

PART ONE

The dome of St. Peter's seen across the Vatican gardens ©Vaticana Photographica Collecta, Roma ... David Seymour, 1948

Pope St. Peter set a precedent for his Church to accumulate wealth, and it led to a series of mediaeval papal forgeries that put the Vatican on the road to great riches.

CHAPTER 1

Early presbyters and Church laws

Things are never as they seem. According to the New Testament, Jesus Christ lived and died in abject poverty, yet his Church today is a multi-billion dollar concern that does not reflect any of the circumstances of its founder. How is it, that such a colossus, ruling in the name of an alleged itinerant preacher who had not even a pillow upon which to rest his head, is now so top-heavy with an earthly fortune that it can rival the might of the most redoubtable financial trusts and the most prosperous global corporations of the world? It is a question that has echoed along the somber corridors of religious history for many centuries, a question that from early times to today has puzzled, confused, and angered untold numbers of believers. How did the Holy Mother Church accumulate so much wealth, and when did it start? That answer is found in the New Testament, a collection of writings made 'official' to Catholicism at the 18-year-long Council of Trent (1545-1563). What is narrated in those texts reveals an original priesthood strategy of purposely amassing riches from the very inception of the Christian religion.

Any discussion on the taboo subject of the Vatican's finances necessarily starts with St. Peter, the man Catholics today call the first pope. It is an extraordinary story, one that has no parallel in the history of world religions. He established a money-making system that set a precedent for the Church hierarchy to follow for centuries to come, and from it an important question arises that is rarely addressed; 'Just who was St. Peter?' The answer to that question is revelatory, and it is found in two different manuscripts that emanate from the Church's inner sanctum, the Secret Vatican Archives. The Prefect of those Archives for many years, Monsignor (later, Cardinal) Angelo Mercati

(1870-1955), was a noted authority of patristic and scholastic literature in subjects pertaining to early Church history. He was a learned man and wrote more than a dozen 'in-house' books on philosophical and theological subjects for the Church. He also 'wrote many long treatises, miscellaneous essays, and shorter articles usually occasioned by the discovery of hitherto unknown documents' (*New Catholic Encyclopedia,* ix, pp. 668-669; Mercati's shorter works were collected as Saggi di storia e letteratura; Rome, 1951).

His job was to analyse old Church manuscripts and publish detailed summaries of their contents for categorizing in the Inner Library. Whileas the majority of his books are unavailable to the general public they are listed in the Vatican's Miscellanea Archivistica (AM, St. Test 165; 1952) and some carry intriguing titles like, *Lives of the Presbyters, The Divine Julius,* and *The Private Libraries of the Popes.* It is his writing called *Peter the Sinner* that attracts our attention, and drawing from that document in the *Confessions of a Vatican Archivist,* it is possible to provide stunning new information about the origins of the Church's fortune. In the region of ecclesiastical, no less than of civil history, our first thought should always be not of what is 'edifying' or 'pious', but what is *true.* Thus, to subsequently bring this story to a conclusion, we need to go back to the early Fourth Century of this era and summarize a series of strange events that took place at that time. Certain laws were passed and powers were given to the churchmen that proved to have had profound ramifications for mankind.

Payment for soapbox operas

In 306, British-born Flavius Constantine (272-337) became King of Briton and then, after a series of victorious battles, Emperor of the Roman Empire. Constantine was a sun-worshipper and a member of the religious order of Sol Invictus, one of two thriving cults of the time that regarded the Sun as the one and only Supreme God (The other was Mithraism). The entire reign of Emperor Constantine was known as the Sun Emperor-ship and Sun-god symbols were prominent throughout the land. Sun images were emblazoned on official coinage of the day and Constantine ordered the construction of a huge stone arch dedicated to the Invincible One, the Sun. It still stands today.

© Photo by James L. Sicard, 1939

This is an old photograph of the Arch of Constantine in Rome. It was ordered to be built by the Emperor as a dedication to Sol Invictus, and was completed two years before his death. There is no mention of Jesus Christ on this monument.

Christian historians give little or no hint of the turmoil of the times and suspend Constantine in the air free of all human events happening around him. In truth, one of Constantine's main problems was that of uncontrollable disorder amongst presbyters and their belief in numerous gods. Presbyters (*presbyteros* in Greek) were a curious body of people who wandered around spinning the public an assortment of yarns 'full of the boldest metaphor and rhetorical artifices of the age' (*Church History*, Socrates Scholasticus (380-450) Jenning's Trans., 1911). They were anciently known as 'capella' and 'capilliatus or capilliatum', depending upon which translation or tense is adopted. The original meaning of their name sheds light on the nature of these men for the word 'presbyter' simply means 'old man', and when contracted, it results in 'preost, an Old English word which today is 'priest'. Rendered into English, the word 'capilliatum' translates to 'having long hair' and 'capella' means 'a dim, dirty fellow' (*A Latin-English Dictionary*, J.T. White and J. E. Riddle, Ginn & Heath, Boston, 1880).

In the formative years of Christianity various fables were publicly 'read out loud' (1 Thess 5:27; Col 4:16) by presbyters to gatherings, exactly as Matthew, Mark, Luke and John are read out in churches today. The transmission of mythology was oral, and rhetoric was the art of the public speaker. The presbyters carried around with them a small collapsible platform upon which they stood when they spoke, and because of this they were variously called *pulpiteers, pleaders,* and '*town criers*' (*Book of the Roman Catholic Church*, Dr. and Bishop Charles Butler, 8 Vols. 1825). The best of the presbyters could read and write and they oversaw other orators who were illiterate and learnt their trade by rote. The more learned among them were called '*episkopos*' (Greek) and this word subsequently became 'biscop' in Old English ('bishop' today). By the end of the Third Century 'the title of biscop (bishop) came at length to be appropriated to the chief among them ... one of these presbyters became the ruling bishop' (*Catholic Encyclopedia,* Farley Ed., ii, pp. 581-589, passim, published under the Imprimatur of Archbishop Farley). This eventually gave each 'dim, dirty, long-haired old man' a special sense of religious importance never originally existing. Presbyters of a lesser standing were assistants of the bishops and sub-servant to them.

Because they were old men, they later came to be called 'elders', and by the mid-1500s, the Church insisted upon calling them 'the reverend fathers'. The word 'reverend' was an epithet of respect originally applied to the God of the Old Testament and was 'never applied to man' (Ps. 111:9, Sinai Bible). This word expanded to 'Most Reverend', 'Right Reverend' and 'Very Reverend', and has been used as a glorified prefix to churchmen's names ever since. The word 'fathers' became 'Fathers' (with an upper-case F), and that subsequently evolved to 'Divine Fathers of the Church', a title falsely giving bishops and presbyters the status of special and dignified founders of the Christian Church. Today the Church itself calls this process, 'ecclesiasticism', which simply means 'an exaggerated attachment to the practices or principles of the Christian Church' (*Catholic Encyclopedia*, Pecci Ed., ii, p. 301).

Bishops and presbyters were beggared entertainers of the public and nothing more (*Confessions of a Vatican Archivist*), to whom an entirely fictitious importance has been given by the later Church. They were heathen opportunists, accepting favours of food, wine, corn, olive oil, wool, shelter and sex in return for their soapbox performance. The low regard in which they were held has been subtly suppressed by modern Church historians and Constantine's efforts to curb the disreputable character of the men now called, 'Church Fathers' has been concealed. They were 'maddened', he said (*Life of Constantine, iii,* 170-73; Eusebius, *The Nicene and Post-Nicene Fathers*, cited as N&PNF, iv, 466-7), and the 'peculiar type of oratory' (*The Dictionary of Classical Mythology, Religion, Literature and Art*, Oskar Seyffert, 1995, pp. 544-546) expounded by them was a challenge to a settled religious order. In a report to the Roman Senate, Celsus, an historian and author, and 'a great authority on these matters' (*Catholic Encyclopedia,* Farley Ed., 'Celsus') called presbyters 'the ulcer of our times' (*Catholic Encyclopedia,* Pecci Ed., i, p. 288). He added:

> To our common misfortune, this presbyter literature weakens the already weakened mind of man still more by laying it open without resistance to all kinds of deceit and delusion, and leads it astray from relatively well-founded thinking, thus stimulating in people, instead of sane judgment, various unworthy properties, such as incredulity, fear, false shame, and hypocrisy. From my point of view, owing to the influence on the general mass of naïve and easily suggestible people, the presbyters are a thousand times more pernicious than all the slobbering dandies who bear so evil a reputation for licentiousness for their conduct of coarse street-corner songs.

> One day a presbyter arrived in town, bringing with him a whole train of assistants, and even, it seemed to me, his own harem. Almost disinterestedly, and without the slightest hurry, he set up his pulpit and read from his scroll. Dozens of illiterate people gathered around one literate man to hear a reading of strange tales and he received a good round sum.

(*Contra Celsus,* written by Origen of Alexandria (c. 251), Bk. I, p. lxvii, and Bk. 111, p. xliv, passim)

Celsus advised the Roman Senate that presbyters were 'charlatans and vagrants, dangerous to civil ideals of the Roman state', and branded their orations on the marvels of ancient gods as absurd. In reality they were ...

> ... the most rustic fellows, teaching strange paradoxes. They openly declared that none but the ignorant were fit to hear their discourses ... they never appeared in the circles of the wiser and better sort, but always took care to intrude themselves among the ignorant and uncultured, rambling around to play tricks at fairs and markets ... they lard their lean books with the fat of old fables ... and still the less do they understand ... and they write nonsense on vellum ... and still be doing, never done.

(*Contra Celsus,* written by Origen of Alexandria (c. 251), Bk. I, p. lxvii, and Bk. 111, p. xliv, passim)

Celsus revealed that the presbyter's manuscripts were ever-changing compilations of ancient myths and fictional tales, and in those early years there was a great diversity of opinion amongst presbyters about what stories should be publicly read. Clusters of presbyters had developed 'many gods and many lords' (1 Cor. 8:5) and numerous religious sects existed, each with differing doctrines (Gal.1:6). Presbyterial groups clashed over attributes of their various gods and 'altar was set against altar' (*Optatus of Minevis*; 1:15, 19, Early Fourth Century) in competing for an audience.

From Constantine's point of view, several presbyterial factions needed appeasing, and he set out to develop one all-embracing religion during a period of irreverent confusion. In an age in which most of our literature accepts the crass ignorance of the times, nine-tenths of Europe were illiterate, and stabilizing religious splinter groups was only one of Constantine's problems. The smooth generalization, of which so many historians are content to repeat, that Constantine 'embraced the Christian religion' and subsequently granted 'official toleration' is 'contrary to historical fact' (*Catholic Encyclopedia*, Pecci Ed., iii, pp. 298-9, passim) and should be erased from our literature forever. Simply put, there was no Christian religion at Constantine's time, and the Church acknowledges that the tale of his 'conversion' and 'baptism' are 'entirely legendary' (*Catholic Encyclopedia*, Farley Ed., xiv, pp. 370-371).

In 313, Eusebius Pamphilius of Caesarea (260-339), commenced the compilation of a series of writings he called *Ecclesiastical History* (*Eccl. Hist.*) and recorded generally unknown knowledge about the development of Christianity. The 18th Century Church called Eusebius 'the first major Christian historian' yet *Ecclesiastical History* was basically a summary of earlier presbyter's writings, 'many of which were false' (*De Antiqua Ecclesiae Disciplina*, Bishop Louis Dupin, Catholic historian, *Folio*, Paris, 1686; *Annales Ecclesiastici*, tome vi, Fol. Antwerp, 1597, Cardinal Caesar Baronius; *Eusebius of Caesarea*, J. B. Lightfoot, World Publ. Co. 1962, NY; in *A Dictionary of Christian Biograph, Literature, Sects and Doctrines*, London 1880). The sixth and seventh books of Eusebius, for example, are based on letters under the name of Dionysius that the Church admits are 'forgeries or inventions of later times' (*De Antiqua Ecclesiae Disciplina,* Bishop Louis Dupin, Catholic historian), yet it still present Eusebius's writings as historical.

Scarcely a pious figure, Eusebius was notorious by nature and became an influential bishop of the early Fourth Century. He was a 'military priest' (*Confessions of a Vatican Archivist*), enthroned by Roman combatant leaders, as were many early bishops, including Martin, Bishop of Tours (d. c. 397) and Philiaster of Brescia (d. c. 397 also). Gregory of Nazinanzus (c. 390) recorded that it was Church practice in the Fourth Century for bishops to be drawn 'from the army or the navy' (*Epistle* and *Procop* (Al 130), Schaff), and that extraordinary confession opposes modern-day presentations of bishop selection. The truth of the matter is that they were rough fighting men, warrior-priests, more warriors than priests, and more soldiers than theologians. In the centuries to come they developed into the pope's private military force and by the time of Pope Gregory (540-604), they were called 'the Militia of Jesus Christ' (*A History of the Popes*, Dr. Joseph McCabe, Rector of Buckingham College; d. 1955; C. A. Watts and Co, London, Book 1). Eusebius was a friend of Emperor Constantine and, important for our treatise, wrote a detailed book called the *Life of Constantine* (c. 335). What he recorded opens up a can of worms for the Holy Mother Church and reveals an entirely different origin to Christianity than that presented by the Church. His records preserve valuable reflections on what really happened in the early decades of the Fourth Century, and the majority of modern-day Christian historians attempt to cover-up the truth about what he said. That is because he reveals the true story of the development of their religion.

CHAPTER 2

The first ecclesiastical council and missing records

It was Emperor Constantine who created Christianity, and how he did it provides an extraordinary story, one that has been constantly suppressed by Vatican censors (*Confessions of a Vatican Archivist*). Church records note that among presbyterian factions, 'strife had grown so serious, vigorous action was necessary to establish a more religious state' (*Life of Constantine*, iii, 26-8, Bishop Eusebius Pamphilius of Caesarea, c. 335) but he could not bring about a settlement between rival god-factions. Constantine 'never acquired a solid theological knowledge' and 'depended heavily on his advisers in religious questions' (*Catholic Encyclopedia,* New ed. xii, p. 576, passim). They warned him that the presbyter's religions were 'destitute of foundation' (ibid) and needed official stabilization. Constantine saw in this confused system of fragmented dogmas the opportunity to create a new and combined State religion neutral in concept, and protect it by law. When he conquered the East in 324 he sent his Spanish religious advisor, Osius of Cordoba, to Alexandria with letters to several bishops exhorting them to make peace among themselves. 'For as long as you continue to contend about your various gods and insignificant questions, it is not fitting that a portion of God's people should be under the direction of your judgment, as you are divided among yourselves' (*Life of Constantine, ii,* 69-71; Bishop Eusebius Pamphilius of Caesarea (c. 335), N&PNF. i, 516-7).

The mission failed and Constantine, probably at the suggestion of Osius, then issued a Decree commanding all presbyters and their subordinates 'be mounted on asses, mules and horses belonging to the public, and travel to the city of Nicaea' (*Theological Tracts,* On Councils, Vol. 3 (of 6), London,

1791) in the Roman Province of Bithymia, a country of Asia. They were instructed to bring with them the *testimonies* ('nonsense on vellum', Celsus) they orated to the rabble, 'bound in hide' (*The Catholic Dictionary*, Addis and Arnold, 'Council of Nicaea', 1917) for protection during the long journey, and surrender them to Constantine upon arrival in Nicaea. Their writings totalled, 'in all, two thousand two hundred and thirty one scrolls and legendary tales of gods and saviours, together with a record of the doctrines orated by them' (*Life of Constantine,* ii, p. 173, Bishop Eusebius Pamphilius of Caesarea (c. 335), N&PNF. i, p. 518, Prof. S. L. MacGuire's trans, Salisbury, 1921).

Thus, the first ecclesiastical gathering in history was summoned and today it is known as the Council of Nicaea. It was a bizarre event that provided many details of early clerical thinking and presents a clear picture of the intellectual phenomena prevailing at the time. It was at this gathering that Christianity was born, and the ramifications of decisions made at that time are difficult to calculate. Because Constantine was a sun-worshipper, he instructed Eusebius Pamphilius to convene the first of the three sittings on the Summer Solstice, June 21st, 325 (*Catholic Encyclopedia*, New ed, i, p. 792), and it was 'held in a hall in Osius's' palace (*Ecclesiastical History*, Bishop Louis Dupin, i, p. 598). When speaking of the conclave of presbyters gathered at Nicaea, Sabinius, Bishop of Hereclea, who was in attendance, said in an account of the proceedings:

> Excepting Constantine himself, and Eusebius Pamphilius, they were a set of illiterate, simple creatures who understood nothing.

(*Secrets of the Christian Fathers*, Bishop J. W. Sergerus, 1685, reprint 1897)

This is another luminous confession of the ignorance and uncritical credulity of early churchmen. Dr. Richard Watson (1737-1816), a disillusioned Christian historian and one time Bishop of Llandaff in Wales (1782), referred to them as 'a set of gibbering idiots' (*Apology for Christianity*, Dr. Richard Watson, 1796; also, *Theological Tracts*, On Councils, Vol. 2 (of 6), London, 1791). After a lifetime of research into Church councils Dr. Watson concluded that 'the clergy at the Council of Nicaea were all under the power of the devil and the convention was composed of the lowest rabble, and patronized the vilest abominations' (*Apology for Christianity*, Dr. Richard Watson, 1796). It was that infantile body of men who were responsible for the commencement of a new religion, and the theological creation of Jesus Christ.

The Church admits that vital elements of the proceedings at Nicaea are 'strangely absent from the canons' (*Catholic Encyclopedia*, Farley Ed., iii, p. 160) and we shall see shortly what happened to them. However, using records that endured Eusebius, 'occupied the first seat on the right of the emperor and delivered the inaugural address on the emperor's behalf' (*Catholic Encyclopedia*, Farley Ed., v, pp. 619-620). There were no British presbyters at the Council (*Catholic Encyclopedia*, Farley Ed., xv, p. 582) but many Greek delegates. 'Seventy eastern bishops' represented Asiatic factions (*Ecclesiastical History*, Bishop Louis Dupin, Vol. i, p. 598), Caecilian of Carthage traveled from Africa; Paphnutius from Egypt, Nicasius of Die from Gaul and Dommus of Stridon made the journey from Pannonia. Important for our story is the fact that a large number of Nabatean Arabs were in attendance, and they were led by Simon of Petra. Shortly we will learn how his name appeared in the New Testament.

It was at that puerile assembly, and under cult conditions, that a total of 318 'bishops, priests, deacons, sub-deacons, acolytes and exorcists' (*Apology for Christianity*, Dr. Richard Watson, 1796) gathered to debate and decide upon a unified belief system that encompassed only one god. By this time a huge assortment of 'wild texts' (*Catholic Encyclopedia*, New ed, 'Gospel and Gospels') circulated amongst presbyters, and they supported a great variety of Eastern and Western gods and goddesses; Ares, Apollo, Hermes, Artemis, Zeus, Athena, 'the Sun and the Moon' (Acts of Philip, 1:1), Mars, Jove, Mithra, Krishna, Bel (Baal), Attis, Odin, Tammuz, Indra, Prometheus, Hercules, Janus, Sin, Dionysius, Bacchus, Jupiter, Diana, Alcestos, the *Divine Julius*, Serapis, Isis, and Osiris.

Up until the Council of Nicaea, Roman aristocracy primarily worshipped two Greek gods, Apollo and Zeus, but the great bulk of common people idolized either Julius Caesar or Mithra. Caesar was deified by the Roman Senate after his death (d. 15th March, 44 BC) and subsequently venerated as the *Divine Julius*. The word 'saviour' was affixed to his name, its literal meaning being 'one who sows the seed', i.e., a phallic god. Caesar was hailed as 'God made manifest and universal Saviour of human life' and his successor, Augustus was called the 'ancestral God and Saviour of the whole human race' (*Man and his Gods*, Homer Smith, Little, Brown and Co., Boston, 1952). Emperor Nero (37-68), whose original name was L. Domitius Ahenobarbus, was immortalized on his coins as the 'Saviour of mankind' (ibid). Because the *Divine Julius* was Roman Saviour and 'Father of the Empire', he was considered 'god' among the Roman rabble for more than 300 years. He was the deity in some Western presbyter's texts, but was not recognised in Eastern or Oriental writings.

Constantine's intention at Nicaea was to 'create an entirely new god for his Empire' (*Confessions of a Vatican Archivist*) that would unite all religious factions under one deity, and presbyters were asked to debate and decide who their new god would be. Delegates argued among themselves, expressing personal motives for inclusion of particular writings that promoted the finer traits of their own special divinity. Throughout the meeting, howling factions were immersed in heated debates, and the names of 53 gods were tabled for discussion; 'As yet, the new God had not been selected by the council, and so they balloted, in order to determine the matter; for one year and five months the balloting lasted' (*God's Book of Eskra*, xlviii, 26-53 Prof. S. L. MacGuire's trans, Salisbury, 1921).

At the end of that time, Constantine returned to the gathering to discover that the presbyters had not agreed on a new deity but had balloted down to a short list of five prospects, namely, Caesar, Krishna, Mithra, Horus, and Zeus. Constantine was the ruling spirit at Nicaea and he ultimately decided upon a new god for them. To involve British factions, he ruled that the name of the mighty Druid god, Hesus (crucified in Britain and later restored to life), be joined with the Eastern saviour-god, Krishna (Krishna is Sanskrit for Christ), and thus a caricature, or the personification of an ideal, Hesus Krishna, would be the name of the new Roman god. A vote was taken and it was with a majority show of hands that both divinities became one God ... 161 votes to 157. Following longstanding heathen custom, Constantine used the official gathering and the Roman Apotheoses Decree to legally deify two deities as one, and did so by democratic consent. A new god was proclaimed and 'officially ratified by Constantine' (*Acta Concilii Niceni*, Colon,

1618). That purely political act of deification effectively, and legally, placed Hesus and Krishna among the Roman gods as one individual composition. That abstraction lent earthly existence to amalgamated doctrines for the Empire's new religion, and when the letter 'J' was introduced into alphabets around the Ninth Century, the linguistic relic of the name became Jesus Christ.

The secret history of the New Testament

Constantine then instructed Eusebius to organize the compilation of a uniform collection of new writings developed from primary aspects of the religious texts submitted at the Council. His instructions were:

> Search ye these books, and whatever is good in them, that retain; but whatsoever is evil, cast away. What is good in one book, write ye with that which is good in another book. And whatsoever is thus brought together shall be called the Book of Books, and it shall be the doctrine of my people, which I will recommend unto all nations, that there shall be no more war for religion's sake.

> (*God's Book of Eskra*, xlviii, 26-53, Prof. S. L. MacGuire's trans, Salisbury, 1921)

'Make them to astonish', said Constantine (*Life of Constantine*, iv, pp. 36-39, Bishop Eusebius Pamphilius of Caesarea, c. 335), and over the next five years, 'the books were written accordingly' (ibid). Eusebius amalgamated the 'legendary tales of all the religious doctrines of the world together as one' (ibid) using the standard god-myths from the presbyter's manuscripts as his exemplar. Merging the supernatural 'god' stories of British Culdean belief with Krishna's life, and elements of Mithraism, effectively joined the orations of Eastern and Western presbyters together 'to form a new universal belief' (*Confessions of a Vatican Archivist*).

To modernize his writings Eusebius appropriated the aggressive spirit of the presbyters of the time and, with words like 'buy swords', and 'fighting', revealed the military aspect of the new priesthood. He built in mythical personalities, such as apostles, with the Church admitting, with the soundest scriptural basis for its conclusion, that 'the whole [Gospel] story of apostles is fictitious' (*Encyclopedia Biblica,* iii, p. 2987). This is an instructive passage, and the same source added this remarkable information about the creation of 'apostles': 'the number twelve was symbolical, corresponding to the twelve tribes of Israel' (*Encyclopedia Biblica,* i, p. 264), who were personifications of the twelve signs of the Zodiac.

Constantine believed that the restructured amalgamation of ancient myths would unite variant and opposing religious factions under one representative story. Eusebius then arranged for scribes to produce 'fifty sumptuous copies ... to be written on parchment in a legible manner, and in a convenient portable form, by professional scribes thoroughly accomplished in their art' (*Life of Constantine,* iv, pp. 36-39, Bishop Eusebius Pamphilius of Caesarea, c. 335). 'These orders', said Eusebius, 'were followed by the immediate execution of the work itself, which we sent him [Constantine] magnificently and elaborately bound volumes of three-fold and four-fold forms' (*Life of Constantine,* iv, 36, Bishop Eusebius Pamphilius of Caesarea, c. 335). Constantine called them the *New Testimonies,* and originally they contained six variant Gospels (*The Various Versions of the Bible*, Dr. Constantin Von Tischendorf (1815-1874), available in the British Library). This is the first mention in world history of the New Testament (c. 331), and other writings were attached in upcoming centuries.

With his instructions fulfilled, Constantine then decreed that the *New Testimonies* would thereafter be called the 'word of the Roman Saviour God' (*Life of Constantine,* iii, 29, Bishop Eusebius Pamphilius of Caesarea, c. 335) and official to all presbyters sermonizing in the Roman Empire. Copies were subsequently distributed to various presbyterial factions who then restructured them in their own way, and that provides a reason why the Gospels today disagree with each other on fundamental doctrinal matters. Constantine then ordered earlier presbyterial manuscripts, and records of the Council, 'burnt' (ibid), and 'any man found concealing writings should be stricken off from his shoulders' (beheaded). As the record shows, presbyterial writings previous to the Council of Nicaea no longer exist, although some fragments survived. In 1890, records of the Council were found in a Genizah at the Seraglio Library in the Topkapi Palace Museum, Constantinople (Istanbul today), and they provide startling ramifications that the Church is yet to publicly address. Included in the cache was a large ancient Bible that contained an original letter written in 'large Latin characters' by Emperor Constantine himself.

Some old documents say that the Council of Nicaea ended in mid-November, 326, while others say the struggle to establish a god was so fierce it extended 'for four years and seven months' (*Secrets of the Christian Fathers*, Bishop J.W. Sergerus, 1685, reprint 1897). Whenever it ended, the savagery and violence it encompassed was concealed under the glossy title, the 'Great and Holy Synod', assigned to it by the Church in the 18th Century. Earlier churchmen, however, expressed a different opinion. The second Council of Nicaea in 785-7 denounced the first Council of Nicaea as 'a synod of fools and madmen' (*History of the Christian Church,* H. H. Milman, D.D., 1871), and sought to annul 'decisions passed by men with troubled brains' (ibid). If one chooses to read the records of the second Nicaean Council and notes references to 'affrighted bishops' and 'soldiery' needed to 'quell proceedings', the 'fools and madmen' declaration is surely an example of the pot calling the kettle black.

The Church of the 15th Century developed an official policy of publicly presenting the ancient '*pulpiteers*' as learned and dignified men, worthy of the highest respect. So vigorously was this opinion enforced that one of the charges upon which Michael Servetus was burnt to death by John Calvin at Champel, on October 27th 1553 was he had spoken disrespectfully of early Christian presbyters (*Servetus and Calvin*, R. Willis, M.D., London, 1877, p. 308).

Bishops, worldliness, and gain

Shortly after the closing of the Council of Nicaea, Emperor Constantine appointed Simon of Petra ruling bishop of the Roman Empire (*Confessions of a Vatican Archivist*). He was a Nabatean Arab, a Semitic people, and bishop of his faction at the Council of Nicaea. Because of its secure location, Petra had earlier been adopted by the Nabatean kings as their capital city, and in 106 it became incorporated into the Roman Empire. The Nabatean Arabs passed out of history with the advent of Islam some century's later (*Encyclopedia Judaica Jerusalem,* 1971, pp. 740-744), but at the time of Constantine they had a dramatic influence on the development of the Christian religion. Researchers add: 'Simon, originally from the rock of Petra, a fortified rock city south of the Dead Sea ... there they had a rock dome upon which they hoarded their wealth' (*The Keys of St. Peter,* Bunson, 1867, also; *Bingham's Antiquities of the Christian Church,* Straker's Edition, 1840; also *New Catholic Encyclopedia,* Farley Ed., x, p. 191, 'the rock').

Simon of Petra is Simon Peter in the New Testament today (*Confessions of a Vatican Archivist*). Simply put, Simon of Petra was a standard naming designation, like Mary of Bethany or Joseph of Arimathea, and it evolved to Simon Peter in variant later translations. In establishing how Simon Peter came to eventually be called simply Peter creates confusion for researchers, and numerous opinions exist. Petra (at one time called, Petta; *Atlas of the Early Christian Church,* H. H. Rowley, Professor of Hebrew Language and Literature, University of Manchester, Nelson (Publ.), 1966), when translated into English, is Peter, and in the Roman Catholic Church today he is Pope St. Peter. Traces of the 'Peter' (Petra; Petta) or 'rock' tradition are found in all four Gospels, and they record the prominent role he played as a 'pillar' in the circle of Constantine's new churchmen (Gal. 2:9).

When the later Church retrospectively made St. Peter the first pope, they attempted to position him of necessity in the First Century, not the Fourth Century (*Confessions of a Vatican Priest*), but he was contemporaneous with the writing of the Gospels. That was after the Council of Nicaea (325), and the Church makes extraordinary admissions to that effect. For example, when discussing Gospel origins, 'the most distinguished body of academic opinion ever assembled' (Preface in *Catholic Encyclopedias*) admitted that 'the earliest of the extant manuscripts [of the New Testament], it is true, do not date back beyond the middle of the fourth century AD' (*Catholic Encyclopedia,* Farley Ed., vi, pp. 656-657). That is some 350 years after the time the Church claims that a divine Jesus Christ walked the sands of Palestine, and here the true story of Christian origins slips into one of the biggest black holes in history. An appreciation of the clerical mindset arises when the Church made this admittance:

> The titles of our Gospels were not intended to indicate authorship ... it thus appears that the present titles of the Gospels are not traceable to the evangelists

themselves ... they [the New Testament collection] are supplied with titles, which however ancient, do not go back to the respective authors of those writings ... the Gospels do not go back to the first century of the Christian era.

(*Catholic Encyclopedia,* Farley Ed., pp. vi, 135-137; vi. pp. 655, 656, *passim*)

For centuries, fabricated Gospels bore Church certification of authenticity now confessed to be false, and while some aspects had an earlier existence they were not representative of Jesus Christ *(History of the Vulgate,* History of the Council of Trent, Paolo Sarpi, Translated by Brent, London, 1676; also, *Ecclesiastical History,* Mosheim, Book 6, London, 1825). In a remarkable aside, the Church further confesses that 'the headings ... were affixed to them' (*Catholic Encyclopedia,* Farley Eds., i, p. 117; vi, p. 656), therefore they are not Gospels written 'according to Matthew, Mark, Luke or John', as publicly presented. The full force of this confession reveals that there are no genuine Gospels and the writings the priesthood use embody the very ground and pillar of Christian foundation and faith. The consequences are fatal to the pretence of Divine origin to the entire New Testament and expose Christian texts as having no special authority. The conclusion is inescapable ... no historic apostolic authors, no historic Gospels.

Dr. Constantin Von Tischendorf (1815-1874), a brilliant and pious German biblical scholar and Professor of Theology, devoted his entire life to the study of New Testament origins, and his desire to read all ancient Christian texts led him on a long camel-mounted journey to St. Catherine's Monastery in the Sinai where he discovered the world's oldest Bible, the Sinaiticus. After a lifetime of dedicated New Testament research, Dr. Tischendorf expressed dismay at the differences between oldest and newest Gospels, and had trouble understanding ...

> ... how scribes could allow themselves to bring in here and there changes, which were not simply verbal ones, but such as materially affected the very meaning and, what is worse still, did not shrink from cutting out a passage or inserting one.

(*Alterations to the Sinai Bible,* Dr. Constantin Tischendorf, Available in the British

Library, London)

After years of validating the false nature of the New Testament, a disillusioned Dr. Tischendorf confessed that modern-day editions have 'been altered in many places' and 'should not be accepted as true' (*When Were Our Gospels Written?* Dr. Tischendorf, available in the British Library, London)

Alarmingly for Christians is the fact that the Church-owned *Encyclopedia Biblica* reveals that a total of 1200 years of Christian history are unknown; 'Unfortunately, only few of the records [of the Church] prior to the year 1198 have been released' (*Encyclopedia Biblica*, Adam & Charles Black, London, 1899). It was not by chance that in that same year (1198) Pope Innocent III (1161-1216) suppressed all records of earlier Church history by establishing Secret Archives (*Catholic Encyclopedia*, Farley Ed., xv, p. 287). Some seven and a half centuries later, and after spending some years in those Archives, Professor Edmond S. Bordeaux (d. 1979), a disenchanted Catholic priest, wrote a book called, *How The Great Pan Died* (Mille Meditations, MCMLXVIII). In a chapter titled, 'The Whole of Church History is Nothing but a Retroactive Fabrication', he said this (in part):

> The Church ante-dated all her late works, some newly made, some revised and some counterfeited, which contained the final expression of her history ... her technique was to make it appear that much later works written by Church writers were composed a long time earlier, so that they might become evidence of the first, second or third centuries.

(*How The Great Pan Died*, Mille Meditations, MCMLXVIII, p. 46)

Here we find internal Vatican evidence of the greatest misrepresentation of all time, for there was no Christian religion until Emperor Constantine created it at Nicaea in the Fourth Century. The Church knows this, and provided its cover story, saying: 'Between the times of the birth of Our Lord and the edicts of Emperor Constantine (d. 337) there is very little documentation to determine the course of the Church' (*Catholic Encyclopedia*, Pecci Ed., ii, p. 44). That is because there is no documentation, no Christ, and no Church.

Henceforth, much of the literature written from that time on was aimed at propagating a fabricated faith to the world and ensuring Roman Emperors were given perpetual places as heads of Church and State. 'After Christianity had become the established religion of the Roman empire at the end of the Fourth Century, the Roman Emperors convened a succession of Councils which were later called Ecumenical, Universal or General' (*Encyclopedia Britannica*, Edinburgh Ed. 1797), and thus developed a series of 19 gatherings over the next 1600 years about which 'considerable doubt exists respecting their genuineness' (ibid). The Church itself admitted that the records of the 'Synod of the 275 Bishops under [Pope] Sylvester' at Rome in 334 are fictitious (*Catholic Encyclopedia*, Farley Ed., ix, p. 225; xiv, pp. 370-371: confirmed in Bishop Jeremy Taylor's book, *Liberty*, and in *Diderot's Encyclopedia*, 1759), revealing that all Church council records should be viewed with the highest suspicion.

The evidence is overwhelming. It is not possible to find in any legitimate historic writings compiled between the beginning of the First Century and the middle of the Fourth Century, any reference to Jesus Christ and the events that the Gospels say accompanied his life. Many people wonder at such an unaccountable omission of what the Church says was the greatest event in world history. The period was rich in prolific writers and voluminous works were produced by such highly-regarded historians as Pliny the Elder, Pliny the Younger, Philo, Flavius Josephus, Cornelius, Titus Livius (Livy), Porphyry, Plutarch, Lucius Seneca, Jewenal, Justus of Tiberias, Epictectus, Tacitus, Suetonius, Cluvius Rufus, Quintus Curtis Rufus, and Roman Consul, Publius Petronius, who lived in Jerusalem at the time ascribed to the life of Jesus Christ. Those great classical scribes wrote about early religious beliefs but never mentioned Jesus or the spectacular events that the Church said accompanied his life. They devote pages and pages to persons and events of no importance, but fail to make a single mention of God incarnating as a man and walking on Earth amongst multitudes to become their saviour. It was as if no such person existed to write about.

This situation arose from a conflict between history and New Testament narratives, and Dr. Tischendorf added this comment: 'We must frankly admit that we have no source of information with respect to the life of Jesus Christ other than ecclesiastic writings assembled during the Fourth Century' (*Codex*

Sinaiticus, Dr. Tischendorf, available in the British Library, London). The Church agreed. In 1947 the Vatican commissioned a priest named Farrer to write a book called *The Life of Christ* and *The Times Literary Supplement* of the day reviewed it as 'a first-rate introduction to the faith'. The author was forced to concede and deplore the dearth of evidence as to the subject of his pen, saying:

> It is amazing that neither history nor tradition should have embalmed for us even one certain or definite saying or circumstance in the life of the saviour of mankind, except the comparatively few events in the four brief Gospels. There is no statement in all history that says anyone saw Jesus or talked with him. Nothing in history is more astonishing than the silence of contemporary writers of the events relayed in the four Gospels relative to Jesus, his disciples and his work.

There is an explanation for their silence ... the construct of Christianity had not yet begun and the 'fable of Christ' was unknown to them (Pronouncement by Pope Leo X (d. 1521) to his cardinals, recorded in the records of Pietro Bembo (*His Letters and Comments on Pope Leo X*, Reprint 1842) and Cardinal Jovius (*De Vita Leonis X*, originally published in 1551).

CHAPTER 3

Powers of acquisition given to the Church

When Emperor Constantine sowed the seeds that grew into Christianity, his new religion became the official creed of the whole imperial structure; and a whole new race of beings subsequently came into existence ... the clergy. These men spread like wildfire, swiftly becoming a vast bureaucracy that outweighed the Roman state itself. They saw as their chief task, the fleecing of the lowly masses of what little material wealth they had, and priests in their thousands raged through the territories in an orgy of theft. Immediately after the closing of the Council of Nicaea, the foundation of the new Roman State religion was finalized and the civil powers began a vigorous campaign to build up numbers by compelling people to embrace Constantine's fabricated system of belief. The Emperor gave St. Peter special powers, issuing official legislation that 'permitted all persons wronged to carry their lawsuits before the bishop' (*Catholic Encyclopedia*, Farley Ed., ii, p. 583). With this permit, St. Peter soon became an influential and powerful personage in the community, the judge and the jury, the voice of Roman authority, and one not of an ecclesiastical nature. He appointed 'several chief orators' (*biscops*) and, of them, Eusebius said that they were 'as much above kings as the soul is above the body ... they were given up to worldliness and gain, and we hear of worse scandals' (*Catholic Encyclopedia*, Farley Ed., iv, p. 583, passim). The Church added that 'the nature of Constantine's bishops makes early Christianity appear as a religion established by criminals' (*Catholic Encyclopedia*, Pecci Ed., ii, p. 197), which is exactly what it was, and it quickly enforced its new concepts with violence.

St. Peter commanded his bishops 'to hearken to' his instructions, hence to 'obey', and demanded of them an *'iusiurandum'* (*Optatus of Minevis*; 3:11-12, Early Fourth Century), which is a military word for 'oath' (*A Latin-English Dictionary*, J. T. White and J. E. Riddle, Ginn & Heath, Boston, 1880). This demand was later called the Canon Rule of Obedience, and St. Thomas Aquinas (1225-74) makes it clear that the 'vow of [papal] obedience is the chief of all vows' in the Christian religion (*Summa Theologica*). Pope St. Peter granted his bishops exemption from the criminal process before a judge and jury, and that contract subsequently developed into a privileged Church Law called the 'benefit of clergy' (*Privilegium Clericale*). In a later chapter we will see how the assertion of ecclesiastical liberties under what we shall now call, 'The Bishop's Oath of Allegiance' dishonestly and 'without fear of punishment' (*Summa Theologica*, St. Thomas Aquinas), added huge property holdings to the Church's portfolio. Until now, there was no indication of the power Constantine's new religion would soon enforce on the populace, but this became visible with a legal event of utmost importance. With Senatorial certification, Emperor Constantine issued legislation commanding his developing priesthood to establish a portfolio of assets, and thenceforward a new phrase of ecclesiastical history was instigated. Count Beugnot, a pious Catholic historian, laments that 'this favour granted to Christianity admitted to its bosom guilty passions which had speedy and pernicious consequences'. Because St. Peter's organization was now an authorized division of the government of the Roman Empire, its structure was privileged with legal rights to acquire property, and some of the wicked methods used under the auspices of 'The Bishop's Oath of Allegiance' are later exposed.

Here we see the origin of the Church's desire to accumulate wealth, and it is still the essence and substance of Christianity today. With this initiate came not only riches, but supremacy, and writers of the time leave no room for doubt that priesthood domination of the culture of the times was accompanied by a serious loss of spiritually that might have derived from Constantine's new religion. Constantine also conferred on his priesthood the right to receive bequests and passed a law enforcing the civil observance of Sun Day (*dies solis,* Sunday), suspending all legal business and military exercises on that day. Thus the new religion was protected and privileged, and the ill-defined boundaries between civil and ecclesiastical jurisdiction led to the gravest evils. The pseudo-belief, triumphant, immediately began to vest itself with the raiment of this world, and the State was its protector.

It soon reached a stage that it became a kind of patrimonium, owned, controlled and administered by a few bishops under St. Peter, and they 'tended to regard themselves as superior to the highest authorities in matters ecclesiastical and to think of the Church as a department of the State' (*New Catholic Encyclopedia*, xii, p. 577). Parallel with mounting greed grew unchecked worldly pride and priestly arrogance: 'They were a conceited body of people and the abuse of religion dangerously undermined the foundations of moral virtue' (*Gibbon's Rome*, ii, p. 272). The two begot lack of charity, which turned soon into blatant intolerance. 'They were haughty, and developed a system denouncing opponents and promoting themselves to a level that is due only to God Almighty' (*De Antiqua Ecclesiae Disciplina*, Bishop Lewis Dupin, Catholic historian (*Folio*, Paris, 1686). Around 1000 years later the superciliousness and greed of the Roman Church eventually brought about a religious revolution today called the Reformation. With the power given to the bishops, the assets of sundry religions were mercilessly expropriated, their clergy dismissed or persecuted, when not civilly or even physically obliterated. 'Tear away without fear, the ornaments of the temples', said Constantine to one, Firmicus Maternus. Ancient temples were forcibly closed, transformed into shrines for the new religion by adding solid silver altars weighing 200 pounds each, or demolished, and many properties were summarily added to the Church's patrimony. The appalling wave of vandalism that then ensured reached its height in the burning of the great library at Alexandria in 389, the destruction of the Serapeum, and the assassination of Hypatia by the murderous bishop of Alexandria, St. Cyril (d. 444). The transfer of political might by Constantine to the bishops having made it easy for Christianity to transform this into the power of acquisition, the new Church set out in earnest to 'promote a policy of swift appropriation of real estates, of highly remunerative governmental posts, and of speculative monetary and commercial enterprises' (*Records of Events*, xxvii, 12-13, Marcellinus Ammianus (c. 330-400), in the Loeb Classical Library).

With the help of St. Peter and his clergy, Constantine left no means untried that would further the promotion of the new order and the suppression of the old. He issued edicts forbidding other religions to assemble or hold meetings, and passed laws demanding that their buildings be seized and become the property of his new Church. In this way, all those who held to doctrines and opinions contrary to budding Christianity were slowly suppressed. He certified an imperial decree which imposed 'condign punishment' (the death sentence) on all people who resisted his demands to attend the new gatherings (*Confessions*, St. Augustine). Scholars and philosophers were silenced and banished, and their works were cast to the flames. Those who refused to accept the new creed were put to death without mercy while others were banished from their homes and their properties seized. In distant country regions people were not so immediately under the control of the police powers of the government, and to avoid persecution many fled the cities to remote rural regions called in Latin, *pagus*. They became known as 'pagans' and the municipalities and townships they established were called *pagus* villages. Forced to escape the sword, flame and torture, they could not be made to accept the fallacious beliefs that Constantine tried to force upon them at the behest of the political and military priesthood. Around a century later, St. Augustine (d. 430), called pagans 'cultured men' (*City of God*), and they resisted to such an extent that the people of the *pagus* were held up to city people as objects of scorn. From the negative comments they became subjected to, they were regarded as irreligious; that is, heathens, because they were seen as a body of people who refused to accept the fabricated religion imposed on them.

To support his creed, Constantine bribed people with gold and silver coins, and heaped honours and favours upon the habitués of his court, who naturally agreed with his wishes. He granted freedom to slaves, and gave gifts of clothing to peasants. This was the origin of 'Christian charity'. It was in larger cities where the new movement made its earliest gains in numbers, for there the civil powers were strongest and most evident. In eight months, hundreds were coerced to attend ecclesiastical gatherings, and the first copy of Constantine's *New Testimonies* was conveyed to those performances on 'a public carriage', personally approved by the emperor himself (*Life of Constantine*, Eusebius, N&PNF). He then had medals struck depicting himself as the 'Supreme Pontiff' and some exist today (*The Catholic Dictionary*, Addis and Arnold, 'Constantine', 1917). It was this same Constantine who drowned his wife in boiling water, butchered a young nephew, murdered two of his brothers-in-law, killed one of his sons, bled to death several men and women, and smothered to death an old Mithraic monk in a well. A century or so later, after St. Augustine failed to convert the populous in Africa, the Church turned to the policy of *Compelle intrare* ('Make them come in'), and force was truculently applied to build up congregations.

Amplifications to Christian texts

Constantine spent his declining years in effeminacy; he wore a blonde wig over his grey hair and his skirt glittered with jewels. His queer actions moved the occupants of the *pagus* villages to mordant irony. He died in 337 and the outgrowth of many now-called pagan beliefs into a new religious system brought many converts. Later Church writers made him 'the great champion of Christianity and it was given legal status as the religion of the Roman Empire' (*Encyclopedia of the Roman Empire,* M. Bunson, 1994, p. 86). Historical records reveal this to be incorrect, for it was 'self interest' (*Smaller Classical Dictionary,* 1910, p. 161) that led him to create Christianity, but it wasn't called Christianity until the 15th Century (Professor Edmond S. Bordeaux, Vatican archivist, *How The Great Pan Died,* Mille Meditations, MCMLXVIII, pp. 45-47). The disreputable character of the first Christian dynasty, the conduct of its clergy and the extraordinary corruption into which Constantine's new Church rapidly fell, are suppressed facts of history. Over the ensuing centuries, Constantine's *New Testimonies* were expanded upon, 'interpolations' (*Catholic Encyclopedia,* Farley Ed., vi, pp. 135-137; also, Pecci Ed., ii, pp. 121-122) were forged in, and other writings added.

For example, in 397, John 'golden-mouthed' Chrysostom (347-407), Patriarch of Constantinople, and before he was deposed and exiled by Empress Eudoxia, restructured the writings of Apollonius of Tyana, a First Century wandering sage, and made them part of the New Testimonies (*Secrets of the Christian Fathers,* Bishop J.W. Sergerus, 1685, reprint 1897, p. 99). The Latinized name for Apollonius was Paulus (*A Latin-English Dictionary,* J.T. White and J. E. Riddle, Ginn & Heath, Boston, 1880), and the Church today calls those writings, the Epistles of Paul. Apollonius's personal attendant, Damis, an

Assyrian scribe, is Demis in the New Testament (2 Tim. 4:10). The Church hierarchy knows the truth about the origin of its Epistles, for Cardinal Bembo (d. 1547), secretary to Pope Leo X (d. 1521), advised his associate, Cardinal Sadoleto to disregard them, saying, 'put away these trifles, for such absurdities do not become a man of dignity; they were introduced on the scene later by a sly voice from heaven' (*Cardinal Bembo, His Letters and Comments on Pope Leo X,* Reprint by A. L. Collins, London, 1842). The Church admits the Epistles are forgeries, saying they were 'greatly interpolated to lend weight to the personal views of their authors' (*Catholic Encyclopedia*, Farley Ed, vii, p. 645).

The collection of canonical (accepted) writings varied dramatically in different ages, and from shortly after the Council of Nicaea in 325 to the decree of the Council of Trent on March 15th, 1546, twenty-one books were added to the 'official' canon and ten deleted. No one list was unanimously accepted and fluctuations and variations in the New Testament showed how indifferent were the stories making-up Christian belief. For knowledge of Jesus Christ one is completely dependent on the New Testament yet the trustees of those writings formerly admit that they 'contain fictions, of which many who know are ashamed' (*Encyclopedia Britannica,* Ninth Edition, Vol. 10, 'Gospels'). The fundamental nature of the New Testament is devoid of every element of genuineness and archival records confirm it as works of falsehood knowingly deceptively presented to the laity. The Christian ministry bases the total of their assertions on narratives that their forefathers personally acknowledged were premeditated forgeries originally created to simply impress the rabble population of the time.

A major economic interest
But the problems of the New Testament don't end there. For a long time now the Church and biblical scholars have presented the Old Testament stories as factual events but this idea is now radically challenged, and it is generally accepted that there is very little archaeological or historical evidence to support the stories of the Bible as factual events. In 1992, and fuelled by the publication of a best-selling book by one of the world's foremost and most esteemed authorities on biblical archaeology, Professor Thomas L.

Thompson, the international media released headline news that 'the first ten books of the Old Testament are fiction'. Those books are Genesis, Exodus, Leviticus, Numbers, Deuteronomy, Joshua, Judges, Ruth, Samuel (1 and 2, combined as one) and Kings (1 and 2, combined as one). It was the findings of the erudite Professor Thompson (Associate Professor of the Marquette University in Milwaukee; currently, Chair of Old Testament Studies, University of Copenhagen; August, 2005) that stunned the religious world and revealed that the Bible is not a factual record of past events. The Professor's conclusions centred primarily on the city of Jerusalem, and his all-embracing findings have the backing of international experts, including the British Museum and Harvard University. Of what the world has been told about the Bible, he said this in his later book:

> The conclusions of those who educated the current generation and formed the foundation for almost all currently written books are no longer accepted or acceptable ... What was presented as the assured results of decades of science and scholarship amount to careless assertions.
>
> (*The Bible in History, How Writers Create a Past*, Professor Thomas L. Thompson, Pimlico, London, 2000)

The financial implications of this knowledge for the Church are profound and with the onset of a new generation, research on the Old Testament has entered a groundbreaking phase that has seen rapid change and innovation in our approach to biblical thinking. The lack of archaeological evidence to support the biblical stories is a serious challenge to both Judaism and Christianity. Professor Thompson provides this learned comment: 'We can now say with considerable confidence that the Bible is not a history of anyone's past' (*The Bible in History, How Writers Create a Past*, Professor Thomas L. Thompson, Pimlico, London, 2000). The arguments against the historicity of the Old Testament are now universally accepted by the academic and archaeological world, and to accept its data as history is a serious error. Thus, decades of archaeological results have revealed that Moses, Abraham, Isaac, Jacob, Solomon, David, and Saul never lived, nor is there any support for the occurrence of an Exodus of 600,000 men and their families. Noah's Ark has never been found, nor Solomon's golden Temple, and there is no verification for the existence of the twelve tribes of Israel, not even in the records of Herodotus (484-430 BC) who never mentioned the Israelites at all. It is just as strange that the 'great cities' that King Solomon was supposed to have built do not exist. The name of Solomon is not recorded by Plato, or by any earlier writer of standing, and, like Moses, appeared originally, and only, in the Bible. Professor Thompson neatly summed up the situation:

> Not only is the Bible's 'Israel' a literary fiction, but the Bible begins as a tradition already established: a stream of stories, song and philosophical reflection: collected, discussed and debated.
>
> (*The Bible in History, How Writers Create a Past* (Professor Thompson, Pimlico, London, 2000)

There is no historical evidence of primary Old Testament characters ever living or the events surrounding them existing in the records of antiquity, and they cover thousands of years. Professor Thompson adds (ibid, p. 99); 'The Bible's language is not an historical language' and concludes: 'The patriarchs of Genesis are not historical' (ibid, p. 190) adding, 'the point to grasp is that the Bible's stories of Saul, David and Solomon aren't about history at all, and to treat them as if they were history is to misunderstand them' (ibid, p. 206).

This rapidly brings us to our point. The bloodline given in the Old Testament descends from Kings David and Solomon and was subsequently used in the Gospels to include Jesus Christ. King David is mentioned 68 times in the New Testament and King Solomon is recorded 12 times. The genealogies in the Gospels say that Jesus Christ was a direct descendant of these intangible kings with his bloodline extending from 'Jesus to Joseph to … David the king. David but generated the Solomon' (Matt 1:6). Professor Thompson added, 'It is not historical realities that created the genealogies', meaning that the dynastic king lists in the Bible are fictitious, and many authors write of the artificial names as if they were historical. To say anybody descended from David is historically unsupportable and a recent spate of books claiming that Jesus Christ was of King David's bloodline has been outdated by archaeological circumstances. Certain authors try to make Jesus Christ heir apparent to the biblical royal house of David, but there was no Davidic succession in the history of the world. A bloodline from a so-called House of Judah never existed because Kings David and Solomon are fictitious characters. This is a truly historic political secret and nullifies claims of authors who accept a surface reading of the Bible as historic.

What does this mean financially? A Judaic Royal dynasty never existed in historical reality, and there is no royal bloodline emanating from a Davidic line because there was no Davidic line. The Gospels are made to say that Jesus Christ was the patrilineal descendant of kings David and Solomon … of Abraham, Jacob and Judah before that. Combined with the lack of archaeological discoveries and admitted Gospel forgeries, references to King David or King Solomon in the New Testament are fictitious and the inclusion of their names in a genealogy developed by the Church for Jesus Christ indicates an intention to deceive. The quest for an historical patriarchal period has proved unsuccessful and Professor Thompson completes the argument:

> There is no room for an historical United Monarchy, or for such kings as those presented in the biblical stories of Saul, David and Solomon. The early period in which the traditions have set their narratives is an imaginary world of long ago. It never existed as such. In the real world of our chronology, only a few dozen very small, scattered hamlets and villages supported farmers in all the Judean highlands. Altogether they numbered hardly more than two thousand persons.
>
> (*The Bible in History, How Writers Create a Past*, Professor Thomas L. Thompson, Pimlico, London, 2000, p. 206)

Professor Thompson added that 'my finding no place for David or his empire in my history of Israel created a scandal'. A final learned statement is drawn from the records of the venerable scholar, and might close our discussion in this chapter: 'The question today is whether the Bible in its stories is talking about the past at all' (p. 205). When the names of Saul, David, Solomon and Moses, and other mythical Old Testament characters are removed from the New Testament, the whole structure of Christianity collapses. The consequences are fatal to the pretence of Divine origin to the entire New Testament and expose Christian texts as having no special authority. This knowledge has a direct effect on the Jesus Christ story and adds another dimension to its fabricated development (*The Forged Origins of Christianity*, Tony Bushby, *Nexus New Times*, vol. 14, No., 4, June-July, 2007). For this reason alone, the story of Jesus Christ must been seen for what it is ... a politically inspired and purposely maintained money-making myth. The real point is that organized religions have a major economic interest in maintaining literal interpretation of both Old and New Testaments, for when the truth about what the Bible really is becomes fully absorbed by the public, the entire edifice of Christianity will be revealed as false.

CHAPTER 4

Pope St. Peter establishes a money-making precedent

Pope St. Peter was not a nice person. It is a little-known fact that, with blasting scorn, Peter is called 'Satan' on two separate occasions in the Gospels (Mt. 16:23; Mk. 8:33). With censure, he is described as materialistic, one who 'savourest not the things that be of God, but the things that be of men' (Mk. 8:33). He used his sword to cut off Malchus' ear (John 18:10), and murdered innocent people to expand his riches. This horrific deed is recorded in the 'Acts of the Apostles', the fifth book of the New Testament, and it will be shown that Church ownership of property, and its enslavement to wealth developed directly from the actions of the first pope. In a fit of anger, Pope St. Peter 'struck down dead' Ananius and his wife Sapphira for giving only half the proceeds of the sale of their property to his new religious movement (Acts of the Apostles, 5:1-11; Sinai, Alexandria, Syriacus, Cantabrigiensis (Bezae), Sarravianus, and Marchalianus Bibles). Those words, as written in the oldest available Bibles, were re-edited in modern New Testaments to read, 'fell down and died', the restructuring of the passage giving the impression that a super-natural power killed Ananius and his wife, thus scripturally releasing St. Peter from any blame in their deaths. For his cold-blooded murders, Peter was arrested and jailed by Herod (Acts of the Apostles, 12:3) but subsequently escaped. British Professor Foakes-Jackson, in his book, *Peter, Prince of the Apostles* (1927, p. 137), added this comment:

> In the oldest authorities [ancient Bibles], Catholic writers either ignore the original passages or cut out phrases from it and piece them together in such a fashion to show him [Pope St. Peter] in primitive innocence ... around the time of Chrysostom [c. 390], the clergy had begun to forge documents and

'traditions' in their own interests.

The seeds of earthly accruement of monies were planted by the first pope and they were to eventually grow into a huge mustard tree that was to obscure the light of Europe for around 1600 years. In priesthood thinking, a biblical precedent was set, and the Vatican's deep involvement with capitalism was high-jacked directly from those New Testament narratives (*The Criminal History of the Papacy*, Tony Bushby, *Nexus New Times*, vol., 14, Nos., 1, 2, and 3, 2007). This was confirmed during the papacy of Achilles Ambrose Damian Ratti who became Pope Pius XI in 1922 (born 1857; pope from 1922-1939). He ardently advocated 'Catholic Action', a form of ecclesiastical militancy that jointly involved the laity and the Catholic hierarchy in a masked political movement that attempted to alleviate matters detrimental to the interests of the Roman Church. Acting on Pius's directives, the Cardinal-Archbishop of Westminster and Catholic Archbishops and Bishops of England and Wales, issued a Joint Pastoral Letter that was published on 25th May, 1934 in *Universe,* a London Catholic weekly. The article was entitled, 'The Call to Action', and this revealing extract is relevant to Pope St. Peter's property dealings in the New Testament:

> In this week of Pentecost we may well remember that Catholic Action is, quite directly, the work of the Holy Spirit Himself ... the book of the Acts of the Apostles is truly the Gospel of the Holy Spirit ... simply the record of the first corporate Catholic Action by the Blessed Pope Peter, in all its pristine vigour, was the model for the activity of the Catholic people in all succeeding ages.

Thus, the reason Pope St. Peter murdered Ananius and Sapphira became the core internal objective of the entire monetary system of the Holy Mother Church, and recounting the New Testament event unmasks the real nature of the Christian religion. In clerical opinion, those narratives (Acts, 5:1-11) provide scriptural support for the priesthood to conveniently quote the relevant passage when challenged about the abandonment of the contrived apostolic tradition of poverty in their pursuit of Earthly riches. The kernel of wealth accumulation was planted in a writing that was later made canonical by the Vatican and from that period forward in Christian history the accretion of assets by churchmen was aggressively pursued. Using Pope St. Peter's slayings as our reference, it is possible to argue that Christianity was inspired into existence specifically to obtain riches for its hierarchy, and support for this opinion is found in the words of a later pope. A decade before his death in 1334, John XXII issued two decretals that condemned the whole Franciscan theory of evangelical poverty. They were *Ad Conditorem Canonum* (1322), and *Cum Inter Nonnullos* (1323) in which the pope asserted from Gospel narratives that Jesus Christ had owned property, therefore the popes could follow his lead. There is no verification of that in today's Gospels, and this papal assurance reveals that modern New Testaments are not identical with earlier versions. The example set by Pope St. Peter became a permanent characteristic of Christian development and subsequently caused irremediable harm to the spiritual interests of the world at large. The lordly assertion of papal power was inspired by the conviction that Peter had founded their Church he was the rock upon which the entire Christian structure must be based. It ignited revolts, provoked uprisings and crusades, caused the founding of the Church's sordid Inquisition, and promoted destructive papal wars which were to scar the Western world for centuries, almost up to our own days.

The attempt to stem priesthood wealth

Around 25 years after Constantine's death, his nephew, Flavius Claudius Julianus (332-363), today called Emperor Julian, was elected Emperor of the Roman Empire, and he immediately issued legislation against the promoters of his uncle's new religious movement in an attempt to curtail their grab for land and power. At that time, Julian was living in Paris, and soon after his election, he returned to London to restructure the Roman government of Briton. Under his reign, he made the leaders and supporters of the new Church ineligible to governmental offices and provided leniency for the populace who took violence in dealing with them. He wept when he heard of famous temples being overthrown; of the priests of Mithraism being killed and their property distributed to the new religious mob. He ordered the bishops to make full reparation for the damage they inflicted on sacred shrines and demanded the demolition of structures that had been built upon illegally seized lands of temples and synagogues (*The Arguments of the Emperor Julian*). Emperor Julian never went to Rome, and this was a common trait among emperors, preferring to rule from safer cities.

No money worries

Around the year 366, a group of presbyters led by Damasus (d. c. 384) left Constantinople for Rome with the intention of establishing a breakaway division of Constantine's new religious movement. There they encountered the Mithraic fathers, 'the chief of [them] the fathers, a sort of pope, who always lived at Rome, was called *Pater Patrum*', and this information is in the Church's own records (*Catholic Encyclopedia*, Farley Ed., pp, 402-404). Today the Church retrospectively calls them (and their predecessors), 'Christian popes', but that is a false claim. Some of the Mithraic fathers adopted the name of the Zoroastrian god, an excellent example being the Pseudo-Christian Pope Hormisdas (514-523), whose name is Persian for Ahura Mazda. Of him, the Church said 'his name presents an interesting problem' and added this curious comment: 'St. Hormisdas owes his canonization to an unofficial tradition' (*The Popes, A Concise Biographical History*, Burns and Oates, Publishers to the Holy See, London, 1964, p. 81). He and his 'considerable numbers of recalcitrant bishops' (ibid) were devotees of Ahura Mazda supporting Mithraic doctrine.

The first attempts by the Roman faction of the new religion to suppress the original Mithraic doctrine and make Constantine's combinative religion Rome's own, came with Emperor Theodosius (d. c. 395). His efforts failed, and the attempted repression of Mithraism was bitterly defended deep into the next century. The followers of Mithra continued to preserve their 1000-year-old belief, and in 436, an angry mob of Alexandrian devotees lynched George the Arian, bishop of the city, for attempting to build a Christian church over a Mithraic cave. The pure version of Mithraism continued unabated, and during the Fifth and Sixth Centuries, it merged with Constantine's invention, and later came to be called Christianity. Around that time, Bishop Victor of Tunnunum (d. c. 589), 'amended' the Gospels (*Chronica*, p. 89-90, Victor of Tunnunum, cited by Dr. Mills, Prolegom to R.V., p. 98), claiming that they had originally been written by 'idiots' (ibid).

The Roman presbyters subsequently elected a 'bishop of Rome' in competition to the 'bishop of Constantinople', and 'the people rebelled against the absurdity of two simultaneous popes' (*The Popes, A Concise Biographical History*, Burns and Oates, Publishers to the Holy See, London, 1964, p. 70; published under the Imprimatur of Georgius L. Craven). The cast-off purple togas and worn-out shoes of the Roman emperors' became the highly-esteemed clothing of the bishops of Rome.

> He strutted in the streets feigning holiness and greatness ... never did you see a peacock flirting its gaudy feathers on a summer's day with more ostentatious pride than does the arrogant bishop of Rome.
>
> (*Fourth Century Rumors About Christ*, P. M. Cozzia-Leone, Archives de Louvre, 1857)

The popes of today do the same thing. Lesser presbyters wore a 'toga picta' bearing a red stripe, and their subordinates dressed in black or dark togas (ibid).

These events take us to the beginning of the Fifth Century and the undertakings of Pope Innocent I (401-417) to enforce papal property seizures in the West. His entire pontificate was spent in securing or asserting the supremacy of his developing See, and, from the safety of his palace in Ravenna, he ordered his troops to seize treasures from the wealthy for his personal collection (*The Popes and their Church*, Dr. Joseph McCabe, Rector of Buckingham College; Watts and Co., London, 1918). Pope Innocent, whose grade of intelligence was such that he wept when his military commander told him that 'Rome had been taken' (in 410, under Alaric), thinking that his pet bantam rooster of that name had been stolen (*A History of the Popes*, Dr. Joseph McCabe, Rector of Buckingham College; d. 1955; C. A. Watts and Co, London, Book 1).

The coffers of the rich

The trade of a priest, especially after he had purchased his bishopric, was an exceedingly lucrative one. Marcellinus Ammianus (c. 330-400), the famous Roman historian and military veteran, speaks with deep scorn of perfumed and silk-clad bishops, of parasitic monks, of vulgarly rich banquets at which '30 secretaries' stand by the pope and tell him the weight or cost of the rare fish or game, of gold-dust strewn upon the marble floors, and so on. The history which has Ammianus has left us is frequently quoted as a witness to the degenerate nature of the Christian hierarchy, and his descriptions of the lifestyle of the higher clergy reflects the group we would call today, 'the jet set'. St. Jerome (347-420), Italian scholar and self-confessed transvestite (*De Viris Illustribus*, 135, D. Vallarsi trans., Verona, 1734-42), adds to our understanding of the curious nature of himself and the priesthood of his time, revealing that they had no understanding of theology:

> One who yesterday was a catechumen (beginner or new convert) is today a bishop; another moves overnight from the amphitheatre to the church; a man who spent the evenings in the circus stands next morning at the altar; and another who was recently a patron of the stage is now the dedicator of virgins ... they gain admission to aristocratic houses and deceive silly women ... they seek ordination simply to see women more freely. They [the priesthood] think of nothing but their clothes, use scent, and smooth out the creases in their boots. They curl their hair with tongs, their fingers glitter with gold rings ... they are bridegrooms rather than clergy'.
>
> (*The Letters of Jerome*, Library of the Fathers, The Nicene and Post-Nicene Fathers, cited as N&PNF; expanded upon in *The Bible Fraud*, Tony Bushby, Joshua Books, Australia, 2001)

In the letters that Jerome writes to these ladies, he warns them that the Roman Church, in clergy and laity, is generally and monstrously corrupt (ibid, *The Letters of Jerome*). He is frank to the point of coarseness. Typical is his letter to the aristocratic maid, Eustochium (Ep. XXII), in which there is not one class of the Christian community which he does not warn her to avoid. However, for the 'bridegrooms' were many wealthy widows dressed in 'red cloaks, with fat bodies, a file of eunuchs walking in front; they have not so much lost husbands as seek them. They fill their houses with guests and flatterers. The clergy ... kiss these ladies on the forehead and putting forth their hands as though to bless, cozen money for their visits ... after a vast supper, these ladies retire to bed with the clergymen for intimacy' (ibid).

Late in the Third Century, Marcellinus Ammianus recorded a further understanding of the nature of the developing Christian priesthood. He called them 'flabby old rogues', and said that once in office ...

> ... they are free from money worries, enriched by offerings from women, riding in carriages, dressing splendidly, feasting luxuriously ... they are never wearied by the sensations of pleasure and delight ... their banquets are better than imperial ones ... they say that they have a divine warrant to fleece their flocks as much as they can, and to pardon one another when they sin ... they are secret thieves who draw gold from the coffers of the rich, and extract silver and coppers even from the rags of the most wretched beggars'.
>
> (*Ammianus,* xxii. 5, O'Neill's Trans, 1898)

More importantly, what concerns us here is that the financial ambitions of the popes to control the income of the West became clearly formulated around this time, and Pope Innocent's successors, Zosimus (d. 418) and Boniface I (d. 422), followed his lead. The temper of the popes hardened, and by the middle of the Fifth Century they were exercising the 'power of the sword' (ibid) in forcibly acquiring property, maintaining the legal right given to them by Emperor Constantine around a century earlier. Furthermore, the popes believed that anybody opposing what was written in Constantine's *New Testimonies* were to be put to death, a demand that is still today a normal and emphatic part of Canon Law (*Public Church Law*), and taught in Catholic Universities.

CHAPTER 5

The cult of the Blessed St. Peter

Around the year 442 the priesthood devised an extraordinary money-making scheme, one predestined to have profound repercussions upon the development of Christianity. The record of this enterprising connivance is found in the writings of Salvianus (d. 456), a distinguished historian of Marseilles, who wrote an open letter to the Church of Rome that now forms part of a book called, *On God's Government* (*On God's Government,* iii, 9, Migne Collection, vol. 53). Salvianus was no cloistered monk or overheated and unbalanced fanatic. For the age he was a writer of cultural distinction, and, living in Marseilles, he was well placed to know the extensive world that he surveys. The writings of Salvianus are numerous and he referred to the 'turpitude of morals' (vileness of principle, words or actions) of the churchmen and their followers. He records that Pope Leo the Great (390-461; pope from 440-461) ordered the construction of a stone enclosure in a cemetery that more than 1000 years later (1506) became the site for the commencement of the building of the largest and most splendid structure in Christendom, St. Peter's Basilica. The workmen covered their crude structure with timber planks and 'town-criers in bright attire' were dispatched to spread the news that the burial place of the Turn-key of Heaven, the Blessed St. Peter, had been found in the Eternal City. The pope celebrated the 'discovery' by naming the 'tomb', *Memoria* (*Secrets of the Christian Fathers,* Bishop J. W. Sergerus, 1685, reprint 1897, p. 169), and renamed Rome, the 'Pardon of Peter' by which it was known for many centuries (ibid, p. 225).

However, Peter never went to Rome and this information has been suppressed by the Holy Mother Church by 'official fabrication of her history'

(*Diderot's Encyclopedia*, 1759). In stark contrast, Bishop Eusebius claimed that Peter died in Britannia or Scotland in 334 (*Metaphrastes ad 29 Junii, Menaloggi Graeceorum*), and archaeological evidence confirms his record. A marble headstone was discovered at Whithorn in Lincoln, and is now called the 'Peter Stone'. It is a rough pillar, around four feet high and fifteen inches wide. An inscription in despoiled Roman capitals reads:

HICIACENT
LOE (VS) S (ANC)
TISACER
DOTES (T)
SIMEON PETRI

The Bishop of Edinburgh, John Dowden, D.D (c. 1894), transcribed these words into English, 'In this place lies *sacerdotes*, Simon Peter', piously adding that '*sacerdotes* may have meant bishop' (*Stuart's Sculptured Stones of Scotland*, pre-1894). It is relevant in our discussion that St. Ninian (c. 355-432), a British presbyter, built a strange little temple at Whithorn shortly after he returned from Rome in 390, and it subsequently gave its name, Candida Casa, or White House, to the bishopric. Thus, according to the records of Bishop Eusebius, Pope St. Peter was buried somewhere in the British Isles, not Rome, and whatever the papal 'marketing division' say about his life, no evidence subsists for him ever being anywhere near Rome; not even in the testimony of Roman historians, Tacitus (c. 56-126) and Gaius Suetonius (70-140). Just as importantly, there was no Christianity in Rome until it arrived from Constantinople with Damasus around 380, some 50 years after Eusebius's dating of St. Peter's death. An embarrassing fact for the Church that is rarely discussed is the existence of a narrative in older versions of the New Testament revealing that Pope St. Peter was a married man with at least two children, a boy and a girl. His wife was Jotape, an Anglethorn, and 'she accompanied him everywhere' (1 Cor 9:4-5; Luke 4:38, Latin Vulgate, trans. R. Challoner; Donay; 1609; 1749, First Revision).

Increasing revenue

With the ploy of a fabricated tomb for St. Peter in Rome, a cult developed and it demanded that believer's of the Church's story journey to Rome and offer prayers to the Blessed Peter at his fake final resting place. Beginning with the English and the Scots, pilgrims from deeply naïve countries were cajoled to travel to Rome, and the 'tomb discovery' provided the Church with a tremendous source of revenue. Roman priests spread a rumour saying that St. Serf, a Seventh Century Scottish saint, heard about the discovery of the tomb and immediately set off to pay his reverential respects. As he approached the coast of Britain, the sea dried up, and he and his 7,000,000 devoted companions crossed to France on dry ground. Shades of Moses! The subjects of the popes were the most degraded and debased people in Europe, ignorant, superstitious and semi-civilized, 'squalid beggars pilfering their beseeched offerings' (*Chronica*, Victor of Tunnunum (c. 589), cited by Dr. Mills, Prolegom to R.V., p. 93), and in this aspect the papacy has had for centuries an open field. Thus, the tradition of pilgrimages was developed (*Pilgrimage to Rome*, Rev. Seymour, 1832), and in addition to encouraging the belief that Peter's tomb was in Rome, the bishops cultivated the myth with undiminished eagerness. This they did, not as upholders of a devout legend, but as skillful promoters of a growing cult that had concrete and far-reaching objectives. Its magnification brought it immense authority, and, with it, money. Today we would call it by the more accurate and prosaic name of Tourism.

That is how pilgrimages to Rome were initiated, later supported mainly, and curiously, by Anglo-Saxons. Popes of the day actively promoted pilgrimages to the 'tomb', and from the start they showed a special predilection for the richest and most powerful personages of the times; that is, individuals who could give them costly presents, land and power. To quote a typical example, Pope Leo the Great records in one of his 173 extant letters how, after 'Peter had spoken' to him from the tomb, 'Emperor Valentinian III (c. 419-455) and his family regularly performed devotions at the tomb, 'such practices yielding a useful respect for the apostle's successors' to whom they offered costly presents and the tenure of land' (*Leo's Tome*; a doctrinal letter). The Church, far from discouraging the dishonest practices, gave its approval.

Witness, for example, the words of St. Gregory of Tours (538-594), who, in his *De Gloria Martyrum*, provided a detailed description of the ceremony he devised in order for the faithful to 'speak' with the Prince of Apostles. The pilgrim was told to kneel down upon the tomb and open a wooden trap door. Then, he inserted his head into the hole, after which, still remaining in that posture, revealed in a loud voice the object of his visit to the saint. Offerings of money were then thrown into the tomb, followed by veneration and obeisance that were offered to St. Peter's successor, the pope. The religious and even political results of this practice upon deeply ignorant nations like the Anglo-Saxons and the Franks who imitated them, can easily be imagined. The well-calculated policy of this cult, once widely established, yielded valuable results for the popes, who were quick to turn the prestige gained into a powerful instrument by which to obtain the submission of men of low or high rank, both in the spiritual and in secular fields (*Pilgrimage to Rome*, Rev. Seymour, 1832). In 1506, construction of a substantial and sumptuous temple taking more than a century to build was commenced near the same site. It is a temple of art, not a church, and it exhibits all the wonders and proportions of the highest efforts of architecture. In 1626, it was sanctified and then dedicated to the murderous Pope St. Peter, not to the worship of God. In 1851, Reverend John Hughes, the Roman Catholic Bishop of New York, conducted his own pilgrimage to St. Peter's and expressed dismay, saying, 'There is no Bible there on its altars'.

Worldly ambition
Around that same time, a strange document called the *Liberian Catalogue* appeared, and it purported to record a lineage of popes 'from St. Peter to Pope Liberius' (366). This was a priesthood forgery, designed to give credence to the Church's claim of an earlier foundation. Seeking to push the origins of uniformity as close as possible to the First Century, this document, forged under the name of Eusebius, drew up a running list of earlier bishops that purported to trace a line back to Mark, and so to Peter. In the sequence of names, however, invented predecessors were consciously falsified into the list and those 'legendary' names were termed by the Church a scribal 'slip' by Eusebius (*Catholic Encyclopedia*, Farley Ed., iv, p. 706), but they were

subsequently transformed into a series of monarchical bishops who never lived in actual history. Catholic historian, Bishop Louis Dupin (d. c. 1725), wrote: 'sadly, the catalogues of Bishop Eusebius are forgeries or inventions of later times' (*De Antiqua Ecclesiae Disciplina,* Bishop Lewis Dupin (*Folio,* Paris, 1686). Various attempts were later made to substantiate the fabricated list but the Church confessed that the genealogy attributed to Eusebius 'had no precise status and could not be deemed trustworthy' (*Annales Ecclesiastici,* tome vi, Fol. Antwerp, 1597, Cardinal Caesar Baronius). By such forged documents does the Church claim 'apostolic succession', and clerical insiders know the assertion is false.

Investigation of the Church's own records shows that the priesthood's claim of a continuous ministerial succession from apostles of Jesus is false, because there were no apostles, and no Jesus Christ until Constantine created the concept at Nicaea in the Fourth Century. Thus, confessed forgery and fraud taint to the core the 'unauthentic' record of Church 'histories', and reveal that the 'successors' of Pope St. Peter are papal fabrications (*The Crucifixion of Truth,* Tony Bushby, Joshua Books, 2004). In the early 1940's, Pope Pius XII (1939-1958) ordered an ancient cemetery under St. Peter's basilica to be scientifically excavated and the team found a series of 21 mausolea facing southward onto a Roman street. The excavations resulted NOT in the discovery of Peter's bones, as claimed by Pope Paul VI on the 26th June 1965, but as the spot designated by churchmen in the 16th Century to be his First Century resting place. Opponents argue that Peter, supposedly crucified as a convicted criminal, was not entitled to burial, but more importantly, Peter never went anywhere near Rome. In these days, should Peter come back to earth and continue to advocate circumcision, the strangulation of bullocks, and the strict observance of the Jewish ceremonial, he would not be permitted to preach in any Christian church, Catholic or Protestant.

The first Catholic Balance Sheet
In the same miserable vein as Pope Leo, Pope Gregory, who also called himself 'Great' (590-604), wrote numerous letters to the vicious and murderous Frankish Queen Brunhilde (567-613), praising her 'devout mind',

saying that she was 'filled with the piety of heavenly grace'. His letters would completely deceive us about the truth of her life if we had not available the historical records that have been fully documented. William Lecky (1838-1903), one of the greatest and most unbiased historians of the 19th Century, fills several pages in one of his books, *The History of the Franks*, with the most revolting details of her tortures, murders, adulteries, thefts, and of every species of corruption. He described her as the 'worst sovereign in history' (ibid), adding that she 'found flatterers or agents in ecclesiastics' (ibid), the pope being one of them. Gregory offered her remission of her sins if she visited the tomb of St. Peter, saying, 'the most Blessed Peter, Prince of the Apostles ... will cause thee to appear pure of all stain before the judge everlasting by granting him which he asked of her' (St. Gregory, Letters, vii, 5, 50, 65 etc.). That was the gift of money, real estate and investitures which she gave to the pope, and they yielded abundant revenues to the Church, a practice that became the papal way of life in upcoming centuries. Here we have documentary evidence in the pope's own hand-writing by which we may judge the personality of a head of the Roman Church. In just 14 years as pope, Gregory became Europe's richest man and its largest slave-holder. In fact, he has armies of slaves working his estates and the few phrases, cut out of their context in which apologists make him disapprove of the institution of slavery, are taken from letters in which he merely gives freedom to a few old slaves who have inherited money and promised to leave it to his Church.

He preached that the end of the world was at hand and induced large numbers of nobles to leave their estates to his Church, since their sons would have no use for them. He farmed and ruled immense territories, and was as shrewd in material matters as he had been credulous in religion. In his letters, he regularly confesses to being 'a miserable sinner', and when the steward of his great estate in Sicily sent him a horse and five asses, he angrily replied: 'I cannot ride the horse because it is a wretched nag, and I cannot ride the asses because they are asses' (II, 32). We will, however, attribute this attitude not to pride, but to the poisonous influence of papal pretensions. He sent a nobleman a necklace made from old chains, fraudulently alleging that it was the very one which had fettered St. Peter in prison, and to wear it at his throat 'which is like as if he were wearing the chains of St. Peter himself'. He added that 'these chains, which have lain across and around the neck of the most Blessed Apostle Peter, shall unloose thee for ever from thy sins'. The gift, of course, was not a free one, 'it cost money, land, and gold' (*Vita Bonifacii*, 14, Willibald; also *Liber Pontificalis*). Not content with this, Pope Gregory had sets of false keys made and sent to aristocratic people as being 'the original keys of St. Peter which remit sins', and the recipients paid in cash or with costly presents for such an honour (St. Gregory, Letters 12-17). Thus, keys became a fundamental element in the Arms of the Vatican known today.

© Rome Picture Library, 1934

Arms of the Vatican.

Under the pontificate of Gregory the Great, the Church accepted valuables in exchange for the sale of future burial sites near the 'tomb' of the Blessed Peter and also charged fees for the induction of clerics into office, for the investment of a bishop, for the drawing up of documents, and so on. These payments invariably involved earthly treasures of money, silver and gold, or deeds of real estate. At that time, the better-paid clerical offices were bought and sold in every country, and they attracted the sons of the new 'nobility'. 'Barbarians who barely abjured Odin', says French historian Bon Louis Henri Martin (1810-83), speaking of his own country at this period in time, 'installed themselves with their wives, soldiers, and hunting dogs in the episcopal palaces' (*History of France*, 15 vols. 1836). Bishops and priests were actively selling Church assets for personal gain and in repeated cases they were accused by the populous of profiteering from gifts given by the public. After having been told of how a priest had secretly sold two silver chalices and two candelabra to a Jew, Pope Gregory issued a series of ordinances decreeing that each Christian community make a written inventory of all its sacred vessels, land and buildings, and send it to him. He demanded precise details of how money gifted to the

Church was being spent, and scrutinized the book-keeping as it came to him. He issued stern prohibitions against 'hidden balances of the Greek sort' (St. Gregory, Letter 47) that led to the production of a Church Balance Sheet of sorts (Note: this statement is extracted from one of Pope Gregory's extant letters, of which there are many).

It is at this time in the history of Catholicism that we see for the first time a papal record of the wealth of the Holy Mother Church. The result was stunning for it showed a surprised Pope Gregory how his Church owned landed property in Sicily, Gaul, Spain, the Balkan lands, the Near East and even many parts of Africa. These properties included not only lands and farms, but also whole towns. St. Peter's Patrimony, as it began to be called, owned Syracuse and Palermo, besides numerous rich estates in Sicily, Southern Italy, Apulia, Calabria and even Gallipoli, although in ruins. The estates in Campania and those of Naples and the Isle of Capri were all producing large revenues. All in all, the Church in Pope Gregory's time owned 23 estates, whose total area comprised of hundreds of square miles, with combined incoming revenues of over a million dollars a year, a colossal sum at that period (*The Vatican Billions,* Baron Avro Manhattan, Paravision Books, London, 1972). These properties were selfishly bequeathed to St. Peter by fearful people in hope of full remission of their earthly sins by the benefactor, not as donations to the Church (*Secrets of the Christian Fathers,* Roman Bishop Joseph W. Sergerus, d. c. 1701). The fact of the matter was that Pope Gregory, as successor of Pope St. Peter was ruling an establishment that owned vast real estate properties and riches of all kind, bestowed upon a dead Arab called Simon of Petra. Less than 300 years after the death of Emperor Constantine, the Church had turned itself into one of the largest land owners of the West. The Patrimony, not a modest sum of liquid money, but the accumulated fortune of a rich Church was destined to become even richer in the centuries ahead.

CHAPTER 6

The offensive that yielded the papacy 1800 square miles of land

The progressive amassment of worldly riches and the tide of corruption continued unabated ... indeed, it gathered momentum, and Pope Gregory had his eye on vast tracts of land in Britain. In June 596 he dispatched 40 'military priests' from Rome to Britain under the leadership of an Italian prelate who designated himself, Augustine (d. 604). His Welsh name was Awstin and he is sometimes recorded as Austin, which, like many matters associated with biblical research, creates confusion. The original purpose of Augustine's mission was 'to bring the Culdee Church to the observance of the Roman Easter' (*Encyclopedia Britannica,* Vol. 11, 1797 Ed.; also, Cumbrian Abbey records, Section 67, part 9), it being an historic fact that some 600 years after the canonical time of the death of the Gospel Jesus Christ, the scriptures and preaching of the British Church did not embrace crucifixion and resurrection in its dogma. The Culdee leaders immediately warned the pope to mind his own business and called him 'an old fool' (extract from one of Gregory's extant letters). The Celtic bishops then received this bitter threat from the pope via Augustine; 'If ye will not have peace with the brethren, ye shall have war from your enemies; and if you will not preach our way of life to the English, ye shall suffer the punishment of death at our hands' (*Catholic Encyclopedia,* Farley Ed., v, pp. 83-4).

The modern Church opined that, 'in the long run it was Gregory's mission to England that had the most momentous consequences of all of his pontificate' (*The Popes, A Concise Biographical History*, Burns and Oates, Publishers to the Holy See, London, 1964, p. 111; published under the Imprimatur of Georgius L. Craven), but did not elaborate upon the true nature of those consequences. In fact, the Christian world was defrauded of historical truth, for in the following year, Pope Gregory, 'the richest man in Europe' (*A History of the Popes*, Dr. Joseph McCabe, Rector of Buckingham College; p. 77; d. 1955; C. A. Watts and Co, London), denounced members of the British Culdee Church as heretics and ordered an armed invasion against them. However, he died suddenly in March 604 and his successors, Sabinian (d. 606), and then Boniface III (d. 607), continued the military build-up, and we should not fail to take into account the fierce spirit of the age. Eventually, under the direction of Pope Boniface IV in 612 (d. 615), the militia of Jesus Christ (still 'Hesus Krishna' at that time) arrived in Britain. The Church admits that Boniface IV 'had dealings with the British Church' (ibid) but carefully avoids revealing the character of those 'dealings'. St. Augustine's threat was subsequently fulfilled 'in the butchery of the Bangor monks at the hands of Aethelfrid the Destroyer at the great battle won by him at Chester in 613' (*Catholic Encyclopedia*, Farley Ed., v, p. 84). It is a notorious fact of Christian history that the Roman Church 'extended its authority over the native British Church by force of arms' (*Encyclopedia Britannica*, 1797 Ed; also Cumbrian Abbey records), and the vehemence of the Catholic massacre of the celebrated monastery of Bangor by the Menai Straits in Northern Wales resulted in the slaughter of 1200 unarmed Culdee monks. British monastic properties were seized by the Holy Mother Church and the offensive 'yielded the papacy about 1800 square miles of land and revenue of about £2,000,000' (*A History of the Popes*, Dr. Joseph McCabe, Rector of Buckingham College; d. 1955; C. A. Watts and Co, London, p. 40; also, *Memorials of Bangor*, Bishop Walcott, 1860).

This information is profound, for suddenly the Catholic claim of a peaceful spreading of its 'Gospel' into Britain becomes historically untrue. Professor Geoffrey Dudley Smith, in his book, *The Religion of Ancient Britain* (1898, p. 168), revealed that during the attempted takeover of the British Church and its income-producing estates, Roman military priests burnt no fewer than 130 volumes of writings 'esteemed by the Culdees' (ibid) that related to their origins and beliefs. Under King Oswy in 664, the yoke of Rome finally imposed itself on the British people and it wasn't until the reign of Queen Elizabeth I nine centuries later (1533-1603) that the revolt against papal intrusion into Britain was fully reversed. The reason for this was that the Roman Church paganised Britain with its lineal successors of the augers, the curiones, the sodales, and the virgines vestales of earlier centuries. During those centuries, popes appointed Italian and French cardinals to rich benefices in England, to canonries or bishoprics which they never visited, but lived riotous life-styles from the incomes derived, collected by their appointed associates, usually family members. In 1351, the aggression of the Roman Church towards the British Church caused the English Parliament to pass the Statute of Provisors, declaring all papal nominations in England null and void. In these views, the mass of the populous concurred, and of the desire to restrict the popes' growing usurpation of the British Church, John Wycliffe (c. 1329-1384), was an ardent spokesman. Wycliffe, an Oxford professor and theologian, was a great thinker of the time, though he expressed his thoughts in crabbed Latin prose, which hides his meaning from almost all who read. While speculating on the problems of Christian theology he was advancing along the path of religious freedom. Wycliffe was critical of not only the Roman bishops, but also of worldly English bishops whose great wealth, he said, should be used to increase the stipends of the lesser clergy, or too relieve the poor.

Early in the 1380's Wycliffe produced the first-known handwritten English-language edition of the Bible, translated from a corrupted Latin Vulgate, which was the only source-text available to him. He openly challenged the 'barren foolishness of the Eucharist' (*Diderot's Encyclopedia*, 1759), the Roman Catholic theory on the change of bread and wine at Communion into the body and blood of a non-existent Jesus Christ, and demanded an explanation for the extraordinary statement that Pope Boniface VIII (1234-1303) made at his impeachment trial:

> There was no Jesus Christ and the Eucharist is just flour and water. Mary was no more a virgin than my own mother, and there is no more harm in adultery than in rubbing your hands together.

(*A History of the Popes*, Dr. Joseph McCabe, Rector of Buckingham College; d. 1955; C. A. Watts and Co, London; also; *The Criminal History of the Papacy*, Tony Bushby, in *Nexus New Times*, vol., 14, No. 2, February-March, 2007, part

2, p. 44).

From that and similar papal pronouncements it is concluded that Christianity was created from premeditated frauds, a plethora of fake and forged documents and books, fictitious Gospels, suppression of early Church records (*Encyclopedia Biblica*, Adam & Charles Black, London, 1899), mass murder of opponents, and is sustained today by false claims and a deceptive presentation of the facts.

Wycliffe challenged the historicity of a virgin birth and a resurrection (*The New History of Great Britain*, R. B. Mowat, Oxford University Press, England, 1923, p. 143), and relentlessly attacked mounting papal decadence. Forty-four years after his death, Pope Martin V (b. 1368; pope from 1417-1431) was so infuriated with the continuing attack on Catholic dogma that developed from Wycliffe's challenge, he ordered his bones dug up, crushed, and scattered in the River Swift. The pope's actions reflect the vagary of an unbalanced mind, riddled with hate and bitterness, and hardly compatible with sanity.

CHAPTER 7

A celestial letter from St. Peter

After the death of Pope Boniface IV in 615, the process of adding more riches to the Church's already vast accumulation went on unabated for another 100 years or so, and by the end of the Seventh Century, the material holdings around Rome and in Naples, Calabria, and Sicily had become immense. The annual revenues from Calabria and Sicily that flowed into the 'Holy See' (that is, 'the holy seat' of St. Peter) amounted to more than 35,000 gold florins annually, but then, to the horror of succeeding popes, the tide turned. In the Eighth Century, when the papacy had so much prosperity that it did not know what it owned, the semi-converted Slavs started to despoil St. Peter's Patrimony, claiming they were doing so in the name of God, *their* God. They called him Allah, telling popes and their subjects, while taking away their possessions, or rather the possessions of their papal masters, that in addition to having changed the landlord they had better also change their religion ... which the vast majority of simple-minded did. In this manner, whole papal dominions were lost and that included Dalmatia, Istria, Spain, the South of France, and the whole of North Africa. To all this Providence, or rather human greed, insult was added to injury when successive Byzantine emperors followed suit and deprived Peter's Patrimony of its vast estates in Sicily, Sardinia, Calabria and Corsica. Within the next few decades, the Holy Fathers had been robbed of such immense estates that their former boundless dominion was eventually reduced to just central Italy, not far away, relatively speaking, from Rome. Notwithstanding such a shrinking of their possessions, the worst devils of all, the Lombards of North Italy, set out to rob the last estate of the Blessed Peter.

What happened next is unbelievable, and its concept and subsequent outcome has no equivalent in the pages of history. As a direct result of a series of forged papal documents, the wealth and power of the Holy Mother Church was soon to dramatically expand and put her on the road to economic benefits so massive as to stagger the human belief system. Attention is now drawn to a remarkable historic papal event that seems to have escaped the notice of Catholic writers. This episode in the development of the Christian Church involves another pope whose 'exact status in the list of popes has never been authoritatively determined' (*The Popes, A Concise Biographical History*, Burns and Oates, Publishers to the Holy See, London, 1964, p. 128). He was Stephen III (IV?) (768-772), and his 'election was followed by an appalling massacre among the supporters of the anti-popes ... it is unlikely that the new pope had any responsibility ... not surprisingly Stephen III has never been counted amongst the ornaments of the Roman Church' (ibid). The Lombards were about to invade when Pope Stephen invoked the help of none other than St. Peter himself. He had the Blessed Peter write in a letter in his own hand, a miraculous appeal direct from Heaven, to the gruff and superstitious Pepin the Short (715-768), king of Italy (King of the Franks). Pope Stephen, amidst great fanfare, sent the celestial letter by a Papal Envoy mounted on a splendidly-caparisoned white horse to be read out to King Pepin. The letter, written in gold on vellum commanded (in summary) Pepin to ...

> ... come ye to the aid of the Roman people, who have been entrusted to me by God. And I, on the Day of Judgment, shall prepare for you a splendid dwelling place in the Kingdom of God ... until that day you shall be the Father of Rome.

(Migne collection of the Latin Fathers, Vol. LXXXIX, col. 1004)

The duped Pepin went down on his knees when the Papal Envoy vouched for the authenticity of St. Peter's signature. How had the letter reached earth, asked King Pepin? The Papal Envoy solemnly explained that the Blessed Peter personally came down from Heaven and handed the letter to his successor, Pope Stephen. The mental limitations of the time are thus shown, and the type of thinking to which we are confronted is that of simpletons.

Devout French Church historian, Claude Fleury (1640-1723), in his famous *Historia Ecclesiastica* (Bk. 17; 43, 20 vols., 1691-1720) could not contain his indignation at the celestial letter, which he bluntly declared 'an unexampled pretense ... in a system of lying wonders', but the fact remained that the letter had the desired effect, and King Pepin defeated the rapacious Lombards in battle. Since they had originally wished to rob the lands of St. Peter, Pepin, besides donating to the pope what he had just preserved and recovered, he added; the Governorship of Ravenna, the Duchy of Rome, the Exarchate, and the Pentapolis, as the surrounding district was then called (*The Vatican Billions*, Baron Avro Manhattan, Paravision Books, London, 1972, p. 28). The pope then conferred on Pepin the title, *Patricus Romanus*, 'Father of Rome'. Thus, the pope obtained this formable increase in worldly possessions and prestige by duping an illiterate monarch and the temporal power of the Holy Father expanded by the deception. These lands added up to a considerable amount of territory encompassing 23 Italian cities, hundreds of villages, estates, castles, forts, and farms ... henceforth owned by ongoing representatives of St. Peter on Earth, the popes. The papacy was now richer than it had been even in the days of Gregory the Great, and the baneful consequences of this enrichment at once became apparent.

The true nature of the Holy Fathers
Those who affect to doubt whether the pope really intended to deceive the King should not forget that the papal office has an unparalleled record of corruption and criminality, and the true history of the popes is one of scandals, cruelty, debauchery, reigns of terror, warfare, and moral depravity. It is deeply-stained in the production of false documents, and today centuries of intrinsic forgeries are used by the Church as the very essence of its projections. Its greatest fraud is revealed in the next chapter, but of the 'celestial letter', erudite Dr. Paul L. Williams, added a summary comment. Dr. Williams, a consultant to the FBI and author of several books including *Everything You Always Wanted to Know about the Catholic Church But Were Afraid to Ask for Fear of Excommunication*, and *The Complete Idiot's Guide to the Crusades*, has taught religion and philosophy at the University of Scranton and Wilkes

University, and this is what he said:

> The worldly power of the Roman Church was greatly enhanced by the famous donation of Pepin the Short in 766. In exchange for the exalted title of *Patricus Romanus* (Father of Rome), Pepin, the King of the Franks, gave to the Holy See all of the Italian cities he had conquered from the Lombards along with all their territories. In this way, Pope Stephen received enormous tracts of land. One, comprising 4,542 square miles, centered about Ravenna. It was later called the Romagna. The other, consisting of 3,692 square miles, lay below Ravenna and stretched into southern and central Italy. It became known as the March of Ancona. The Holy Father got one of the greatest real estate deals in human history. For a mere title, he had come to possess almost all of modern Italy.
>
> (*The Vatican Exposed*, Dr. Paul L. Williams, Prometheus Books, New York, 2003, p. 13)

Yet here we touch only the lighter fringe of the dark story of the making of the papacy, and note just how superficial is the Christianity of the popes. The success of the heavenly missive spurred its schemers to new efforts and around that time another infamous Christian deception was introduced to the world. It took the form of a large ornate timber chair that was passed off as the very chair upon which St. Peter sat, a further inducement to Pepin and his successors to grant popes their protection and additional property if need be. The incentive was a powerful one, since a king of the Franks, if crowned sitting on the Chair of St. Peter would be invested with an authority surpassing that of any other temporal ruler ... except the pope. The fake chair of St. Peter was later embossed in gold, and it became one of the most precious relics of the Church. Upon instructions from Pope Alexander VII (1655-1667), it was exhibited inside an ornate bronze structure specially designed and built by Italian sculptor Gian Lorenzo Bernini (1598-1680). The propaganda value of the chair was immense, and it was displayed in Rome until modern times as the true chair of the Prince of Apostles.

In the late 1960s, its falsity was exposed after it was analyzed by a commission of scientists. Following carbon 14 and other radiological tests, they confirmed that the chair belonged to around the year 800, the time of

Pepin and Charlemagne. In 1970, Pope Paul VI (1897-1978; Giovanni Battista Montini), faced a dilemma … should he apologize for a priesthood fraud that drew vast revenues from the faithful pilgrims for more than 1000 years, or should he remain silent. Should he put the chair back in St. Peter's Basilica, or display it in the Vatican Museum? That was a personal problem of a pope of the 20th Century, but those from the Eighth to the 19th Centuries had been concerned only with magnifying the cult of the Blessed Peter, and so enhance their power and wealth.

CHAPTER 8

The great papal forgery

The story of the existence of a Christian religion in the Roman Church before the time of Constantine has been grossly and deliberately falsified, and major ecclesiastical forgeries, and counter-forgeries, by means of which this was done, begin about the period we have now reached. Two of them, the *Acts of the Martyrs* and *Lives of the Saints* are 'impudent fabrications, perpetrated by Roman Christians between the Fifth and Eighth Centuries in order to give a divine halo to the very human origin of their religion' (*The Popes and Their Church*, Dr. Joseph McCabe, Rector of Buckingham College; Watts and Co., London, 1918). But the best deception was yet to come.

Around the year 771, the most elaborate fraud ever perpetrated against mankind was set in motion by the same Pope Stephen III (IV) who hoodwinked King Pepin the Short, and it provided spectacular additional riches to the Church for the next 1000 years. It emerged from nowhere and took the form of the production of a series of false documents that were forged in the name of Emperor Constantine (d. 337) or misleadingly associated with him. It was called the Donation of Constantine and the fact that the documents first appeared at the Abbey of St. Denis where Pope Stephen spent the winter of 770 is evidence that the pope was personally involved in its fabrication. The falsehood harked back to a pretended origin with Emperor Constantine and Pope St. Sylvester (d. c. 335) and was a series of retrospective directives boldly used by popes to dupe King Charlemagne (c. 742-814) and Christendom into accepting false papal claims of right of ownership and sovereignty over a great part of Europe … the fake documentation, in fact, made the Holy Mother Church the inheritor of the former Roman Empire. Let the *Catholic Encyclopedia* bear the clerical witness:

> This document is without doubt a forgery [the Donation of Constantine], fabricated somewhere between the years 750 and 850. As early as the 15th century its falsity was known and demonstrated. Its genuinity was yet occasionally defended, and the document still further used as authentic, until Baronius in his *Annals Ecclesiastici* admitted that the 'Donation' was a forgery, where-after it was soon universally admitted to be such. It is so clearly a fabrication that there is no reason to wonder that, with the revival of historical criticism in the 15th century, the true character of the document was at once recognized ... the accounts given in all these writings concerning the persecution of Sylvester, the healing and baptism of Constantine, the emperor's gift to the pope, the rights granted to the latter, and the council of 275 bishops at Rome, are entirely legendary ... the document obtained wider circulation by its incorporation with the 'False Decretals' (840-850).
>
> (*Catholic Encyclopedia*, Farley Ed., v, pp. 118, 119, 120; xiv, p. 257; xiv, pp. 370-371)

The 'False Decretals' is the name given by the Church to around 100 fake papal letters that appeared suddenly in the Ninth Century and became integrated with the Donation of Constantine. They are a heterogeneous collection of fictitious documents claiming to be early decrees of Councils and popes. Their seeming purpose was to give a legal basis to the complaints of the clergy in the Empire, appealing to Rome against the misdeeds of high prelates or, of civil authorities. This was in order to achieve their real aim: to obtain additional power for the popes by giving to the abbots, bishops and clergy general authority over civil jurisdiction in all the provinces, thus establishing a legal basis for evading the orders of the provincial secular rulers.

Birth of the Papal States

The Donation of Constantine had tremendous influence upon the territorial acquisition of the Church, and a cursory glance at its origins, contents and meaning will help to elucidate its importance. The fabrication was a successful attempt to strengthen the pope's temporal powers and add wealth in general to the priesthood. It was definite, precise and spoke in no uncertain terms of the spiritual and political supremacy which the popes had been granted as inalienable right. The result was that the Holy Mother Church obtained important privileges, among them immunity from the operation of the secular law, which put her out of the reach of the jurisdiction of all secular tribunals. In this fashion the clergy acquired not only a peculiar sanctity which put them above ordinary people, but a personal inviolability which gave them an enormous advantage in their dealings or disputes with the civil power. In view of the profound repercussions of these forgeries, the most spectacular in the annals of Christianity, it might be instructive to glance at the main clauses of the Donation of Constantine:

> Constantine gives up the sovereignty over the four Patriarchs of Antioch, Alexandria, Constantinople, Jerusalem … and Rome, the provinces, cities and towns of the whole of Italy, and of all the Western Regions, to Pope Sylvester and his successors … the Emperor has signed them with his own hand and placed them on the tomb of St. Peter.

These clauses, the most important and carrying the greatest consequences for Western history made succeeding popes the territorial sovereigns of Rome, Italy and the Western regions; that is to say, of Constantine's original Roman Empire, which comprised France, Spain, Britain and indeed the whole territory of Europe, and beyond. By virtue of fake documents, the old Roman Empire became a fief of the Holy Mother Church, while emperors turned into vassals and popes into suzerains. Their age-old dream, Roman dominion, became a reality, but a reality in which it was no longer the Vicars of Christ who were subject to the emperors, but the emperors who were subject to the Vicars of Christ. With it, the papacy, having made its boldest attempt of world dominion, succeeded in placing itself above the civil authorities of Europe, claiming to be the source of all ecclesiastical and secular power, as well as the real possessor of lands ruled by Western potentates, and the supreme arbiter of the political life of all Christendom.

Thus, thanks to a series of fabrications, forgeries and distortions carried out through several centuries and of which the Donation of Constantine was the most spectacular, the popes not only obtained a vantage ground of incalculable value from which to extend their spiritual and temporal power, but rendered themselves practically independent of all secular authority. Even more, they saw to it that the statutes of emperors and kings, no less than the civil law of nations, be undermined, greatly weakened and indeed obliterated by their newly appointed omnipotence.

The pope claims the Americas

Pope Stephen also claimed that all islands and lands as yet undiscovered were the property of the Roman Pontiff. It was on the strength of such tenets that in 1155, the first Englishman to become Pope, Nicholas Breakspeare (Hadrian IV (sometimes Adrian IV); 1115; pope from 1154-9), sold the hereditary lordship of Ireland to King Henry II (1133-89). Shortly after Christopher Columbus (1492-1503) discovered the New World (1492-1503), the reigning pontiff, Pope Alexander VI (1431-1503; pope from 1492-1503) immediately issued a full-blooded written claim of 'sovereignty' over the newly-discovered lands. In modern parlance, the pope claimed that the Americas, with all they contained, were the absolute and rightful property of the Holy Mother Church (For more details, see chapter called, *The Popes and the Discovery of America*, by Baron Avro Manhattan in his book, *2000 Years of World History*). The original document, besides its extraordinary intrinsic importance, is a fascinating study of papal thinking and deserves to be better known. Called *Hakluytus Posthumus*, it was published in English by R. Eden in 1577, and later, in 1625, was republished by William Stansby for Henrie Fetherstone in London. This celebrated document was written, not so much to re-assert in the plainest possible terms the papal right to ownership of the New Lands, since that was taken for granted by all popes using the Donation of Constantine as their authority, but to prevent Spain and Portugal from taking over the territories without having first been apportioned to them by their owner, or, rather, their landlord, Pope St. Peter's successor. Pope Alexander subsequently leased the Americas to Spain and Portugal, following secret bargaining for treasures from the Spanish and Portuguese crowns.

The fraudulent takeover of the former Roman Empire

This remarkable deception is almost beyond comprehension but it provides details of clerical thinking and presents a clear picture of the intellectual phenomena that prevailed at the time. The document, with one master stroke, put popes above kings, emperors and nations, made them the 'legal' heirs to vast territories, which the forgery granted to them, lock, stock and barrel, and gave to St. Peter and his successors all lands to the West, and beyond, indeed the whole world. Using the forgeries as his reference source, Pope Innocent III (1161-1216), at the Fourth Lateran Council in 1215, proudly stated to the assembled delegates; 'The Lord left to Peter the government not only of all the Church but of all the world' (*The Age of Faith*, Dr. Will Durant, vol. 3 of *The Story of Civilization*, Simon and Schuster, 1950, p. 762). The Holy Mother Church subsequently became a worldly ruler over vast territories that it called States of the Church, or Papal States, and though pretending to affect only matters spiritual and causes ecclesiastical, the new theocratic priest-kingdom soon had all Europe strangled as if in the tentacles of a giant octopus.

And so it came to pass that, thanks mostly to the cult of the Blessed Peter, the Church, which had collected vast amounts of temporal wealth prior to the time of King Pepin, now crowned her earthly possessions with additional territorial dominions. The Papal States had truly come into existence and here popes reigned as absolute temporal rulers until 1870. These landholdings, which had originally formed the first nucleus of papal possessions, theoretically were given legal status by Pepin in 766 and became a concrete and accepted reality in 767. In 774 the Donation of Constantine was confirmed by Pepin's successor, Charlemagne. The establishment of the Papal States provided the Church with a territorial and juridical base of paramount importance. From thereon it enabled her to launch upon the promotion of an ever-bolder policy directed at the accelerated acquisition of additional lands, more gold and the greater status, prestige and power that went with them.

The first spectacular materialization of the Donation of Constantine was seen later when Charlemagne, the most potent monarch of the Middle Ages, granted additional territories to the Papal States and went to Rome in the year 800 to be solemnly crowned by Pope Leo III (795-816) as the first Emperor of the Holy Roman Empire. His 'empire', however, was not holy, not Roman, and not an Empire, but its conception and culture created the foundation of the Europe we know today. The Donation of Constantine was fraught with incalculable consequences, not only for Italy, France, Germany, England, Ireland and practically the whole of Europe, but also for the Americas and for the Near and Middle East. Indeed its full extent found admittance even in Russia, for it exists in the Kormezaia Kniga, the *Corpus juris Canonici* of the Graeco-Slavonic Church, which was translated from the Greek by a Serbian or Bulgarian in the 13th or 14th Century (*The Vatican Billions,* Baron Avro Manhattan, Paravision Books, London, 1972).

Lord James Bryce (1838-1922), British jurist and statesman, summarized the 'Donation of Constantine' fraud with comments as to the mental and moral qualities of the priesthood that it reflected. He said it was the 'most stupendous of medieval forgeries, which under the name of the Donation of Constantine commanded for eight centuries the unquestioning belief of mankind. Itself a portentous falsehood, it is the most unimpeachable evidence of the thoughts and beliefs of the priesthood which framed it' (*Holy Roman Empire,* Bryce, Ch. vii, p. 97, Latin text, extracts, p. 98). It is significant that after the appearance of the Donation of Constantine the papal chancery ceased to date documents and letters by the regnal years of the Emperors of Constantinople, submitting instead those of Pope Stephen II's (III, 752-757) pontificate, then to that of his brother, Paul I (757-767), and then Stephen III (IV) (768-772).

It was the purest form of fraud, and many were those who rebelled against it. Its conception and execution are of immense significance in understanding how the Church became so rich, for it inherited the Roman Empire by the fabrication of a forged document. In 1152, an historian named Wetzeld wrote a letter to Emperor Frederick in which he declared:

> That lie and heretical fable of Constantine's having conceded the imperial rights in the city to Pope Sylvester, was now so thoroughly exposed that even day labourers and women in the fields are able to confute the most learned on the point, and the pope and his cardinals dare not venture to show themselves

for shame.

(*Ap. Martene,* ampl. Coll. ii, p. 556)

The public exposure of the falsity of the Donation gathered momentum until the middle of the 15th Century, when three men succeeded, more than others had earlier done, in exploding the myth on historical grounds, proving that the fact of the Donation of Constantine, no less than the document, was a fraudulent invention. They were Reginald Peacock, Bishop of Chichester, Cardinal Cusa, and, above all, Lorenzo Valla, who proved in a court of Law that popes had no right whatsoever over any land in Europe and had not even the right to possess the States of the Church in Italy or Rome itself. In 1440, after Lorenzo Valla's public exposure of the false nature of the Donation of Constantine, the Holy Inquisition ordered his death, but he narrowly escaped by fleeing into hiding.

Pope paid in pure gold

The popes knew that the Donation of Constantine was a blatant fabrication but used it for centuries as a 'marketing machine' to promote their financial schemes. The significance and consequences of its appearance were portentous for the whole of the Western world and the social structure and political framework were of the Middle Ages were molded and shaped by its contents. The financial advantages for the Church were immense. For example, the inhabitants of the 'donated' territories were ordered to pay yearly contributions to the pope because they were told that the land belonged to the Blessed St. Peter. For centuries, papal abuse was rife and the popes were anything but slow in capitalizing on the fraud. Using the Donation of Constantine as his authority, Pope Clement IV (1265-1268), sold millions of South Italians to the king of Naples and Sicily, Charles of Anjou (1227-85), for a yearly tribute of 800 ounces of pure gold to the coffers of St. Peter; neglect of payment carried with it excommunication and interdict, with all that they implied.

Once rooted in tradition and strengthened by the credulity of the times, the dubious seedling of the Donation of Constantine grew into a mighty oak tree under the shadow of which papal authoritarianism thrived. From the birth of the Carolingian Empire around the year 800 onwards, the gifts of Pepin, the Donation of Constantine, and the False Decretals were assiduously used by pontiffs to consolidate their power and wealth. This they did, until, with the remarkable and immense 'Pseudo-Areopagitell Forgeries' and the Forged Decretals of Gratian, issued early in the Thirteenth Century (*Catholic Encyclopedia*, Farley Ed., iv, p. 671), and the arbitrary exercise of spiritual and temporal might, these documents became the formidable foundation stone upon which the Holy Mother Church was eventually to erect its political and territorial claims, the rock upon which stood the whole papal structure of the Middle Ages. The Church retained the 'sovereignty' and revenues from the deception and flatly refused to give up the fruits of the swindle. Italian patriot bayonets finally cancelled the 'Donation of Constantine' forgery in 1870, and the stolen territories of Peter's Patrimony were restored to United Italy.

CHAPTER 9

New tombs of St. Peter

The reference in the Donation of Constantine to the Emperor personally placing the signed document on the 'tomb of St. Peter' provided the Church with the impetus to maintain the cult of the Blessed Peter, and the 'tomb' was constantly reconstructed to cater for the pilgrims' cash. During the 17-year rule of Pope Gregory IV (828-844) a large bronze casket was built and placed under the timber boards already existing in the cemetery. Within it were human bones that were imposed upon Christians as those of the Blessed Peter himself. Later, the Saracens sacked the ports of Ostia and Portus, and then sailed up the Tiber and invaded Rome. The soldiers smashed the casket and threw the bones into the Tiber. Later, another and much larger tomb was built and, for the first time, enclosed by walls and roofed. It too, housed human remains, not only of St. Peter but also of St. Paul. Under Pope Leo IV (847-855), St. Peter's tomb was dramatically restructured and re-furbished with a sumptuousness which lead German historian, Ferdinand Gregorovius (1821-91), to estimate that the Roman treasury at this time was richer than in the days of Leo X (d. 1521), the Renaissance pope who spent millions, mostly on his own pleasures. Of the new tomb, Dr. McCabe said:

> The new High Altar of St. Peter's was plated with gold ... not merely gilded, for we read of one plate weighing 216 pounds ... and decorated with jewels and enamels. A silver ciborium weighed 1,606 pounds; a golden cross, studded with jewels, weighed 1,000 pounds ... an immense silver chandelier, with 1,345 separate lamps, hung from the ceiling and lit all these new splendors and the purple hangings, the mosaics, and ornaments ... and statues, lamps, altar-vessels, and tapestries were strewn everywhere.

(*A History of the Popes*, Dr. Joseph McCabe, Rector of Buckingham College; d. 1955; C. A. Watts and Co, London, p. 103).

Silver plates covered a newly-developed lower area, around which pilgrims could 'pay reverence at the glorious tombs of the twin prince Apostles' (*Catholic Encyclopedia*, Farley Ed., xii, pp. 86, 94). It was subsequently destroyed and the valuables stolen. Another more-lavish tomb was then built but was later stripped by Pope Calixtus II (d. 1124) who, to avoid impending charges of murder, fled to Constantinople with 'silver panels from the doors', 'thick plates of gold' that had covered the altar, and 'a solid gold statue' (*A History of the Popes*, Dr. Joseph McCabe, Rector of Buckingham College; d. 1955; C. A. Watts and Co, London).

The Church defined pilgrimages as 'the idea of wandering over a distance to discharge some religious obligation. Once theophanies are localized, pilgrimages necessarily follow ... the hardships of the journey, the penitential garb worn, the mendacity it entailed made a pilgrimage a real and efficient penance' (*Catholic Encyclopedia*, Farley Ed., xii, pp. 85-98). However, pilgrimages were not what the Church today makes them out to be:

> At first a mere question of an individual traveling a short distance of a few paces to a suspected site was sufficient to develop into pilgrimages properly organized by groups. The initiators were clerics ... invented a method of almsgiving ... naturally with all this there was a great deal of corruption and abuse ... in many cases the journey has proved a scandal and caused serious harm ... for certain pilgrimages were not always undertaken for the best of motives ... pilgrimage-making degraded into causes of vice ... they make their pilgrimage away from God and to the devil.

(*Catholic Encyclopedia*, Farley Ed., xii, pp. 85-98)

The reality of the matter was that the Church organized pilgrimages to the 'tomb' specifically for profit, and by the 16th Century they developed into a huge money-making industry (Cardinal Pietro Bembo, *His Letters and Comments on Pope Leo X*, Reprint 1842).

Blatant priesthood embezzlement

In all times, pilgrimages have been a source of profit, and evidence of this can be seen in the bitter struggle between churches and monasteries over possession of relics that could attract a hoard of pilgrims ... or the well-known invention and false presentation of such relics (like the chair of St. Peter, aforementioned). The tradition started centuries earlier by Emperor Constantine's mother, Helena (c. 248, d. c. 328), 'unquestionably a British princess' (*Epistola,* Melancthon, 1497–1560, p. 189). Immediately after the Council of Nicaea, Constantine, in his campaign to entice people to accept his new belief system, circulated a rumour among the rabble saying that his mother had 'discovered' some remarkable relics that make pale into triviality the 20th Century discovery of Tutankhamen's tomb-treasures. Helena 'found' two sealed clay jars, one containing the precious last breath of Hesus Krishna and the other, beams of light from the Star of Bethlehem. Helena's public showings of her 'treasures' were displayed in Constantinople with great fanfare and coincided with Emperor Constantine's announcement that *New Testimonies* were being written:

> Great mobs of ignorant rabble, slaves and seamen, the lowest populace, peasants, drunks and hoards of women ... lined up to view the fabrications and the presbyters schemed to this end and devoured the people's means.

(*Catech,* xviii, 7-8; also Schaff, *History of the Christian Church*)

After Empress Helena's success in displaying 'fraudulent impossibilities' (*Secrets of the Christian Fathers*, Bishop Joseph W. Sergerus, (d. c. 1701), 1685, reprint 1897), a tendency quickly developed throughout Europe for churchmen to magnify whatever 'treasure' they could find, with extravagant claims appearing without foundation in truth. Thus, from the time of the Council of Nicaea, trickery figured prominently in priesthood incomes and became an integral part of Church practice. Less than 60 years after Helena's death (c. 328), Emperor Theodosius, in his famous Code of Laws (c. 384), tried to stop the growing fraud, and issued a decree forbidding churchmen to manufacture and sell false relics (*Code of Theodosius*, vii, ix, 17; also, *Catholic Encyclopedia*, Farley Ed., xii, pp. 734-738). His commands were circumvented, and the 'discovery' and production of 'saintly items' developed into priesthood devices that were 'concerned with commercial transactions for greed and gain ... many unprincipled persons found a means of enriching themselves by a sort of trade in these objects of devotion, the majority of which no doubt were fraudulent' (*Catholic Encyclopedia*, Farley Ed., xii, p. 737). Augustine (d. 430) denounced the frauds, and called them 'the cult of the dead men ... but the pope commanded the service of the police in silencing critics' (*A History of the Popes*, Dr. Joseph McCabe, Rector of Buckingham College; d. 1955; C. A. Watts and Co, London, vol. 1, p. 44). The unashamed deceptions were never rebuked or prevented by pope or priest, but, rather, were industriously stimulated by them for the rich revenues they produced, and the dishonour to the human mind wrought upon the public by 1600 years of priestly impostures should be questioned.

After Constantine announced the 'discovery' of a timber cross, the priesthood claimed it as a 'true cross', adding that 'its wood was cut up into small relics and scattered throughout Christendom' (*Catholic Encyclopedia*, Farley Ed., iv, p. 524; xii, p. 736). This assurance is out of harmony with later Church declarations for in 395, Bishop Ambrose displayed the 'true cross', fifteen-foot high, in his church, and the ignorant lined up to buy fragments pared from it. Eventually, the last small remnant was preserved in a silver receptacle, and the rabble paid money to walk past it in awe. Other churchmen profited from the idea, Chrysotom and Paulinius of Nola, for example. In 629, Emperor Heraclius staged a public exposition of another 'true cross' at Rome after he claimed to have 'recovered' it from the Persians into whose hands he said it had fallen in 614 (*Catholic Encyclopedia*, Farley Ed., iii, p. 105). Heraclius spent the rest of his life living off sales made from 'sacred fragments of the true cross' (ibid). Nearly 1000 years later, Genevan religious reformer John Calvin (1509-1564), declared that enough 'fragments of the true cross' had been sold to construct a large ship (*Institutes of the Christian Religion*). As a matter of record, 62 'true crosses' were displayed to the naive public by churchmen between 326 and 680 and upon computation, it seems that they multiplied themselves even more miraculously than the two fishes and the five loaves of bread. However, the reality of the issue is this: 'The tradition of the finding of the Cross of Christ is held to be a mere legend, without any historical reality' (*Catholic Encyclopedia*, Pecci Ed., ii, p. 328). In a remarkable disclosure, an orthodox reference work, *Oxford Dictionary of the Christian Church* (1994) fails to record an alphabetical entry under C for 'Cross' but rather documents an extraordinary confession in bold capital letters on Page 710, titled, THE INVENTION OF THE CROSS (*Oxford Dictionary of the Christian Church,* p. 842 in the 1997; also, *Catholic Encyclopedia,* Farley Ed., iv, p. 524). The international Christian panel frankly concedes that the Christian cross upon which the Church maintains that Jesus historically suffered was 'invented', and today it is 'the epitome of the Gospel'.

In such an atmosphere of lawlessness fake relics came to abound and the faithful parted with their cash to view the frauds. It was not allowable for a church to be built or consecrated without a box of bones or other fetid human scraps deposited under the altar, and they were placed there in grand ceremonies in which believers contributed a donation. The decree of the second council of Nicaea 787, reaffirmed by the Council of Trent in 1546, forbade the consecration of any church without a supply of relics (*Catholic Encyclopedia,* Farley Ed., xii, p. 737). Thus the ancient superstition of morbid relics was sanctioned and its observance made mandatory under Canon Law. To this very day, the Vatican maintains the most macabre library in the world in which it keeps bags and envelopes stuffed with skull fragments, ashes, bones, pieces of old clothing, and other bizarre items all pertaining to belong to a saint. 'Because churches and chapels are inaugurated every month somewhere in the world, the priest-librarian is kept busy filling envelopes with pinches of dust or fragments of bone which are then mailed in registered letters' (*The Vatican Papers*, Nino Lo Bello, New English Library (a division of Hodder and Stoughton, Ltd.), Kent, 1982). An unceasing demand was created, and the market supply was (and is) more than equal to pious demand. For example, an assemblage of macabre collections are found in Church records and this instance is just one: 'At the beginning of the ninth century the exportation of bodies from Rome had assumed the proportions of a regular commerce, and a certain bishop, Deusdona, acquired an unenviable notoriety in these transactions' (*Catholic Encyclopedia*, Farley Ed., xii, pp. 737-8). He and his 'unscrupulous rogues' (ibid) were selling human remains to churches to display as those of martyrs, and body parts 'discovered near a church or in the catacombs' brought the greatest price (ibid). Of this bizarre practice, British-born American author John William Draper (1811-82) said 'The pretence reflects the debauchery of morals and mind which made possible these scandalous practices of the Christian priesthood' (*The Intellectual Development of Europe*, J. W. Draper, i, p. 328).

The use of sacrilegious tricks to manipulate crowds of slaves and poor people on a money-shedding pilgrimage was an ingrained feature of Christianity and subsequently developed into epidemic proportions. In the 15th Century, the Church publicly presented two forged missives attributed to Virgin Mary, and the faithful were summoned from all over Europe to hear the 'revelations' read to them. One purported to be a letter in answer to another addressed to her by Ignatius in the early Second Century in which she confirmed all things learned by her correspondent from 'her friend', the apostle John. She bided him hold fast to his vows, and added as an inducement, 'I and John will come again together and personally pay you a visit'. Crude copies of the letters were reproduced in their hundreds and sold to a gullible pubic. Nothing was known of the letters until Church orators (bishops) in 1495, firstly in Rome and later in Paris, read them to the public in town squares. By a curious accident, the proclamations were made at a time when the pope was publicly challenged about forgery in the New Testament. This controversy raged for two centuries, and gave unending trouble to later popes, especially, Gregory X111 (1502-1585), and Alexander VII (1599-1667). Late in the 17th Century, the kingdom of Spain was thrown into complete disorder by the debate, and demanded papal clarification. Embassies were sent to Rome with a view to engage the pope in official discussions about the virgin birth and resurrection narratives applied to Jesus Christ, demanding that the forgeries be terminated by a papal Bull. The pope, however, fled the controversy, and sort to cover his retreat by 'uttering nothing except ambiguous words, he would not make a decision, and evaded giving a conclusion' (*Idem*, cent xvii, part ii, vol. ii, p. 302). By this time the 'New Learning' (*Catholic Encyclopedia*, Farley eds., v, p. 442; ix, p. 335; xv, p. 376) had been introduced into Catholicism (c. 1588), and the forgeries associated with this extraordinary event are discussed in Chapter 12.

Misappropriation of the truth

Christianity's hilarious and weirdest form of deceit, relic fraud, continued unabated. For the edification and mental stultification of the faithful, Abbot Martin (c. 1498) obtained for his monastery in Alsace the following inestimable articles: 'A spot of the blood of the saviour; one arm of the apostle James; part of the skeleton of John the Baptist, and a bottle of the Mother of God's breast milk' (*The Intellectual Development of Europe*, J. W. Draper, ii, p. 57). But perhaps none of those impostures surpassed in audacity that offered by a monastery in Jerusalem that presented to the beholder one of the fingers of the Holy Ghost and the tongue of St. Anthony, miraculously still flapping in prayer (*Conflict between Science and Religion*, J. P. Draper, p. 270). Displayed at the same monastery were wings and tail feathers of the same Holy Ghost that had, from time to time, shed off or were pulled out when, disguised as a Dove, it (or he, or she) came down and perched on the shoulders of delighted Christians. Also brought to light in that era were a number of priestly tricks such as hollow statues of wood or brass, with hidden apertures from which priests whispered oracles or maledictions and the tailoring of special blue and white garments presented in expensive public showings as those once belonging to Virgin Mary. Such drivel is part and parcel of Christianity, and has been since the day Constantine created it.

The Church, like so many others, exploited the good faith of the pilgrims to the extent that, in 1523, German painter and engraver, Albrecht Dürer (1471-1528), wrote to Pope Clement VII (1478-1534) in his own hand and criticized the deceitful commerce in Church-organized pilgrimages. The fraud was not confined to Europe and the British priesthood also profited from the deception. In England at the time of Henry VIII (d. 1547), Mary's girdles, and packets of her powdered breast milk, were publicly displayed with great fanfare in eleven towns and villages and the Queen herself purchased one of the girdles as a gift for Catherine of Aragon on her marriage to Henry. During the plague of 1531, Henry VIII bought a vial of water used to baptize Jesus and a tear that Jesus shed over Lazarus, hoping the liquids would avert the plague. The Church said that the tear had been preserved in a phial by an angel who gave it to Mary Magdalene along with a phial of the sweat of St. Michael when he contended with Satan (*Henry*

VIII, Hackett, pp. 11, 234). The Cathedral of Arras in France also possessed some 'highly venerated and remarkable relics, to wit, some manna that fell from Heaven in the year 371 during a severe famine, and a holy candle that was presented by Virgin Mary to Bishop Lambert in 1105 to stop an epidemic' (*Catholic Encyclopedia*, Farley Ed., i, p. 752). The Church claimed that the candle had burned continuously from 1105 to 1713 without being diminished, and English theologian and deist, Anthony Collins (1676-1729), in his celebrated *Discourse of Free Thinking*, expressed doubt whether the clergy would permit a careful scrutiny to be made of the phenomenon.

A large collection of Church fetishes are recorded by Dr. Joseph McCabe (d. 1955) who revealed that every church in Europe once displayed some type of 'relic' for 'believers to gaze at in rapt awe, and to kiss and fondle, these ghastly and ghoulish, false and forged, bloody scraps and baubles of perverted piousity' (*Intellectual Growth*, Bloomsbury, 1927). A few may be admired: At Leon the chief treasures shown to the public were canisters of powdered breast milk and lockets of hair from Virgin Mary. That was Leon's set-off to the rival attraction at Soissons, a neighbouring town that had secured a tooth shed by infant Jesus, presented to the Church by the 'tooth-fairy'. Exhibited in Spanish churches in the 19th Century was enough of Virgin Mary's milk to feed a dozen calves and sufficient hair to make 100 wigs. There were the teeth of Christ in quantities to outfit a dentist and one monastery at Charroux boasted that it had the complete set. In Italy, France and Spain, enough sets of baby-linen once worn by infant Jesus were shown to have opened a second-hand baby's clothing shop. In all such miraculous presentations like that, history must step out that fiction may step in and the public display of bogus relics raged right into the 20th Century.

In Rome in the mid-1870's, the priesthood commissioned the creation of a timber doll of the child saviour, 'Sanctissimo Bambino' whose power in curing the sick was made a world-wide sensation by the Vatican's public relations division (Sacred Congregation of Propaganda). This hand-carved wooden doll was wrapped in swaddling clothes and crowned on its head with a sparkling royal tiara. Its public showings achieved more income for the Church than the combined fees of the three top physicians in Rome (*Romanism at Home*; J. Kirwin, being Letters to the Hon. Roger B. Taney,

Chief Justice of the United States, printed in Edinburgh by Johnstone and Hunter, M. DCCC. LII, p. 77). These pathetic farces have been part and parcel of Christianity for 1600 years and without them the Church would not be what it is today.

Also in Rome, its greatest church displayed Christ's manger-cradle made from a 19th Century packing case, and seven churches claimed they had his authentic umbilical cord. The childishness and grossness continues, with a number of churches claiming that they had his foreskin, removed at circumcision, and kept as a souvenir by Mother Mary. One church even had the miraculous imprint of his little bottom on a stone upon which he had sat. Mary herself left behind enough wedding rings, shoes, stockings, panties and skirts to fill a museum, and one of her fake shifts was still on display in the Chartres Cathedral in 1935. A northern French church displayed Aaron's rod, and the 'canon of common-sense' reveals that eight European churches simultaneously exhibiting severed heads as those of John the Baptist were unashamedly deceiving the public. The same can be said for three human skulls displayed in 1929 in the cathedral of Cologne as those of the Wise Men who followed the Star of Bethlehem. In the neighbouring church of St. Maurice, bones from a whole cemetery were excavated, laid out with exequial pomp on the church floor, and presented as those of the 'unhistorical' (*Concise Dictionary of the Christian Church*, Oxford, 1996, p. 329) saint and his Theban Legion of 10,000 martyrs. In fitting competition were the spoils of the adjoining graveyard, yielding the bones of St. Ursula and the remains of her 11,000 virgin martyrs. They were openly displayed to the public, despite Vatican admissions that the story of St. Ursula has 'no claim to authenticity' (*Catholic Encyclopedia*, 1914, 'St. Ursula'). The miraculous bones of St. Rosalia (c. 1160) exhibited in Palermo in 1930 were those of a goat, and the faithful filed past these deplorable pretences in ignorant respect (*Associated Press* dispatch, August, 1930). Likewise, early in the 1980s, 'the Vatican quickly destroyed the relics of one saint when Church archaeologists discovered that her ribs, unearthed over 200 years ago in a catacomb and preserved in the Vatican since then, were the bones of a large dog' (*The Vatican Papers*, Nino Lo Bello, New English Library (a division of Hodder and Stoughton, Ltd.), Kent, 1982).

The ministry treasury of the Cathedral of Aix-la-Chapelle, or Aachen, where in a silver-edged tunic and a blue mantle, Charlemagne (d. 814) and originally enshrined some 'holy thorns', 'includes a large number of relics, vessels, and vestments, the most important being those known as the four 'Great Relics', namely, the cloak of the Blessed Virgin, the swaddling-clothes of the infant Jesus, the loincloth worn by Our Lord on the Cross, and the cloth on which lay the head of John the Baptist after his decapitation. They are exposed every seven years, and venerated by thousands of pilgrims' (*Catholic Encyclopedia*, Farley Ed., i, p. 92). Processions were held inside ancient edifices to honour relics including what churchmen said were the heads of apostles St. Peter and St. Paul, shown for the adoration of the faithful (*Herald-Tribune*, April 19, 1930). What may not the Holy Mother Church squeeze from a people whom she makes believe that she carries in her purse the keys to heaven and hell, and that she can, at pleasure, admit them to the bliss of the one, or shut them up amid the eternal miseries of the other?

The 'Church Hoax' published in newspapers

A later repentant summary from the Church throws a ray of light on the scale of the centuries of priestly impostures: 'That they cannot by any possibility be authentic will be disputed by no one; more than 700 such relics have been enumerated' (*Catholic Encyclopedia*, Farley Ed., iv, pp. 540-541) but the actual number is 'not hundreds, but thousands' (*The Story of Religious Controversy*, Dr. Joseph McCabe (d. 1955), Rector of Buckingham College). The foregoing solemn vouching for antique fakeries provoked a deal of sceptical ridicule throughout the world, even among the faithful (*Associated Press* dispatch, April 19, 1930, *Vera icon*) and the frauds 'helped to further Christianity' (*Catholic Encyclopedia*, Farley Ed., xiv, pp. 339-341). False miracles and fraudulent relics were primary priesthood devices for stimulating the faith of the ignorant and superstitious masses, and gave them cause to open their wallets. It seems certain that 'the law of demand and supply' prevails in regard to 'miracles' as well as to other Church commodities. These frauds were sanctified by the Holy Mother Church, which is, in reality, an illegitimate organization and, together with the 'fictitious accounts' of the supposed martyrdom of early churchmen (*Catholic Encyclopedia*, Farley Ed., xii, p. 219; also *Catholic Encyclopedia*, Farley Ed., vii, pp. 644-647; ANL. i, 46), they provide unending evidence of the iniquitous nature of the Christian religion. The sordid debasement of the human mind to the degree of gullibility; the dishonesty of the false pretences that gave credit to those farcical objects for purposes of extortion from silly dupes of religion; the vastness of the grand larceny thus perpetrated in the name of Jesus Christ, is beyond orderly comment.

An apologetic overview of the debauchery of morals and mind which made possible these scandalous practices for financial gain is affirmed by the *Catholic Encyclopedia*: 'Naturally it was impossible for popular enthusiasm to be roused to so high a pitch in a matter which easily lent itself to error, fraud, and greed for gain, without at least the occurrence of many, grave abuses' (*Catholic Encyclopedia,* Farley Ed., xii, 'Relics', pp. 734-738). Church inventions were common holy stock in trade and were still being used in recent times, complete to displaying dead shaven monkeys as 'demons' in the 1940s. A large freestanding gold cross in a Marseilles church was secretly hinged at its base and, with the use of thin wires when lights were dimmed, bowed down, as if paying reverence to Jesus. Statues of Jesus and Mary were endowed with pretended supernatural powers with eyes that would wink, heads that nodded, or limbs rising up and down. The crucifix of Boxley, in Kent, for example, lifted its head, opened its lips and eyes, and when examined in London, was found to be a puppet-like dummy with an internal spring-loaded mechanical system operating its movements. It was exposed in British newspapers under the headline, 'Church Hoax', and subsequently displayed to a deriding public. These scams excite little more than a smile of contempt, but for centuries shameless impostures have been palmed off on an ignorant populace by impious churchmen who would degrade a naive and unsophisticated people by charading behind the banner of God. Surely, the pope and his cardinals, when secure behind locked doors, and with exclusive access to suppressed information in the Secret Vatican Archives, must laugh in their sleeves at the credulity of Christians prostrate on their knees before false relics and carved images of people who never existed.

The most cherished female saint

Then came the consummation and solemn Infallibility of the Pope accrediting 'the most precious relics' with the newspaper headline saying: 'Pope Celebrates Easter Mass. Relics of the Passion surrounded him, a reputed fragment of the cross, with a piece of the spear which pierced the side of the saviour, and the Veil of St. Veronica … were displayed from the balcony above the Papal Altar' (*Herald-Tribune*, April 21, 1930). That public display, however, further revealed the crude nature of Christianity and overtly exposed the fraud of St. Veronica's Veil. The relic was based on a fictitious 12th Century tale of a non-existent First Century woman who offered Jesus a linen cloth to wipe his face as he was carrying his cross. On wiping his sweating face, the supposed authentic likeness of the features of God on Earth was miraculously impressed upon the cloth. The lucky lady then …

> … went to Rome, bringing with her this image of Christ, which was long exposed to public veneration. To her were likewise traced similar relics (other forgeries) venerated in several churches of the West. To distinguish at Rome the oldest and best known of those images, it was called 'vera icon' (true image), and that ordinary language soon made 'veronica' … by degrees; popular imagination mistook this word for the name of a person.
>
> (*Catholic Encyclopedia*, Farley Ed., xv, pp. 362-3)

Thus, St. Veronica emerged from the canonizing division of the Church and the world witnessed myth-in-the-making. Ready-made through a confessed fable and a fake veil, the Church of Christ had supplied its faithful with one of the most cherished female saints of the Calendar, and his Holiness especially displayed and vouched for that fake on March 19, 1930, when he preached his crusade against Russia (*Associated Press* dispatch, April 19, 1930; *Vera icon*). This outrageous fraud was not perpetrated in a Third World country or by Slippery John, a cardinal in New York City, but at the Vatican in Rome, and by the Holy Father himself. Is there anything peculiar to the papacy today that is not intended to deceive?

Think not that those deceptions were discarded in shame by the Church after their fraudulent origin and financial purposes were exposed to public obloquy and ridicule. This method of deluding people has not been surrendered by the Holy Mother Church, and is still used to increase a superstitious reverence for the ghostly power of the Church. It is practiced, where it can be, in all shapes and forms in our own day, for in full blaze of world attention and publicity of the Twentieth Century, God's own Vicar vouched for the authenticity of another hoax, the Shroud of Turin.

CHAPTER 10

The bishop and the platter of gold

Adding to the trickery of pilgrimages, fake relics, and forged documents, were the weapons of interdiction and excommunication, used with increasing frequency to compel the faithful to pay under practically any pretext. In an interesting old book about Church council meetings published in Great Britain during the 18th Century, we read of a bishop of Wales who excommunicated his king. The king later asked for the excommunication to be lifted and the bishop agreed, but at a price ... he was to be given a thick, sculptured plate of pure gold the size of the bishop's face (*Councils of Great Britain*, Haddan and Stubbs, undated, vol., i, pp. 207-8). Besides such trivia for developing riches, more serious abuses became common practice, and the Church saw in the denunciation of heretics another major source of income. A heretic was simply a person who 'held a different view' (*The Bible Fraud*, Tony Bushby, Joshua Books, Australia, 2001), but to stamp out opposition to the papal story, Pope Gregory VII (d. 1085) ruled that the 'killing of heretics is not murder' (ibid). His edict demanding 'extermination' of nonbelievers was later promulgated by St. Thomas Aquinas as one of the unchangeable laws of the Church of Rome (*Summa Theology*, St. Thomas Aquinas (1225-1274), Vol. iv. p. 90).

The authorities, lay or ecclesiastical, were compelled under pain of excommunication 'to seize all the heretic's property, goods, lands and chattels, to arrest him and throw into prison' (*Fundamental Ecclesiasticism*, M. Magdal, 1422, Ludwick I, xi, pp. 457-69). The custom appears to have fully developed around the time of St. Bernard of Clairvaux (1090-1153) who was a ruthless denouncer of heretics. He became the terror of any dissenter and he was only one of a series of extirpators for nearly 1000 years. Thanks to this principle, the Church obtained vast estates and substantial wealth when prosperous individuals were, as happened often, accused of heresy and condemned ... sometimes in collusion with temporal authorities. The seizing of property became a source of untold riches for prelates, bishops and popes who pretended orthodoxy, so that very often no one knew with certainty whether the accused had been arrested because of their deviation from the faith or because of greed for their riches on the part of their anonymous denunciators.

Later, Pope Innocent III (d. 1216) issued specific instructions concerning this abuse. The *Corpus Juris*, the official law book of the papacy, gave the details: 'The possessions of heretics are to be confiscated. In the Church's territories they are to go to the Church's treasury' (ibid, c. 10). This papal injunction was carried out everywhere the Church ruled. Thus, for instance, following the edict to the authorities of Nîmes and Narbonne, in 1228, Pope Gregory IX (1147-1241; pope from 1227-1241) ordered that any heretic or excommunicated person 'shall be forced to seek absolution by the seizure of all his property' (Ordun. Ann. 1228). Thanks to such decrees, the Church could obtain vast estates and a substantial fortune merely by accusing a rich man of heresy ... and did ... for centuries.

The battle for control of Vatican wealth

Apologizing for centuries of pandemonium caused by popes, and giving a smear of whitewash to their actions, the Vatican admits that at the time of Pope Alexander II (1061-73) 'the Church was torn by the schisms of anti-popes, simony, and clerical incontinence' (*Catholic Encyclopedia,* Farley Ed., i, p. 541). The development of a multiplicity of popes simultaneously operating in confliction with each other started when Damasus (d. c. 384) left Constantinople and established a breakaway division of Constantine's new religious movement in Rome. He became 'bishop of Rome' in competition with the 'bishop of Constantinople', and this was first recorded example of 'simultaneous popes' (*The Popes, A Concise Biographical History*, Burns and Oates, Publishers to the Holy See, London, 1964, p. 70; published under the Imprimatur of Georgius L. Craven) operating within Christianity. The ongoing existence of multiple popes is a little-known episode in Christian history and provides clear evidence of the existence of powerful factional opponents scheming to gain solitary control of the riches and income of the Holy See. 'The Church was disturbed many times in her history by rival claimants to the papacy ... the strife that originated was always an occasion of scandal, sometimes of violence and bloodshed' (*Catholic Dictionary*, Virtue and Co, London, 1954, p. 35). Initially, rival Imperialist popes were elected by noble French families to rout out Roman ecclesiastical vice and subsequently new elements appeared in a variety of ways that endured for centuries. In modern times, the Church labeled them anti-popes, 'devils on the chair of St. Peter' (*Catholic Dictionary*, Virtue and Co, London, 1954, p. 35), claiming that they were unlawfully appointed. That distinction, however, is purely arbitrary for each multiple pope was canonically elected at official conclaves. This extraordinary confession from the Church:

> At various times in the history of the Church illegal pretenders to the Papal Chair have arisen, and frequently exercised pontifical functions in defiance of the true occupant. According to [Cardinal] Hergenrother [d. 1890], the last anti-pope was Felix V (1439-49). The same authority enumerates twenty-nine in the following order ... (naming them).
>
> (*Catholic Encyclopedia*, Farley Ed., i, p. 582)

Each opposing papal hierarchy was supported by formidable military factions and the subject of popes warring against each other is a topic too vast to even summarize here. Their struggles for power were conducted with amazing bitterness and the word 'schism' is not strong enough to describe the depth of the fury that raged for centuries within the Christian religion. Catholic historians admit that 'even now it is not perhaps absolutely certain from the two lines of popes who was pope and who was anti-pope, or which anti-pope was a legal anti-pope' (*Catholic Encyclopedia*, Pecci Ed., iii, p. 107; also, *Catholic Dictionary*, Virtue and Co, London, 1954, p. 35). This is luminous clerical reasoning, but there is more to this peculiar side of Vatican history and it is found in a book called *Secrets of the Christian Fathers*, written in 1685 by Roman Bishop Joseph W. Sergerus (d. c. 1701). He provides evidence from Church archives at his disposal that at some periods in papal history there were four popes occupying the papal chair(s), each in a different building, city, or country, operating independently with their own cardinals and staff, and holding their own canonical councils. He names them, and one example from twelve quadruple sets of popes is that of the self-declared Pope Benedict XIV (1425) who, for years, rivaled popes Benedict XIII (1427), Clement VIII (1429), and Martin V (1431). Church historians today ingeniously refer to the fourth member of the quadruple groupings as 'a counter anti-pope' (*The Popes, A Concise Biographical History*, Burns and Oates, Publishers to the Holy See, London, 1964), adding that 'this is not the place [in Church reference books] to discuss the merits or motives of the multiple claimants' (*Catholic Encyclopedia*, Pecci Ed., iii, pp. 107-8; *Catholic Dictionary*, Virtue and Co, London, 1954).

The introduction of the word 'anti-pope' was a retrospective move by the Church to eliminate the reality of simultaneously-serving popes and thus provide itself with a singular continuous ministerial succession of popes from St. Peter to Benedict XVI today. However, the lineage should have only gone back to Emperor Constantine (d. 337), the founder of Christianity, the original 'Supreme Pontiff' (*The Catholic Dictionary*, Addis and Arnold, 'Constantine', 1917). Investigation of the Church's own records, however, reveals that the priesthood's claim of an unbroken papal continuity back to the First Century is false. Christian historian, and the first prefect of the embryonic Vatican Library, Bishop Bartolomeo Platina (c. 1495), admitted that direct lineage 'was interrupted by repeated periods; after Nicholas 1 (867), an interregnum of eight years, seven months, and nine days, etc, etc'. Those breaks are piously called 'vacations' and are recorded by Bishop Platina as totaling '127 years, five months and nine days' *(The Lives of the Roman Pontiffs,* Bishop Platina; also, *Catholic Encyclopedia*, Farley Ed., xii, pp. 767-768). However, Platina failed to record the 'vacations' that occurred in the centuries preceding Nicholas I, for 'unfortunately, few of the records (of the Church) prior to the year 1198 have been released' (*Encyclopedia Biblica*, Adam & Charles Black, London, 1899). Clerical insiders know writings purporting to record the lineage of popes are false, saying:

As for the pretend catalogues of succeeding bishops of the different assemblies from the days of the apostles, exhibited by some ecclesiastical writers, they are filled up by forgeries and later inventions. Thus diocesan bishops came in, whose offices are considered as corruptions or dishonest applications, as dictated by the necessities of the Church, or of instances of worldly ambition.

(*The Authentic and Acknowledged Standards of the Church of Rome,* J. Hannah D.D., 1844, p. 414)

However, humanitarian and biblical scholar Desiderius Erasmus (d. 1536), got it right when he stated, 'succession is imaginary' (*Erasmus,* in *Nov. Test. Annotations,* Fol. Basil, 1542), simply because its modern-day portrayal is contrary to recorded historical fact.

French gold in the Church of Rome

When French pope, Urban II (Odo of Chatillan, 1040-1099; pope from 1088) returned to Rome in 1093 from exile in the Norman south, he needed to borrow money to pay for lodgings in the city. Why? The Vatican (which now begins to find mention), and the Asinarian Station (later renamed, the Lateran Palace) had been reduced to rubble by a series of bitter battles between warring armies of the multiple popes (*The Popes and their Church,* Dr. Joseph McCabe, Rector of Buckingham College; Watts and Co., London, 1918, p. 44), and the papacy, to its great grief, faced the prospect of existing in poverty. However, the structures were rebuilt before the Third Lateran Council in 1179, not as they are known today, and subsequent popes had new palaces to occupy. It is not recorded how the rebuilding program was funded, but it is known that Urban paved his way back to Rome with French gold.

In 1124, an influential and opposing faction elected Lambert of Bologne as Pope Honorius II (1124-1130) and the Church maintained two rival popes, each bitter and warring opponents and both living murderous, debauched, and luxurious lifestyles. There is no doubt that Honorius was determined to buy or force his way into the papal chair and he succeeded, preserving his position for the term of his life. Upon his death, two new popes, Anacletus II (1130-38) and Innocent II (1130-1143) were elected and consecrated on the same day by opposing clerical factions. Before his election Peter Pierleoni (Anacletus II) had been military leader of a rival army whose family fought (in total) for 50 years for control of the Vatican, a confrontation subtly called by the Church today, 'The Fifty Year War'. If we can believe his enemies, he disgraced the papal office by gross immorality and his greed in the accumulation of lucre. When Pierleoni died, his faction elected Victor IV to the papal chair (*Catholic Encyclopedia,* Farley Ed., i, p. 447), and the Church remained in bitter conflict still under divided control of two popes, neither possessing a Bible, and each operating independently (*Confessions of a French Catholic Priest,* New York, Mathers, 1837).

The true significance of records of such a military force in Christianity nullifies the modern-day presentation of the 'sweetness and light' that the Church today says it brought to the world. The extent of papal transgression is expanded by this passage in the Pecci Edition of the *Catholic Encyclopedia*:

> At the time of Gregory VII's elevation to the papacy (1073-85), the Christian world was in a deplorable condition. During the desolating period of transition the terrible period of warfare and rapine, violence, and corruption in high places, which followed immediately upon the dissolution of the Carolingian Empire, a period when society in Europe seemed doomed to destruction and ruin. The Church had not been able to escape from the general debasement to which it had so signally contributed, if not caused ... the tenth century, was the saddest perhaps, in Christian annals.
>
> (*Catholic Encyclopedia,* Pecci Ed., ii, pp. 289, 294, passim; also Farley Ed, vi, pp. 791-5)

The chief paradox of our age is the survival of the Church of Rome, and the history of its money-making schemes is bewildering. One ancient glimpse of the condition of Christianity around this time (c. 1200-1300) will suffice, and it is found in the writings of Bishop Bonitho (d. c. 1260; *Ad Amicum,* vii). He said that it was an 'old custom' of the Roman Church to employ 'sixty or more' laymen to dress up as priests, complete with mitres, and pretend to be the hierarchy of the Church. They presented themselves to ignorant pilgrims as cardinals, and promised silent prayers in exchange for money. Bishop Bonitho said that these venerable rogues had wives, mistresses, or male partners, yet at night they raped or seduced the pilgrims who slept near the building that eventually grew into the structure today called St. Peter's Basilica.

From the tenth and eleventh centuries the accretion of Church riches gathered momentum ... that is, it became systemized. Indeed, it became a fixed feature of the administration of the Holy Mother Church (*Petrus Cluniacensis*, lib, v., epist, xxix, (Peter, Abbot of Cluny), c. 1310). Up until around that time the accumulation of Church wealth had been carried out in a somewhat haphazard fashion, but things were soon to change with the growth of Vatican riches gathering momentum. The sudden development of a papal system of taxation demands was introduced by the Avignon popes (1305-1403, generally), and additional forms of revenues were created, benefices, for example. A tribute was demanded in recognition of papal suzerainty over various vassal kingdoms, and rent from the Papal States was dramatically increased.

Prostitutional income from the nunneries

Simultaneously with the accelerated growth of Church riches, a new factor appeared on the scene amidst the ruins of the classic, and the new emerging cultures; the monastic communities. These, the nuclei of which had come to the fore in original obscurity, now transformed themselves into associations of pious individuals determined to personally ensure the riches of heaven by the abandonment of the riches of the earth. But the anonymous hermits and nuns who sustained themselves upon locusts, fruit and spring water, found it increasingly difficult to follow such a strict mode of life. The legacies of the pious, the presents of parcels of lands, estates and goods from newly converted rich individuals, and the thanksgiving of repentant sinners, all contributed within a few centuries to make the monastic movement in Europe custodians of earthly riches and administrators of earthly goods. The popes imposed the *Census*, a tax paid by monasteries and also churches were taxed. Thus the Holy Mother Church soon found herself, not only on a par with the political and military potentates of the world, but equally a competitor with these amassers of riches, from her high prelates, consorting with top officials of the imperial court, to the monastic communities, springing up with ever more frequency in the semi-abandoned hamlets of former Roman colonies. The tradition of supposed poverty became an abstraction; at most, a text for sermons or pious homilies. And, while single heroic individuals preached and observed it, the Church triumphant, congregating with the principalities of the Earth, not only ignored it; she shamelessly stultified its injunctions, until, having become embarrassed by it, she brazenly disregarded it, abandoning both its theory and, even more, its practice.

The monasteries were corrupted, and nunneries were not cloisters for the seclusion of withered old maids or young ladies renouncing the vanities of the world, but 'luxurious lounging palours for the priests ... the walls were gemmed with brilliance, set off by folds of black velvet richly damasked in gold' (*Diderot's Encyclopedia*, 1759). They were, in fact, 'brothels filled with the choicest prostitutes, lean with fasting, but full of lust' (*A History of the Popes*, Dr. Joseph McCabe, Rector of Buckingham College; d. 1955; C. A. Watts and Co, London). This wasn't a new development for the Church, as descriptions of nunneries being busy brothels were recorded centuries earlier in the *Annals of Hildesheim* (c. 890), and the *Annals of Hincmar* (Archbishop of Rheims, c. 905). Later in time, a considerable number of the girls were destined to become 'hearth-girls' ... a euphemism for the concubines kept by the Christian priesthood. Later still, (the 14th-17th Centuries), they were called 'Cathedral-girls' because they sought their customers in cathedrals, and the revenue generated by them was the property of the bishops (*A History of the Popes*, Dr. Joseph McCabe, Rector of Buckingham College; d. 1955; C. A. Watts and Co, London).

In 1554, a special papal representative, Andrew Avellino (b. 1521), 'was commissioned to reform a nunnery at Naples, which by the laxity of its discipline had become a source of great scandal. Certain wicked priests were accustomed to have had clandestine meetings with the nuns' (*Catholic Encyclopedia*, Farley Ed., i, p. 472). Christian reformer, Martin Luther (1483-1546), wrote of a fishpond at Rome, situated near a convent of nuns which, having been cleared out by the order of Pope Gregory, disclosed at the bottom, over 6000 infant skulls. He also records that a nunnery at Neinburg in Austria, whose foundations, when searched, disclosed the same relics of feigned celibacy and chastity.

CHAPTER 11

Paying for the release of a soul

And then there was the scandal of Indulgences. Originally an Indulgence was one of the most innocuous instruments of the spiritual armory of the Church, but things changed with the crusades (1096-1571) pushing Indulgences to the forefront as a means of accumulating massive riches for a thousand years. Indulgences developed into machinations whereas believers paid money the priesthood to secure them from the threat of burning in Hell, or the release from their sins of murder, polygamy, sacrilege, and perjury. For cash, property, or some penitential act, a pardon was conveyed, or a release from the pains of purgatory, guilt, or the forgiveness of sins was granted to any person who bestowed wealth upon the Church.

Within Catholicism, the practice of selling Indulgences became widespread, particularly when they were applicable to the dead, thus tempting, as it were, members of families to pay for the release of the souls of their beloved from the flames of purgatory. 'Here … the love of money was the chief root of the evil; Indulgences were employed by mercenary ecclesiastics as a means of pecuniary gain' *(Catholic Encyclopedia*, Farley Ed., vii, p. 787). St. Bernard of Champagne (1090-1153), the dissolute son of Lord Tescelin and Aleth of Montbard, fulminated against a Church he deemed 'atheistic', and complained that 'pardoning of sins in exchange for money' (Indulgences) was not Gospel dogma. In his onslaught, he spared neither priest, bishop or pope, accusing them of worshipping Mammon instead of God. In his treatise *On Customs and Duties of Bishops,* he thundered against bishops who 'grew fat on the revenues from bishoprics' and did not hesitate to castigate papal Legates. He declared the Roman Curia 'a den of thieves' (ibid) and described them as 'rapacious men who would sacrifice the well-being of people for the gold of Spain' (ibid).

The immensity of the riches that Indulgences brought to the Church over the centuries is incalculable and they contributed to the development of priesthood corruption and decadence. Their trading for valuables became such a scandal that it turned into a universal, well-organized abuse which operated at all levels of the clergy, its chief exponent and proponent being the papacy itself. An English account which appeared around 1370 enumerated the widespread racket of Indulgences offered by churches in Rome, the following being a typical example:

> We learn, that at St. Peter's, from Holy Thursday to Lammas (1st August), there was a daily Indulgence of 14,000 years, and whenever the Vernicle was exhibited, there was one of 3,000 years for citizens, 9,000 for Italians, and 12,000 for pilgrims from beyond the sea. At San Anastasio there was one of 7000 years every day, and at San Tommaso one of 14,000, with one-third remission of sins for all comers.
>
> (*A History of Auricular Confessions and Indulgences in the Latin Church*, H. C. Lea, vol. iii, London, 1896)

The sale of Indulgences took sundry shapes and forms, and produced a massive income. If the privilege of granting Indulgences was accorded to the shrine of some saint, it resulted in the increase of pilgrims attempting to partake in the spiritual treasures of that saint, and since, after each visit, huge sums of money were invariably left behind, the Indulgence became *ipso facto* a money-spinner of incalculable importance. This reached such absurd proportions that at one time no less than 800 Indulgences-plenaries, accompanied by appropriate offerings, were attached to St. Peter's in Rome.

The pope's urgent call for funds

The Church had scarcely a pope more dedicated to expensive pleasures, or to whom money was so anxiously sought, than the fat and amiable Pope Leo X (Giovanni de Medici, born, 1475; pope from 1513-21). Pope Julius II had earlier bestowed Indulgences on all who contributed toward building

St. Peter's at Rome, and Leo X rapidly expanded the doctrine. The year after his election he sold the archbishopric of Mainz and two bishoprics to a rich loose-living young noble, Albert of Brandenburg for a huge sum and permitted him to recover his investment by the sordid traffic in Indulgences which a few years later inflamed Luther. Lord Bryce (1838-1922), British jurist, author and statesman, summarized the mental and moral qualities of the priesthood that Indulgences reflected. He said that its concept was 'a blatant fraud against the naive ... a portentous falsehood and the most unimpeachable evidence of the true thoughts and beliefs of the priesthood which framed it' (*Holy Roman Empire*, Lord Bryce, h. vi, p. 107, Latin text, extracts, p. 76).

To replenish the coffers and maintain his 'luxuriant abundance' Leo expanded the sale of Indulgences into a major source of Church revenue and developed a large body of priests to collect the payments. After detailing how people should come to the Indulgence Seller, the pope declared:

We have therefore fixed the following rates:

Kings, queens, and their sons, archbishops and bishops and other great rulers shall pay, upon presenting themselves to places where the cross is raised, twenty-five Rheinish guilders.

Abbots, prelates of cathedral churches, counts, barons, and others of the higher nobility and their wives, shall pay, for each letter of indulgence, ten such gold guilders. Other lesser prelates and nobles, as also the rectors of famous places, and all others who take in, either from steady income or goods or other means, 500 gold guilders, should pay six guilders.

Other citizens and merchants, who ordinary take in 200 such gold florins, shall pay three florins.

Other citizens, merchants, and artisans, who have their families and income of their own, shall pay one such guilder; those of lesser means, pay only one-half of a gold florin.

(Martin Luther, *Wider Hans Worst* (1541), Weimar)

In forming his plans, Pope Leo was assisted mainly by his relative Laurentius Pucci, whom he made cardinal of Santaquatro, and John Tetzel, a former military officer of the Teutonic Knights in Prussia. They appointed a series of retailers to keep pace with the disposal of goods given to pay for Indulgences and he and his team then set off on a mission through Italy to entice more sales. The pope exercised every option to increase his wealth, selling favours and opportunities to anyone who had enough coin to jingle in the purse that swung heavily at his side. This picturesque overview of his trip is drawn from *Diderot's Encyclopedia*, and provides one reason why Pope Clement XIII (1758-69) ordered all volumes to be burned immediately after its publication in 1759, and decreed arrest for Diderot should he ever enter Rome (*The Censoring of Diderot's Encyclopedia and the Re-established Text* (NY. 1947), D. H. Gordon and N. L. Torrey; also, *Oxford Concise Dictionary of the Christian Church,* E. A. Livingstone, 2000):

> The Indulgence-seekers passed through the country in gay carriages escorted by thirty horsemen, in great state and spending freely. The Pontiff's Bull of Grace was borne in front on a purple velvet cushion, or sometimes on a cloth of gold. The Chief Vendor of Indulgences followed with his team, supporting a large red wooden cross; and the whole procession moved in this manner amidst singing and the smoke of incense. As soon as the cross was elevated, and the Pope's arms suspended upon it, Tetzel ascended the pulpit, and with a bold tone, began, in the presence of the crowd, to exalt the efficacy of Indulgences. The Pope was the last speaker, and cried out: 'Bring money, bring money, bring money'. He uttered this cry with such a dreadful bellowing that one might have thought that some wild bull was rushing among the people, and goring them with his horns.

(*Diderot's Encyclopedia*, 1759; expanded upon in *D'Aubigné,* J. H. Merle, 1840, Church historian; also, *History of the Great Reformation,* 3 Vols. London)

The pope and the priests associated with him falsely represented their topic, and exaggerated the value of Indulgences so as to lead people to believe that 'as soon as they gave their money, they were certain of salvation and the deliverance of souls from purgatory' (ibid).

So strong was the Protestant Movement's opposition to the sale of Indulgences that Pope Leo X issued a bull called *Exurge Domine,* its purpose being to condemn Martin Luther's damaging assertions that 'Indulgences are frauds against the faithful and criminal offences against God'. Around 45 years later, the 18-year-long Council of Trent pronounced 'anathema against those who either declare Indulgences to be useless or deny that the Church has the power to grant them' (*Catholic Encyclopedia,* Farley Ed., vii, pp. 783-4). The immense wealth the Church went on collecting in this manner finally reached such proportions that her economic stranglehold upon all and sundry was no less massive than her spiritual dominion, and almost paralyzed whole countries. During the reign of Francis I (1515-47), for instance, just 600 abbots, bishops and archbishops controlled so much land throughout France that the Church's income equalled that of the French State itself (*A History of the Popes from the Close of the Middle Ages,* Dr. Ludwig Pastor (1854-1928), German historian of the papacy, Vol. IV (of XVI), par. I, p. 589). And, France was not an exception; practically every other country in Western Europe was in a similar situation.

The bridge to purgatory is down!

The use, abuse and misuse of Indulgences should not make us lightly condemn them as unimportant, or their absurdities induce us to underestimate the tremendous power they had ... or rather, the tremendous power of the cumulative effect of their employment by both the Church and the popes. Indulgences grew in number and power with the passing of time until finally they became so unlimited that even the pious began to doubt their efficacy. Believers suggested that the asking price of a pardon of 20,000 years from the pains of purgatory was overvalued by 'the avarice of the people who were selling them' (*A History of the Popes,* Dr. Joseph McCabe, Rector of Buckingham College; d. 1955; C. A. Watts and Co, London). But then there was a major catastrophe for the Holy Mother Church ... the bridge to purgatory collapsed. The Christian priesthood, in Naples, Rome, Florence and Ireland, sent out urgent demands for money for repairs so as souls of the deceased could pass over. The following extract is just one example of the artifices used by the priesthood to deceptively obtain money, and is reproduced verbatim from a letter sent by Mr. James Kirwan, a British barrister and layman of the faith, to the Hon. Roger B. Taney, Chief Justice of the United States:

> There lived a poor man in one of the cities of Ireland who made his support by selling beer. He was honest, and punctual in his payments, and won the entire confidence of the brewer. He died; and, as the priest stated, his soul went to purgatory. His widow carried on the business, and sent for one barrel of beer after another, until she was in debt to the brewer about one hundred pounds. The brewer, who was a Papist, went to her beer-shop to make enquiry as to the cause of this large indebtedness. 'And have you not heard of the terrible accident that has happened?' said the woman. 'What is it?' asked the brewer. 'The bridge to purgatory is broken', was the reply, 'and it takes a great deal of money to repair it; and Father O'Flanagan is very faithful in collecting money to repair it, bless his soul; and when the bridge is finished, so that my poor husband can get across, then I will strive to pay you all'.
>
> Sure am I that the fiction of purgatory is made to yield millions every year to the priests, and in ways no more justifiable than that adopted with the poor lady that sold beer. But if there is a class of persons living that deserves a good long residence in purgatory, priests are the men. And should they go there, and should the bridge break down, I would not give Father O'Flanagan a penny to rebuild it.
>
> (*Romanism at Home*; Kirwan, being Letters to the Hon. Roger B. Taney, Chief Justice of the United States, printed in Edinburgh by Johnstone and Hunter, M. DCCC. LII, (1852), pp. 171-4)

Such are the ways and the manner in which the priesthood seek to deceive, delude, and prejudice the minds of believers of their story.

The toll-gate of the Church

The absurdity to which the swindle of Indulgences was carried can be gathered by the fact that no less than 9000 years, plus 9000 quarantines for every step of the *Scala Sancta*, or holy staircase in Rome, were transferable to the souls of the dead. The *Scala Sancta* is a 15th Century 'made to order' fake relic housed in the Vatican and comprises 28 white marble steps which the popes falsely present as the stairway which Jesus Christ ascended and descended at his trial before Pontius Pilate. These Indulgences were granted by the authority of Pope Pius VII (1742-1823; pope from 1800-1823) and supported later by Pope Pius IX (1792-1878; pope from 1846-1878). The depth of this fraud is seen in the fact that these stairs are in Rome but according to the Gospels, Jesus never went to Rome ... the canonical story was set in Jerusalem. The Stations of the Via Crucis, also in Rome, were so rich in Indulgences that, according to Bishop Ferraris, an eminent authority on the subject, a Christian could, within one year, gain 49 plenaries (absolutes) and more than 1,000,000 years of partials (parts only). These unashamed deceptions were never rebuked or prevented by pope or priest, but, rather, were industriously stimulated by them for the rich revenues they produced, and the dishonour to the human mind wrought upon the public by centuries of priestly impostures should be seriously questioned.

CHAPTER 12

Protecting Church revenues

The worldly interests of the Church are involved in keeping up its delusions and in withholding people from contact with everything that would, in the least degree, tend to dissipate them. For example, the pretended holiness and piety of popes as publicly presented today is not represented in the records of history, and that provides proof of the dishonesty of the Church's own portrayal. Pious Catholic historian and author, Bishop Frotheringham (1877), extended this summary of Christian leaders up to his time:

> Many of the popes were men of the most abandoned lives. Some were magicians (Occultists); others were noted for sedition, war, slaughter and profligacy of manners, for avarice and simony. Others were not even members of Christ, but the basest of criminals and enemies of all godliness. Some were children of their father, the Devil; most were men of blood; some were not even priests. Others were heretics. If the pope be a heretic, he is *ipso facto*, no pope.
>
> (*The Cradle of Christ,* Bishop Frotheringham, 1877; see also, *Catholic Encyclopedia*, Farley Ed., xii, pp. 700-703, passim)

For centuries, the priesthood was resented by the laity and when better economic conditions re-awakened the mind of a developing European Middle Class, there was widespread rebellion against them. Many popes were forcibly removed from Rome, and it became standard procedure for Romans to drag statues of popes through the mud after their death (*The Criminal History of the Papacy*, Tony Bushby, in *Nexus New Times*, vol., 14, No. 3, April-May, 2007, part 3, p. 53). In the 14th Century, a more-intelligent community was developing, and they were openly challenging the Christian story at its very core. People wanted evidence to support papal claims about Jesus Christ, and there 'was a silent spread of suspicion in the intelligentsia, even in the clergy themselves ... for many, despite papal Bulls, were disbelievers' (*Confessions of a French Catholic Priest*, New York, Mathers, 1837). Thinking-people were making threatening enquiries as to the genuineness of the Gospels, and publicly questioned the role of the Church. The popes saw this exposure as a threat to not only their hedonistic lifestyles, but to their vast incomes and embarked on a policy to eliminate the truth of Christian origins from the public eye. They were intent only upon their own interests, not those of God, and cultivated a system of cover-ups more assiduously than writers of Christian history dare to openly reveal.

To protect their frauds and deceptions from exposure, the papacy employed obscurantisms as it sought to hide the fabricated nature of its god, and dishonestly establish a basis for claims of a 'revealed' origin to their religion. In 1415, Pope Benedict XIII (Pedro de Luna, 1394-1423) ordered the destruction of all copies of two Fourth Century books that contained 'the true name of Jesus Christ'. A battle raged in the Church as to whether he was a legitimate pope or not, but he created four new cardinals to specifically single out for condemnation a Latin treatise called *Mar Yesu*, and then issued instructions to destroy all copies of the mysterious *Book of Elxai*. No editions of these writings now publicly exist, but Church archives record that they were once in popular circulation, and known to the early Christian priesthood. Knowledge of these writings survived in extracts published from them by St. Epiphanius of Salamis (315-403), 'an honest, but credulous minded zealot ... who collected a rich abundance of genuine traditions from what seemed a worthless mass (*Dictionary of Christian Biography,* Smith and Wade, undated). St. Epiphanius constantly called the creation now known as Jesus Christ, 'Hesus Krishna', and was puzzled by the unhistorical nature of the Christian god. Today, the Church calls the Saint's revealing comments, 'The Riddle of Epiphanius'.

The pontiff who could fill the Sistine Chapel with sacks of gold

The name 'Hesus Krishna' also appears in ancient New Testaments, and in old versions of the Talmuds of Palestine and Babylonia. For this reason, Pope

Alexander VI (1492-1503) ordered all copies of the Talmud destroyed, for if the truth about Jesus Christ was made public, the process of the deconstruction of Christianity would necessarily begin immediately. Had this happened, the dissolution of the Christian Church would have preceded the Fatima prophecy of its downfall (by 2015) by some 500 years. In amazement, Pope Alexander exclaimed: 'Almighty God! How long will this superstitious sect of Christians, and this upstart invention, endure?' (*Diderot's Encyclopedia*, 1759). It was this same pope who openly boasted that he could fill the Sistine Chapel with sacks of gold. He ordered the Council of the Inquisition to burn all Jewish writings, and the Spanish Grand Inquisitor, Tomas de Torquemada (1420-98), was personally responsible for the elimination of 6000 volumes at Salamanca. In 1550, Cardinal Caraffa, the Inquisitor-General procured a Bull from the Pope repealing all previous permission for priests to read or own the Talmud that he said contained 'hostile stories about Jesus Christ'. Bursting forth with fury at the head of his minions, he seized every copy he could find in Rome and burnt them. In Cremona, priest Vittorio Eliano bitterly testified against the Talmud, and 10,000 Hebrew books were burned under his rage. His brother, Solomon Romano (1554) also burnt thousands of Hebrew scrolls and in 1559 every Hebrew book in the city of Prague was confiscated. The mass destruction of Jewish books included hundreds of copies of the Old Testament and caused the irretrievable loss of many original hand-written versions. In an attempt by the Church to cover-up damaging information about the real nature of Jesus Christ, the Inquisition burnt at least 22,000 volumes of the Talmud (*Diderot's Encyclopedia*, 1759).

Around the same time (1501), Pope Alexander VI established the *Index Librorum Prohibitorim* (*Index of Prohibited Books*), by which the Roman Catholic Church, for centuries, policed the literature available to the world. It was perhaps the most dramatic form of censorship known to the world and was overseen by official Vatican censors. The *Index* was a catalogue of forbidden reading which continued to have official Church sanction well into the 20th Century. More comprehensive rules were developed at the first period of the Council of Trent in 1546 (*The Vatican Censors,* Professor Peter Elmsley (1773-1825), Principal of St. Alban's Hall, Oxford), and books hostile to the Church were condemned under 10 separate headings. Seven years later, a

Congregation of the Index was set up in Rome that for centuries regularly issued catalogued lists of new books forbidden by the Church to be read. Thus, regulated reading was established, and hardly a classic escaped ... no good book was left out of the Index.

On the pain of excommunication, generations of students, scholars, the general public, bishops and cardinals too, were forbidden to read or own books listed on the *Index*. That fearful restriction kept candid and important knowledge away from the mainstream populace and restricted public access to truths that had survived. Printers and bookshops were at mortal risk of discovery by the Inquisition whose leaders were vigilant for any sort of public theological impropriety. Thus, books written challenging the validity of Christianity never reached the mass-market audience and many valuable historical tomes were destroyed. The last edition of the *Index* appeared in 1948, and contained the names of 5000 banned books. In 1966, Pope Paul VI finally discontinued it and relegated it to the status of an historical document. In January 1998, the Vatican revealed the infamous *Index* and publicly admitted that its own Bible was once on the black list, originally suppressed by Pope Damasus at the First Council of Constantinople in 381-3.

How a pope replenished his treasury

Priesthood extremes outraged the general populous and when Leo X captured the papacy in 1513, his extravaganzas shocked even blasé Italy. In Germany, the story of the pope's financial transactions shared in the anger of Luther's revolt (October 1517), and the people of Europe 'shook with cynical laughter' (*Weimarer Ausgabe,* Weimar, 1883) at the pope's blatant grab for money. To replenish his treasury Leo created 1353 new and saleable offices, for which appointees paid a total of 889,000 ducats (US$11,112,500 in 1955). He nominated 60 additional Chamberlains and 141 squires to the 2000 persons who made up his ménage at the Vatican, and received from them a total of 202,000 ducats. In July 1517, he named 31 new cardinals, chosen 'not of such as had the most merit, but of those that offered the most money for the honour and power' (ibid). Cardinal Porizetti, for example, paid 40,000 ducats and altogether Leo's appointees on this occasion brought in another half a million ducats for the treasury. Some cardinals received an income from the

Church of 40,000 ducats a year and lived in stately palaces manned by as many as 300 servants and adorned with every art and luxury known to the time. A favourite satire that developed around Leo was called the *Gospel according to Marks and Silver*, which said:

> In those days Pope Leo said to the clergy: 'When Jesus the Son of Man shall come to the seat of our Majesty, say first of all, 'Friend, wherefore art Thou come hither? And if He gives you naught in silver or gold, cast Him forth into outer darkness'.

It was Pope Leo X who made the most celebrated statement in the history of the Christian Church. His declaration revealed to the world papal knowledge of the Vatican's false presentation of Jesus Christ as an historical divine being and unashamedly exposed the puerile nature of the Christian religion. At a lavish Easter Friday banquet in the Vatican in 1514, and in the company of 'seven intimates' (*Annales Ecclesiastici*, Cardinal Caesar Baronius), Leo made an amazing announcement that the Church has since tried hard to invalidate. Raising a chalice of wine into the air, Pope Leo toasted:

> How well we know what a profitable superstition this fable of Christ has been for us and our predecessors.

The pope's pronouncement is recorded in the diaries and records of both Cardinal Pietro Bembo (*His Letters and Comments on Pope Leo X*, Reprint 1842) and Cardinal Jovius (*De Vita Leonis X*, originally published in 1551), two associates who were witnesses to Pope Leo's celebratory confession.

The pontiff on a white elephant

Perhaps the greatest marvel ever seen in Rome was the pomp and ceremony associated with a regally-attired Pope Leo riding around the city on a white elephant draped with burgundy silk fringed with gold and purple tassels. Like King Charlemagne some 700 years earlier, the pope was given the rare animal as a gift, and like Charlemagne's monster at his court in Aachen, it actually lumbered across the Alps to the enclosure of its new papal owner. It was Pope Leo who announced to the scholastic world that he would financially reward any person who should procure for him ancient manuscripts, and sometimes he dispatched envoys for the sole purpose in co-operating in the search or the removal of old texts already known to exist. 'His agents, on occasion, stole manuscripts or asserted papal pressure for their removal when they could not be purchased' (*Christian Forgeries,* Major Joseph Wheless, USA Judge Advocate, Idaho, 1930). This was the case with the first six books of Roman historian Tacitus's (c. 56-126) *Annals,* originally found in the monastery of Corvey in Westphalia in 1455 and subsequently removed under Leo's instructions in 1516. In the same discovery was a full collection of Senator Pliny's (the Younger, c. 112) letters and they too were taken to the Vatican. Leo gave the purloined manuscripts to Filippo Beroaldo with directions to censor the handwritten texts, and then publish them in a convenient printed form. Existing today is a letter written by, or for Leo, to his agent Heitmers after *Annals* and Pliny's letters had been rewritten and republished, saying:

> We have sent a copy of the revised books in a beautiful binding to the abbot and his monks that they may place them in their library as a substitute for the original manuscripts taken from it.
>
> (*The Vatican Censors,* Professor Peter Elmsley (1773-1825), Principal of St. Alban's Hall, Oxford)

It is not known what changes were made to Tacitus's records, as the originals are not publicly available for comparison. Importantly, there are 'six missing pages' (*Diderot's Encyclopedia,* 1759) in his writings, and they purport to describe the years of the reign of Roman Emperor Claudius' (41-54). The reader may wonder why those pages were removed, and the possibility exists that Pope Leo personally ordered their suppression. Maybe they carried information about Claudius's gift of 'twenty acres of ground and detached buildings on the crest of the Esquiline mount' (Viminalis Hill in Rome) to the royal Welsh Silures. It was called *The Palatium Britannicum* or, 'The Palace of the Britannia' (in some translations, 'The Palace of the British'), and, because of a series of inter-marriages, its inhabitants were founders of not only the British monarchy, but the British Church. If so, that information would have been sensitive to Church portrayals of its origins for it would have revealed the family lineage of Emperor Constantine, and why he included the names of two of his blood-line descendants in his *New Testimonies*. It may also explain why a specific royalist movement is working today towards the ultimate restoration of a prince of Welsh blood to the throne of Britain. However, this book is an overview of the Church's fortune, so we shall leave this matter for a later discussion.

Dollars and sense (or nonsense)

All in all, Leo spent 4,500,000 ducats during his pontificate (US$56,250,000 in 1955) and died owing 400,000 more. Shortly after his death, Church censors set into motion publishing actions that effectively changed world history, and provided for themselves a series of deceptive publications that are today used in learning institutions around the world (*The Propaganda Press of Rome*, Sir James W. L. Claxton, Whitehaven Books, Belgrave Square, London, 1942). The Vatican's Censoring Office altered the 'true name of Jesus Christ' to read 'the Lord' in subsequent revisions of not only the New Testament, but all Church writings. As was the case with the Bible, so also were damaging writings of early presbyters modified in centuries of copying, and many of their records were 'rewritten or suppressed' (*Index Expurgatorius Vaticanus*, edited by R. Gibbings, B.A., Dublin, 1837). Adopting the decrees of the Council of Trent, 'reckless of truth to the highest degree' (*Diderot's Encyclopedia*, 1759), the Church subsequently extended the process of erasure and ordered the preparation of a list of particular information to be expunged from original Church writings (*Delineation of Roman Catholicism*, Rev. Charles Elliott, D.D., p. 89; also, *The Vatican Censors*, Professor Peter Elmsley (1773-1825), Principal of St. Alban's Hall, Oxford).

In 1562, a special censoring office called *Index Expurgatorius* was established and its purpose was to prohibit publication of 'erroneous passages of the early presbyters that carried statements opposing modern-day doctrine'. When Vatican archivists came across, 'genuine copies of the Fathers, they corrected them according to the *Expurgatory Index*' (*Index Expurgatorius Vaticanus*, edited by R. Gibbings, B.A., Dublin, 1837. For a full and accurate account of the *Indices*, both *Expurgatory* and *Prohibitory* the reader is referred to Rev. Mr. Mendham's work, *The Literary Policy of the Church of Rome*, Second

Ed., 1840; also, *The Vatican Censors,* Professor Peter Elmsley (1773-1825), Principal of St. Alban's Hall, Oxford). That Church record provides researchers with 'grave doubts about the value of all patristic writings released to the public' (*The Propaganda Press of Rome,* Sir James W. L. Claxton, Whitehaven Books, Belgrave Square, London, 1942), and reveals a Church cover-up of immense proportions.

But the deception doesn't stop there. Former swineherd and Inquisitor General, Felice Peretti (1521-1590) was elected Pope Sixtus V on April 24, 1585. In 1587, he established an official Vatican publishing press, and we catch the spirit of the times when we read the pope's own words:

> The press will combat the deceit of heretics and the malice and ignorance of printers and publishers, and literature that has been the cause of much evil to us. Authors are everywhere, and they are worse than their own writings, which I don't mean as a compliment to either ... they must be interpreted into harmlessness.
>
> We shall seek to print our own account, a logical analysis of the books which deserve to hold the attention of the public. Church history will be established and will be a considerable part of our report. In general, we shall let nothing escape us which is worthy of the curiosity of people.
>
> (*Diderot's Encyclopedia,* 1759)

It was because of such revelations that the Church sort to suppress all volumes of *Diderot's Encyclopedia.*

In April 1588, Pope Sixtus V put into motion one of the most infamous papal deceits in Christian history ... he rewrote the Vulgate and created a different Catholic belief the Church officially called, the 'New Learning' (*Catholic Encyclopedia,* Farley eds., v, p. 442; ix, p. 335; xv, p. 376). It was a strange feat of literary dishonesty and proof of its execution is found in the Church's own records. After issuing a Bull declaring that he was the only appropriate person to provide a 'proper' Bible for the Roman Church, Sixtus took up the task to rewrite all biblical texts used by the Vatican. He claimed that the New Testament was without a god, saying:

> In the Gospel and the whole of Holy Scripture, there is not one word of Christ spoken of as god. Therefore, by the fullness of the apostolic power within me it must be amended as to be unquestioned by the upper ten thousand, and in all public and private discussions.

(*Diderot's Encyclopedia*, 1759)

Sixtus set to and personally rewrote both the Old and New Testaments in his own hand. For 18 months he laboured night and day, imposing his personal theological views and 'adding new concepts and sentences to his liking' (Cardinal R. F. R. Bellarmine, the pope's advisor; also, *The Vatican Censors*, Professor Peter Elmsley (1773-1825), Principal of St. Alban's Hall, Oxford). He passed days and nights in a continued frenzy, for he was insomniac. He lay with his eyes open, without speaking, eating or stirring. He was obsessed with his new creation and blatantly ignored the advice of his Jesuit consultant, Cardinal Roberto Francis Romulus Bellarmine (1542-1621), that the changes to Church belief were 'inadvisable and difficult to understand'. The pope created a new version of the Jesus Christ story, and it later caused even pious churchmen to lie on its behalf.

In 1988, Roman Catholic scholar, Peter de Rosa, published a powerful book called *Vicars of Christ*, and added this comment:

> A Bible had been imposed with the plenitude of papal power, complete with the trimmings of excommunication, on the whole Church ... and it was riddled with errors. The academic world was in turmoil. Protestants were deriving much pleasure and amusement from the predicament of the Roman Church.

(*Vicars of Christ*, Peter de Rosa, Crown Publishers, New York, 1988)

The pope then issued a command that no printer, editor, or bookseller was to deviate by one jot from his new Vulgate. Anyone contravening the Bull was to be excommunicated and only the pope could absolve him.

The Sixtine Vulgate Bible, as it became known, was subsequently printed and issued along with another papal Bull threatening excommunication for violations of the commands that variant readings should not be printed in subsequent editions, and that the edition must not be modified. This Bull demanded that the new Bible 'be received and held as true, lawful, authentic and unquestioned in all public and private discussions, readings, preaching and explanations'. Sixtus's own words raise serious ethical and political questions about the propriety of deception by a Church leader. A false born-again religion had been written 'to order', and perhaps Catholicism survived by absorbing it. Words describing Jesus Christ as 'the son of God' then appeared in the Gospels (Mark 1:1), and the modern-day family tree tracing a 'messianic bloodline' back to King David was invented for the occasion, as were the now-called 'messianic prophecies' (51 in total). The prevailing vogue with Church writers was then to express and cultivate a deeply reverential feeling for everything written in the New Testament, and entrenched themselves behind false divine sanctions. The Gospels are not unique divine revelations, and if their acknowledged forgeries were deleted, the blood and substance of the Christian religion would go with them. When the New Testament in the World's oldest Bible (Sinaiticus, c. 380) is compared with a modern-day New Testament, a staggering 14,800 later editorial falsifications are identified, and these forgeries are revealed by a simple comparative exercise that anybody can, and should do.

In 1595, Pope Clement VIII published a decree declaring that 'the writings of all Catholic authors since 1515 should be corrected, so as not only to blot out doctrines not approved, but to add to, where necessary' (*Delineation of Roman Catholicism*, Rev. Charles Elliott, D.D., p. 89, 1844; also, *The Vatican Censors,* Professor Peter Elmsley (1773-1825), Principal of St. Alban's Hall, Oxford). In a rare moment of honesty, the Church freely admitted that it sold its soul in the 'perversion of the truth originating in publishing surreptitious or supposititious papal bulls, briefs and transcripts originating in the deceitfulness of one party and culminating in the damage of another party (*Catholic Encyclopedia*, Pecci Ed., iii, pp. 224-5; mollified in the Farley Ed., v, p. 781), and those falsifications made Christianity what it is today. *Falsus in uno, falsus in omnibus* ... 'Untrue in one thing, untrue in everything'.

CHAPTER 13

The Vatican's marketing machine

On 22nd June, 1622, Pope Gregory XV (d. 1623) issued a papal bull called *Inscrutabila Divine* by which the Church instituted for itself a new promotional division called the Sacred Congregation of Propaganda. Shortly thereafter, Gregory summoned 13 cardinals and 2 prelates to announce his intentions to formalize a 'special department of pontifical administration' (Pope Gregory XV), initially established around four decades earlier by Pope Gregory XIII (d. 1585). Cardinal Santorio was its first President and Prefect, and weekly progress meetings were held in his Palace. Originally, his new department had been charged with the task of combating the international spread of the doctrines of Protestantism by printing and distributing works of propaganda in many languages that were designed to damage opponents' claims against Catholicism. 'Indeed, one of the chief duties was to sow jealousies and hatred among their people toward all who are not Papists' (*Romanism at Home*; J. Kirwin, being Letters to the Hon. Roger B. Taney, Chief Justice of the United States, printed in Edinburgh by Johnstone and Hunter, M.DCCC.LII, (1852), p. 171). The intrinsic importance of the duties of the Sacred Congregation of Propaganda, and the extraordinary extent of its authority, including the huge territory under its jurisdiction, caused the Cardinal Prefect of Propaganda to be called the 'red pope'.

After 300 years of operation, the Sacred Congregation of Propaganda developed into a massive internal organization, issuing strictly party line misinformation to an unsuspecting public. As a general principle, the territory of Vatican propaganda was conterminous with countries that were non-Catholic in government, and emigrants were specifically targeted. The Holy

Mother Church produced its dictatorial literature by establishing a publishing division called the Propaganda Press that initially operated from Rome (*The Propaganda Press of Rome*, Sir James W. L. Claxton, Whitehaven Books, Belgrave Square, London, 1942). It printed disinformation, both retrospective and contemporary, that was distributed to the public in the form of apostolic letters, creeds (*The Christ Scandal*, Tony Bushby, University Press, USA, 2008; see Entry, 'Fake Apostolic Letters and Creeds', p. 264), brochures, pamphlets, bulletins, and Church-established newspapers. A Society of Cardinals called Propagandists oversaw distribution of the information by means of Church delegations, dioceses, vicariates, prefectures, simple missions, colleges, and universities, and by this method, Vatican false information subsequently reached 'an international market' (*Catholic Encyclopedia,* Farley Ed., xii, pp. 456-460; there are almost 6000 words about the establishment and extent of the Church's Propaganda machine in this section of the *Catholic Encyclopedia*).

© Archives de Historé. Photo by Alain Fachini, 1908

This is the Palace of Propaganda, Piazza Di Spagna, Rome, circa 1900, and shows the ground floor windows heavily-reinforced with steel bars. The inscription directly above the front door on the first floor reads:
COLLEGIVM VRBANVM DEPROPAGANDA FIDE
and above that is a crest displaying the papal keys.

An extra US$20,000 for the Holy Mother Church

One of the first jobs of the Holy See' new marketing and promotional division was to establish a department that for around the next 400-years wrote, and published false information about the lives and 'miracles' of people now called 'saints'. Ioannes S.J. van Bolland of Belgium (d. c. 1665), accepted a commission to establish a Catholic publishing Society known as the Bollandists, and it was still industriously carrying on its dishonest labours in the 1930s. Its official task was to publish 'books containing the lives and acts of every saint in the Holy Roman Calendar' (*Catholic Encyclopedia*, Farley Ed., ix, pp. 129-130), and the saint-library of the Society subsequently grew to over 150,000 volumes. The Church said that that 'monumental work, the *Acta Sanctorum* of the Bollandists, has become the foundation of all investigation in hagiography and legend' (*Catholic Encyclopedia*, Farley Ed., ix, p. 129), and it is entirely fictional. Irish Archbishop James Ussher (17th Century) was right when he described it as 'packed with the most stupid lies' (*The Celtic Church in Scotland,* John Dowden, D.D, Bishop of Edinburgh, 1894, p. 75).

Arranged in order of dates of their 'feast days', so numerous was the contents of the *Acta Sanctorum* that up to the month of October over 25,000 'officially authenticated' (ibid) saints were created, and the 'lying wonders of falsified fiction' (*Christian Forgeries,* Major Joseph Wheless, USA Judge Advocate, Idaho, 1930) recorded in those volumes were, without exception, presented by the Holy Mother Church as actual verities of its past. Major Joseph Wheless called them 'a collection of sinister lies of priestcraft and unimpeachable evidence of the fraudulent pretensions of the Church of Christ' (ibid). The approbation with which 'miracles' were applied by the Bollandists to unhistorical people, and the peculiar sanctity attributed to them by the Church, is sufficient to show the juvenility of Christian development. It is this sort of mentality that we are constantly confronted with in all areas of Christianity. It is a fact of Christianity that modern-day access to the *Acta Sanctorum* is not easy to obtain, and one suspects that the Church is withholding these volumes because of the embarrassment their invented nature would cause if released into the hands of judicious modern-day researchers and authors.

The first saint created by a pope was St. Swidborg (c. 752) who boasted that he 'dreamed dreams' while sleeping. The pope described Swidborg as 'a fool, but his supernatural favour' should be revealed to the people, for 'miracles are necessary to evince faith' (*Secrets of the Christian Fathers,* Bishop J. W. Sergerus, 1685; also *Catholic Encyclopedia,* 'Saints'). Shortly thereafter, the second council of Nicaea (785-7) decreed that 'he who goeth about to wrought a miracle should do so without limitation; he maketh the mark of the true church'. Spates of churchmen subsequently 'attested to miracles' (*Encyclopedia Biblica,* 'Saints') and were publicly exhibited as 'spouses of Jesus Christ' (ibid). Gala street parades called 'circuses' were held for them and 'peasants cringed at the sight of the miracle-men dressed splendidly and feigning greatness while riding in gilded carriages' (*Petrus Cluniacensis,* lib, v., epist, xxix, (Peter, Abbot of Cluny), c. 1310). The processions circled endlessly around the streets and 'fools in bright attire were paid to make strange gestures and attract public attention. They could not have given a grander spectacle to God himself; salutations being exchanged, the whole procession moved towards the church where admiration that is due only to God Almighty is given to them' (ibid).

During the 12th to 14th Centuries, the Church developed a formal procedure of honouring past 'miracle-makers' and during that time ...

> ... a vast number of incredible and false miracles, as well as other fables, have been forged and invented by the worst of churchmen ... and these sonnets grieve me ... they are unworthy of God and man ... the stories of saints were written by false brethren who had an iron mouth and a leaden heart ... the miracles of Benedict contains not less than twenty-four lies ... to this day I could never see one story which I could allow to be told.
>
> (*Petrus Cluniacensis,* lib, v, epist, xxix (Peter, Abbot of Cluny), c. 1310)

In finding a miraculous reason to glorify and then canonize a Third Century presbyter, Dionysius of Paris, the 14th Century Church settled on the marvel that 'he walked two miles with his severed head in his hands' (*Elliott's Delineation of Romanism,* 1884, p. 553). In 1592 'a French ecclesiastic, after reading of Dionysius' dilemma, gravely observed that the saint had found some difficulty in first setting off. 'I can easily believe that', replied a gentleman who was present, 'for in such cases it is only the first step that is any trouble' (ibid).

Around 200 years ago, in 1802, an old family grave was found containing a cadaver and a bottle 'supposed to contain the blood of a martyr'. The relics were enshrined in an altar in the Vatican, and the erstwhile owner of the remains was duly and solemnly canonized as Saint Philomena, but that was 'by mistake', and thus were fooled two infallible Holinesses, Gregory XVI and Leo III (*Christian Forgeries,* Major Joseph Wheless, USA Judge Advocate, Idaho, 1930). Papal infallibility was again fooled with an embarrassing instance being that of the holy Saint Josaphat, under which name and due to an odd slip of inerrant inspiration, the great Lord Buddha, the 'Light of Asia', was duly certified as a Christian saint in the Roman Martyrology (*Catholic Encyclopedia*, Farley Ed., iii, p. 297).

The Holy Mother Church describes her *Catholic Encyclopedias* as 'the exponent of Catholic truth' (Preface), and its ponderous tomes are full of sundry examples of 'inspired and truthful histories of saints and martyrs'. However, the Church itself admits the falsity of the strange tales of its saints, and two particular cases of certified saint-records are worthy of mention. With respect to the purported miracles and wondrous acts of probably the most notable female saint, St. Catherine of Alexandria, the Church candidly apologizes:

> Unfortunately these acts have been transformed and distorted by fantastic and diffuse descriptions, which are entirely due to the imagination of the narrators who cared less to state authentic facts than to charm their readers by recitals of the marvelous.

(*Catholic Encyclopedia*, Farley Ed., iii, p. 445)

Speaking of another case, that of St. Emmeram who died in Bavaria around 600, the Church said: 'The improbability of the tale, the fantastic details of the saint's martyrdom, and the fantastic account of the prodigies attending his death, show that the writer, infected by the pious mania of his time, simply added imaginary details supposed to redound to the glory of the martyr' (*Catholic Encyclopedia*, Farley Ed., v, pp. 405-406).

The Church itself questioned such key instances implicitly carried with it assurance that all recorded saintly miracles are infected with the same taint of fraud and freely confessed that the holy saint-tales, like so many other supernatural fictions used to impress believers, are fake stories that 'belong to the common foundation of all legends of saints' (*Catholic Encyclopedia*, Farley Ed., i, p. 40). The Protestant movement later termed a phrase about the dubious doctrine of Catholic saints; 'Many things became known about them after their deaths which were not known during their lives' (*Elliott's Delineation of Romanism*, 1884, p. 553-7). The Church agreed, saying, 'needless to say that they [the legends] do not embody any real historical information, and their chief utility is to afford an example of the pious popular credulity of the times' (*Catholic Encyclopedia*, Farley Ed., i, p. 131). The Council of Trent ruled that 'respect is to be placed in the saints and the marvelous operations of their miracles', and today the Church continues to peddle their crude untruths as articles of Christian faith.

The Church acknowledged the 'holiness' of the fabricated miracles, and retrospectively applied the title 'saint' to earlier churchmen they originally called 'holy fools'. Saints were called 'Fools in Christ' simply because their lives 'could not be easily distinguished from the retarded, the demented and like' (*Historical Dictionary of the Orthodox Church*, Entry, *Fools in Christ*, p. 133). Thus the category of Christian saints became a brotherhood or guild of fools. Indeed, for centuries the Church held an annual Feast of Fools, but, as people became more enlightened, it became embarrassing for the Church, and the celebration was suppressed by decree at the Council of Basle in 1435. It seems that the merriment had practically died out by the time of the Council of Trent (1545-1563), but even today, lives of Church people are examined for supposed evidence of supernatural sanctity and/or sham miracles performed during their lifetime (e.g., Pope John Paul II). At least two allegedly genuine and fully authenticated miracles need to be proven to have been performed by the candidate while alive or worked by his or her relics after death before the name was certified as a saint to the Calendar.

The Church publicly pretends to appear very careful and conscientious in its processes of certifying saints. A fairly modern instance showing how clerical scrupulosity may be cited is that of the Venerable Mary de Sales, who died in 1875 (*Catholic Encyclopedia*, Farley Ed., ix, pp. 749-61). No miracles were satisfactorily proved to justify making her 'saint' but her sanctity was finally established and she 'was decreed Venerable after a payment of US$20,000 by her family, and in 1897, her Beatification was decreed' (*Christian Forgeries,* Major Joseph Wheless, USA Judge Advocate, Idaho, 1930).

CHAPTER 14

'The Bishop's Oath of Allegiance' and its effect

An earlier chapter raised the reality of Pope St. Peter's directive to his bishops 'to hearken to' (*Optatus of Minevis*; 3:11-12, Early Fourth Century) his demands and, originating from his orders, developed what we call in this book, 'The Bishop's Oath of Allegiance'. Before they receive the mitre or the pallium, claimed by the Church to be made from the wool of 'holy sheep', they are obliged to swear an oath upon their souls … as followers of not Jesus Christ, but of Pope St. Peter. This is what they pledge:

> Heretics, schismatics, or rebels against our lord the Pope, or his successors, I will persecute and fight against to the utmost of my power.

This spirit of persecution is taught in canon law and in 1929 an attempt was made by the Church to have its canon laws enforced by Civil Law but this was flatly refused by Mussolini. Should the bishops disregard this oath, Church management included this passage: 'If a bishop shall have been negligent or remiss in purging his diocese of heretical pravity, as soon as this is made apparent by sure evidence, he shall be deposed from his Episcopal office, and in his place shall be substituted a fit person who will and can confound the heretical pravity'.

The Holy Mother Church subsists on the principle of an oath to 'our lord the Pope', not Jesus Christ, and the bishops became the chief police officers of the pope for enforcing canon law, and for inflicting its pains and penalties. The reality of the purpose of the Church of Rome is one of a vengeful and persecuting spirit which it has exhibited as its main characteristic since Pope St. Peter 'struck down dead' Ananius and his wife Sapphira for giving only half the proceeds of the sale of their property to his new religious movement (Acts 5:1-11). The effects of this oath, and of this threat to keep up its remembrance, the world knows. To prove their fidelity to their oath, and to retain their mitre upon their brow, they have in cruelty out-Heroded Herod, and out-Neroed Nero. The bishops of St. Peter and his successors have been butchers of any opponent, and that includes Protestant Christians. They have stained their garments in blood in the annihilation of the pious Cathars, the Knights Templar, and the men and women the Church labeled 'witches'. This sign on a church door in Scotland in June 1676 summarises the Church priorities: 'No preaching here this Lord's day, the minister being at Gortarchy burning a witch'. Then there was St. Dominic's establishment of the Church's dreaded Holy Inquisition (c. 1221), with its terrifying armory of tribunals, tortures, secret police, informers, and fiery executions. Its structure developed into official Church Law that lasted for 599 years and was vigorously upheld to specifically suppress opinions contrary to Church dogma. A glaring instance of extremism in enforcing Christian concepts is found in a newspaper of less than 200 years ago:

> Witness the horrible crucifixion of females so minutely detailed by Baron De Grimm, who was an eyewitness of them during his residence at Paris, and which were suppressed not by the interference of the clergy, but by order of the Catholic Lieutenant of Police. Let anyone consult the *Edinburgh Review* of September 1814, p. 302, *et seq.*, and he will find detailed instances of the most horrible fanaticism, which occurred in the streets of Paris.
>
> (*Delineation of Roman Catholicism*, Rev. Charles Elliott, D.D., London, 1844, p. 27)

Crucifixion of women was a regular event in the history of Christianity and records exist of instances in earlier times. This example appears in *The Criminal History of Christianity,* published by Free-Thinking Press in Connecticut, USA:

> On 27th September 1275, a 32 year-old French lady named Dorèt was crucified at a church near Mende in Southwest France for alleged prostitution. Her death was ordered and conducted by zealous Italian bishop, Balucci (d. 1301, aged 62), who was assisted by four priests. After suffering for three hours and

fifteen minutes on a cross fixed to the church fence, Dorèt was finally killed with a sword stab to the right side of her chest, and then burned. Balucci was responsible for the crucifixion of eight young ladies in similar style who were 'providing survival income' by prostitution for their children. He subsequently received a promotion in Rome and spent the last twenty years of his Christian life in an administrative role in the hierarchy of the church.

(*The Criminal History of Christianity,* Dr. James W. L. Saunders, Free-Thinking Press, Connecticut, USA, 1969, pp. 79-80)

Additional instances of Church murders are found in 19th Century newspapers held in the British Library Newspaper Division at Colindale in London, and were rampant in countries where the Bible stood foremost in the list of heretical books and the authority of the Holy Mother Church was predominant.

Enriching the Church from the confessional

The following story, often published to the confusion of Catholics, reveals the powerful effect 'The Bishop's Oath of Allegiance' had in achieving riches for the Church, and this event happened just eight generations ago (c. 1851):

> Nor, sir, is there any security for property in Rome. It is constantly confiscated, on the merest pretexts, to the Church; and when not confiscated, it is alienated to the 'Holy See' in a great variety of ways. Two instances [space only permits one example, ed.], in proof of this, were narrated to me there, and by a man of high position. A Roman of wealth married to a lady of foreign birth, and by whom he had a large family of children. After a life of love and harmony, he died, leaving his property to his widow and children, by a will duly authenticated. Although regardless of the priests in health, he sent for one when dying ... who confessed him, and anointed him, and 'fixed him off' for Purgatory or Paradise. A few days after his death, that priest swore before the tribunal having jurisdiction in such cases, that the dying man confessed to him a great sin, and to atone for which he wished his entire property, contrary to his will, to go to the Church. And on the oath of that priest, the will of the deceased was set aside ... his property was turned into the treasury of the

Church, and his widow and children were turned out penniless on the world. Thus nothing is necessary to deprive any family in Rome that has lost its head, of its property, but the oath of a priest.

And if you had seen them in crowds, as I have, that it would be an easy matter to get a priest in Rome that would swear to anything. Absolutions from perjury that enriches the Church are easily secured.

(*Romanism at Home*; J. Kirwin, being Letters to the Hon. Roger B. Taney, Chief Justice of the United States, printed in Edinburgh by Johnstone and Hunter, M. DCCC. LII, p. 125)

This is another way the Church made so much money, by deception and theft. Around that same time, printed copies of the oath itself were distributed by anti-Catholic groups, and the world became aware of the true purpose of the money-making ambitions of the Christian priesthood. The famous Cardinal Nicolas Wiseman (1802-65), English prelate and cardinal, was catechized in reference to the oath; and although the policy of bishops is not to answer questions, he was compelled by public pressure to reply. He did not deny taking such an oath, but asserted that when he administered to British bishops, the above clause was omitted. He lied, for the veracity of Nicholas of Westminster's full admission that the clause was in the oath that he had taken 'in reverence to his lord and master', the pope.

CHAPTER 15

Maintaining priesthood profits

Catholic historian, Dr. Ludwig Freiherr von Campersfelden Pastor (1854-1928), a devout German author, spent many years in the Vatican where he wrote a 16-part collection of documents he called, *A History of the Popes from the Close of the Middle Ages* (1886). He was a simple-minded author and confessed that discoveries made in his researches brought confusion upon him (Preface; *A History of the Popes from the Close of the Middle Ages,* Bishop Forbes's trans. 1937). He wondered why he was denied access to particular writings that he knew were held in the Secret Archives, and opined that he wasn't allowed to see them because they contained a wonderful Christian truth beyond the comprehension of believers. In a way he was right. In 1881, and on the principle that the Catholic Church had nothing to fear from the truth, he influenced Pope Leo XIII (d. 1903) to open the Secret Archives to biblical scholars. However, when Pastor sought certain manuscripts, he learned that they had been earlier withdrawn, and relocated to another part of the Vatican. The existence of this high-security facility is confirmed on page 290 of the *Catholic Encyclopedia* (1912 Ed):

> There is a 'special archive' on the third story of the palace, where is also the archive of the *Congregation for Extraordinary Ecclesiastical Affairs.* This archive admits no investigator, and questions on particular points addressed to it by scholars have failed to receive pertinent answers ... the volumes of this archive contain very interesting information.
>
> (*Catholic Encyclopedia,* Farley Ed., xv, p. 290)

In early volumes of *Catholic Encyclopedias* (1907-14), a major section records comprehensive information about the Secret Vatican Archives and provides a list of documents (*Catholic Encyclopedias,* Farley Ed., xv, pp. 288-9) revealing the extent of those archives in 1912. However, updated *Catholic Encyclopedias* (1976) mention the Secret Archives only once, and in relation to Monsignor Angelo Mercati, (1870-1955), Prefect of those Archives. The reference is to Mercati's proposal that the Church divides the Secret Archives into two major divisions of ten separate sub-divisions, and rename them the Archives of the Castel Sant' Angelo (*New Catholic Encyclopedia*, xiv, p. 552).

While popes were writing new Bibles and suppressing the true history of the origin of their business (for there is no other word for it), unsuspecting devotees were crawling up the fake *Scala Sancta* in Rome, fervently clutching their rosaries while others were prostate on their knees before black statues of Mary and her baby boy. However, forces were developing that would soon present the Vatican with the deepest financial crisis in the history of Catholicism, and take the European division of the Holy Mother Church to the point of extinction.

PART TWO

The dome of St. Peter's seen across the Vatican gardens ©Vaticana Photographica Collecta, Roma ... David Seymour, 1948

The Vatican has built up a vast fortune of material possessions over the centuries but it is not generally known that much of its modern wealth derived from investments in war industries.

CHAPTER 16

The Church suffers a set-back

As the Holy Mother Church headed towards the end of the 19th Century, she was to suffer a set-back of immense proportions. On the 2nd September, 1870, Napoleon III, having gone to war with Prussia, was soundly defeated at Sedan and Pope Pius IX (Giovanni-Maria Mastai-Ferretti; born 1792, pope from 1846-1878) lost his main protector. By the end of the same month (September 20), the Piedmontese army, under Victor Emmanual II (1820-78), the 'honest King' of Sardinia and Piedmont, possessed itself of Rome and the adjacent Papal States, and declared the Eternal City the capital of a newly formed United Kingdom of Italy.

© ACB Picture Gallery

This is an anonymous lithograph of King Victor Emmanuel of Savoy, circa 1870. He was the son of Charles Albert of Sardinia, and was proclaimed the first king of Italy at Turin in February 1861. The King was intensely anti-clerical and was successful in confiscating the ill-gained Papal States.

After the fall of the Empire, the vast territories that the Church had previously owned for a whole millennium were reduced to the microscopic state of the present-day Catholic headquarters. The

Papal States, with 15,774 square miles and 3,000,000 tax-paying inhabitants, were removed from the Vatican's Balance Sheet and vanished forever from the map of Europe, and from history. The Church, with the exception of 108 acres of the Vatican City, no longer had any earthly European dominion to rule and its temporal sovereignty ended.

© Museo di Roma

This extraordinary picture shows Pius IX addressing his troops at the Campo di Annibale and is one the Vatican would rather you did not see.
This photograph was taken in 1868, and shows Pope Pius IX on stage (dressed in white, and slightly right of centre) addressing the Catholic army before their dispatch into battle. The attempt by the Church to hold on to real estate gained from the forged Donation of Constantine was bitterly defended in armed conflict until the very end, and in this encounter the pope's troops were soundly defeated, resulting in great loss of life.
It was the beginning of the end of the Papal States.

The Italians had wrenched away the Church's real estate in legitimate warfare and the weakened pontiff 'immured' himself within the walls of the Vatican in protest against the 'political theft' (*Catholic Encyclopedia*, Pecci Ed., iii, p. 313), obdurately refusing to set foot outside its boundaries. The pope was now seen wearing a gilded cardboard tiara instead of the richly-jeweled headpieces of his illustrious predecessors.

The new government shrewdly invited the Italian people to declare in a plebiscite whether they wanted to remain under the rule of the Vatican. More than 360,000 voted against the popes and less than 12,000 for them. 'Everywhere the forces of anti-clericalism were in the ascendant … and the new criticism [against Catholicism] in Germany and elsewhere threatened to undermine the foundations of the Christian faith' (*The Popes, A Concise Biographical History*, Burns and Oates, Publishers to the Holy See, London, 1964, pp. 439-440; published under the Imprimatur of Georgius L. Craven). Thus, Popes Pius IX, Leo XIII (1878-1903), Pius X (1903-1914), Benedict XV (1914-1922), and Pius XI (1922-1939), grew sombre and went underground, confining themselves to the Vatican, never 'officially' coming out. By no word or act would they seem to recognize the spoliation of their States, and especially not the seizure of the Eternal City. They branded the Italian royal family and the Government 'bandits', and for 59 years remained within the Vatican and its gardens, in spite of the scarcely veiled jeers of many English controversialists at the 'Prisoners of the Vatican'. This papal regime led to the most grotesque incidents at Rome and excited the disdain of educated Italians, matters we shall leave for another time.

The Vatican joins the Billionaire Club of America

Yet in that same year (1870), while the papacy was being reduced to oblivion in terms of earthly power, status, territory and income, the dispossessed pontiff, Pius IX, having earlier convened the first Vatican Council (December, 1869; prorogued on October 20, 1870, and never reassembled), used his spiritual puissance with one single stroke to elevate himself above all men and, indeed, above all human reason itself. He did so by declaring himself 'infallible', something which no man had ever dared do. It caused huge dissension amongst the faithful and bitter opposition by many bishops. A short time later, and under the newly-introduced Law of Guarantees of 1871, Count Camillo, Victor Emmanuel's Prime Minister and architect of Italian unification, offered to recognize the pope's sovereignty over the Vatican, the Lateran and the Castel Gandolfo, allowing him to retain certain essential services such as, for example, the right to have troops for the protection of his property. As an indemnity for the loss of the Papal States, the new Italian government offered the Vatican an annual payment of 3,250,000 lire as 'a perpetual and inalienable income', but Pius IX refused the offer. The Catholic Church in Europe was now all but financially ruined, but things were different in America, where the bride of Christ was already a member of the exclusive Billionaire's Club. US President Ulysses Grant (1822-85), in his 'Annual Message to Congress' in 1875, pointed out that the value of Roman Catholic real estate in America at that time was in excess of US$1,000 million. Advocating a tax on Church property, he said;

> By 1895, without check, it is safe to say this property will reach a sum exceeding three billion dollars. So vast a sum receiving all the protection and benefits of Government without bearing its proportion of the burdens and expenses of the same; it will not be looked upon acquiescently by those who have to pay taxes. In a growing country, where real estate enhances so rapidly with time, as in the United States, there is scarcely a limit to the wealth that may be acquired by corporations, religious or otherwise, if allowed to retain real estate without taxation. The contemplation of so vast a property as here alluded to, without taxation, may lead to sequestration without constitutional authority and through bloodshed. I would suggest the taxation of all property equally, whether church or corporation.
>
> (*Messages and Papers of the Presidents*, vol. vii, pp. 334-5)

The term 'billion dollars' used throughout this story means 'one thousand million dollars' (US$1000,000,000), and the President's estimate of the wealth of the Church being US$3 billion within 20 years of his address was just petty cash to what was to happen during the next 112 years. By 2007, the riches of the Holy Mother Church were to develop to a staggering amount ... and the moral principals of the Catholic hierarchy were to show themselves for what they really were. Dr. Joseph McCabe, Rector of Buckingham College (d. 1955), revealed in one of his many books that five years before the President's dating (1890) the Holy See owned one-fifth of the whole of the wealth of the US and one-fourth in 1906. 'During those sixteen years the value of Church property generally rose by 85.1 per cent, but that of the Catholic Church rose by 147.7 per cent (*The Papacy in Politics Today,* Dr. Joseph McCabe, Rector of Buckingham College; Watts and Co., London, 1937, p. 173). The Holy See agreed, saying 'it had been a period of astonishing expansion for the Church in America' (*The Popes, A Concise Biographical History*, Burns and Oates, Publishers to the Holy See, London, 1964, p. 440; published under the Imprimatur of Georgius L. Craven), and 'the basic factor of the sudden growth of fantastic wealth of the Church of Rome in America cannot be fully understood' (*The Papacy in Politics Today,* Dr. Joseph McCabe, Rector of Buckingham College; Watts and Co., London, 1937). Excluding the revenue of Protestant churches, the income of the Roman Church at that time (c. 1937) was 'assessed by Catholic writers at US$800,000,000 a year' (ibid), or around US$15,000,000 per week.

Birth of a new Vatican financial empire

Back in Europe, successive popes believed that the former Papal States were rightfully theirs and argued for compensation through Vatican lawyer, Francesco Pacelli, brother of Cardinal Eugenio Pacelli, the future Pope Pius XII. They claimed that some of the territories were donated to them by King Pepin the Short (715-768), and later supported by his father, King Charlemagne (c. 742-814). Modern Catholic writers fail to recall that, as historians have revealed, the Holy See had obtained its Papal States by blatant mediaeval forgeries, the fake heavenly missal of St. Peter, and the Donation of Constantine. To this territory the papacy had no just title, nor any legal record of the 'donation' on which it bases its claim of compensation. The Church produced a document known as the 'Fantuzzian Fragment', which professes to give the terms of the 'donation', but investigators agree that it was a shameless modern forgery. However, the Catholic Church, a religion which purports to concern itself with the things of heaven, negotiated with Italy's Fascist leader, Prime Minister and Head of the Government, Cavaliere Benito Mussolini (1883-1945) in the business-like manner of a good go-ahead commercial concern. For 920 days, the pope and the Vatican's Secretariat of State, Cardinal Pietro Gasparri, acting for 'the Lord, our Pope' ('The Bishop's Oath of Allegiance'), bargained for sound, solid, earthly investments in the form of cash, real estate, and income-producing government bonds. No mention of evangelical poverty here; even less about selling one's riches and giving the proceeds to the poor. The Vatican's negotiating team, while resigning themselves to the loss of the Papal States, insisted upon their pound of flesh and bargained for a just financial settlement. The Catholic hierarchy demanded payment for what they considered was lawfully theirs and, after 110 conferences with Mussolini's ministers, 26 with Mussolini himself, and 21 rewritings of a document that came to be called the Lateran Treaty, the Catholic hierarchy wrested from a reluctant Fascist Government a financial settlement, along with a variety of guarantees and measures of protection. It was one of the most tainted bargains of modern times and a fit inauguration to decades of wealth accumulation for the Holy See. The pope would support Fascism provided Mussolini supported the Holy Mother Church ... and he did, but not for religious reasons. The Fascist-Catholic union was an event of the utmost importance for Europe and the West and one of paramount interest to our present scrutiny.

On February 11, 1929, with the signing of the Treaty between the Vatican and the Italian Government, the fortunes of the Church were dramatically reversed. But Mussolini's followers were seething, claiming that he had 'Vaticanized Italy ... and resuscitated the pope's temporal power'. They revealed the fact that the inhabitants of Italy had repudiated the popes' rule by thirty to one, and 'Down with the Pope' was chanted in the streets of Rome (*The Papacy in Politics Today,* Dr. Joseph McCabe, Rector of Buckingham College; Watts and Co., London, 1937). However, the deal had been done, and what was soon to happen to the Holy Mother Church is one of the greatest business success stories of all time. In return for sovereignty, the Vatican relinquished claims to the lands that were seized by the national government in 1870 and agreed to establish diplomatic relations with the Italian government. With the signing of the Treaty in the Lateran Palace, built near the ancient site near where Pope Leo III crowned Charlemagne Holy Roman Emperor in 800, Italy recognized the sovereignty of the Holy See. It was now based in what was called the Vatican City State and it covered an area slightly less than one square mile. Within that Sovereign State, with its 50 palaces and office buildings, the pope became the absolute ruler of religious, judicial and legislative power.

© Archival Film Library, photograph by Felici, 1929

The most significant event of Pope Pius XI's reign was the signing of the Lateran Treaty. Here the Vatican's Secretariat of State, Cardinal Gasparri (seated left) and Benito Mussolini (seated right) pose in the Lateran Palace with their entourages after the signing of the Treaty.

The final section (of three) of the Lateran Treaty was called the 'Financial Convention' and it provided for a payment to the Vatican of some two billion lire plus a parcel of Consolidated State Bonds at a value around 25% greater than the cash payment, bearing interest at 5% per annum. The settlement was in fact 59 years of accrued annual payments, plus accumulated interest of the 'perpetual income' the Italian Government had originally offered the Church in 1870. Comparing 1929 exchange rates with today's equivalent, this figure has been estimated at around US$90 million and as part of the settlement, Pope Pius XI (Achilles Ambrose Damian Ratti, 1857-1939; pope from 1922-1939) received an undisclosed sum for his personal 'privy purse' (*Rich Church, Poor Church*, Martin Malachi, G. P. Putnam's Sons, 1984, p. 31).

A 1984 equivalent figure of the settlement was estimated at approximately US$500 million (*In God's Name, An Investigation Into the Murder of John Paul I,* David Yallop, Bantam Books, New York, 1984, p. 95) and a corresponding 2007 figure was put at around US$1000 million. The ratification of the Lateran Treaty provided for financial restitution for the former papal principalities lost to the Church and thus what came to be called the 'Roman Question' was 'now definitely and irrevocably settled' (official Vatican communiqué, February, 1929).

© Archival Film Library, photograph by Felici, 1929

This is the last page of the Lateran Treaty. It carries the seals and signatures of both Cardinal Gasparri (top) and Benito Mussolini (bottom).

Some five months after signing the Treaty, Pope Pius XI emerged triumphant from the Vatican. On July 25, 1929, Italian newspapers announced:

> Pius XI today became the first pope the leave the Vatican since 1870. He blessed a crowd of some 3000 from a specially erected altar on the Basilica steps. He then moved out of St. Peter's Square in a magnificent procession led by the Swiss Guards.
>
> Since he came to office seven years ago, Pius XI has worked to end the quarrel with the Italian Government. Yesterday's historic occasion was supported by the Italian Court and the aristocracy. The Government arranged for full sovereign honours, so the Italian army was lined up on the Basilica steps and all along the limits of the Piazza Rusticucci.

Whatever one may think of the determination of Pius XI to fund his Church, one cannot help but recall the words of Cardinal Roberto Francis Romulus

Bellarmine (1542-1621), who noted some three centuries earlier that, 'the papacy almost eliminated Christianity'. The same could be said for the 59-year void of non-public popes.

CHAPTER 17

The man with the Midas touch

It was an amazing consummation of one of the strangest chapters in the history of the Christian religion. With the signing of the Lateran Treaty the pope had solved the Vatican's budgetary woes, yet he put his Church in league with some of the darkest forces yet to come into the 20th Century. He was to later say, 'I seem to have allied myself with Satan'. Fascist Italy subsequently paid the Vatican the monies and also agreed to pay the salaries of all parish priests in Italy, funded by the taxpayer. Thus, on February 1929, the independent Vatican State, as it stands today, came into being … Catholicism was declared 'the official religion of Italy' and Mussolini, an atheist and womanizer, guaranteed to introduce compulsory Catholic religious preaching into all State High Schools. He also recognized the bodies of monks and nuns as juridical personalities with an indefinite power to accumulate property and, in a particularly venomous clause insisted upon by the pope, introduced truculent penalties upon all criticism of the Catholic religion in print or orally. Soon after signing the Treaty, the pope confessed that Mussolini was a heretic and was using religion to protect his usurped power. Mussolini's Fascist movement bent over backwards to give special dispensations to the Holy See on matters of taxation and the Church was now flush with cash and resplendent with tax free property rights, but the pope's demand that Canon Law be incorporated and enforced through Civil Law was refused by Mussolini. At that time, Church laws had recently been updated (1918) and within them are embodied papal claims and fundamental Christian principles which no civilized country in the World would permit. For example, the Holy Mother Church reserves the right to put apostate

Catholics to death, and any person who denies Roman Catholic doctrines must also be put to death (*Public Church Law*). The spirit of persecution is taught in Canon Law which is made up of council decrees, and the bulls and decretals of popes. Thus writers like Bushby are under sentence of death in the law of the Roman Catholic Church and its thirst for the blood of people revealing embarrassing truths threatens the moral basis of our modern civilization.

Included in the Lateran deal Mussolini gave ownership to the Holy See of the following valuable properties outside the 108 acres of Vatican City, as recorded in various Articles of 'The Lateran Treaty of 1929':

The Basilica of St. Paul and its Monastery

The edifice of S. Callisto, adjoining Sta. Maria in Trastevere

The Papal Palace of Castel Gandolfo

The Villa Barberini in Castel Gandolfo

The Convent buildings in Rome attached to the Basilica of the Twelve Holy Apostles

The churches of San Andrea della Valle and Carlo ai Catinari

The Palaces of the Cataria, of the Cancelleria, of the Sacred Congregation of Propaganda Fide in the Piazza di Spagna of the S. Offizio with its annexes, and those of the Convertendi (now the Congregation of the Eastern Church) in Piazza Scossacavelli, the Vicariato and more.

Physically the Catholic Church had been reduced to the tiniest State in the world; an independent ecclesiastical machine and working theocracy now reduced to a parcel of land smaller than an international golf course. The revenue the Vatican received, although large, was small in view of the thousands of square miles of prime real estate lost, particularly the rich Romagna countryside and its huge income. Yet the millions paid to the Vatican were the seeds of billions that were to be accumulated in the following decades. The Holy Mother Church's traditional way of accumulating riches of Earth had to be discarded; from now on it would multiply its millions in the same way as contemporary society, that is by merging with great industrial and financial concerns, trusts and corporations of the world, and thus become a mammoth colossus in her own right. It turned out to be the greatest financial achievement of the 20th Century.

The year 1929, therefore, became a milestone in the annals of the Catholic Church for as the Lateran Treaty closed one door, it opened another, that being a major new financial era. Within the structure of the Treaty were major benefits for the Vatican, not least the economic ones. As Dr. Williams observed:

> On the day of the ratification of the Lateran Treaty, Pius XI made two moves that would alter forever the future of Roman Catholicism. First he created a new financial agency called the Special Administration of the Holy See. The sole function of this agency was to safeguard the 'donation of Mussolini' so that the church's newly found wealth would not be channeled into the pockets of friends and associates of Vatican officials or dissipated on social causes, such as feeding the starving masses or providing shelter for the dispossessed. Second, the pope appointed Bernardino Nogara, the financial wizard who reorganized the Reichsbank, as the manager and director of the new agency with complete control over investments.
>
> (*The Vatican Exposed*, Dr. Paul L. Williams, Prometheus Books, New York, 2003, pp. 33-4)

In appointing Nogara (1870-1958), Pope Pius XI hit the jackpot. Few individuals were more influential in the history of the Roman Catholic Church than Nogara, confirmed at the time of his death (1958) by Cardinal Spellman, who said; 'Next to Jesus Christ, the greatest thing that has happened to the Church was Bernardino Nogara' (Cardinal Spellman, quoted in, *In God's Name, An Investigation Into the Murder of John Paul I*, David Yallop, Bantam Books, New York, 1984, p. 98). Nogara was a Roman Catholic layman who never entered Holy Orders, not even the lay order of a religious brotherhood. He originally trained as a mineralogist in Turkey and subsequently played a leading role as a member of the Italian delegation that negotiated the peace treaty between Italy, France, Britain and Germany. He was fluent in eight languages and his fellow workers recalled his fastidious dress sense. They also spoke of his prodigious memory, his acumen, and his studious disposition. Earlier, from 1924 to 1929, his financial skills came to full play in his efforts to reorganize the Reichsbank in order to stabilize Germany's postwar financial problems. In this capacity he performed an amazing feat of fiscal juggling by reaping the payment of 2.5 billion Deutschmark for annuities from a loan of 800 million Deutschmark (*Rich Church, Poor Church*, Martin Malachi, G. P. Putnam's Sons, 1984, p. 25).

It was the beginning of a period when the Vatican's future wealth would surpass beyond imagination, its riches of the past. As part of his employment contract Nogara insisted that any investments he chose to make should be free of religious or doctrinal considerations, and the pope agreed. For his personal assistants, Nogara chose the Marquis Enricho de Maillardoz, Count Enrico Galeazzi, and four top accountants from leading Italian financial institutions. He established his headquarters on the fourth floor of the Lateran Palace next to the private apartment of the pope, and Nogara became the only Vatican official with free and unannounced access to the Holy Father. With his talented committee he initiated a brand-new policy which has characterized Vatican strategies ever since ... that being one of international investments, gold trading, currency speculation, real estate purchases, Stock Exchange dealings, and the acquisition of shares in companies whose products were inconsistent with Catholic preaching. It was a step which, although taking the Vatican along the dangerous road of global speculation, financial unknowns, and political risks, nevertheless within an astonishingly short time, yielded immense dividends.

© Film Library of the Museo di Roma; Photograph by David Seymour

Count Enrico Galeazzi, Director-General of the Administrative and Economic Services of the Holy See, at his desk in the Lateran Palace shortly after the pope established his new Vatican bank.

The creation of the 'Special Administration of the Holy See' was not entirely a novel one, being the offspring of an elderly parent, the 'Administration of the Goods of the Holy See' originally established by Pope Leo XIII in 1878. This had been instituted to deal with the sudden downturn in the financial affairs of the battered papal economy after the loss of its temporal dominions in 1870. Nogara not only had the Midas touch, he was a shrewd negotiator and gifted in the art of persuasion. As Dr. Williams observed:

> As the world fell into the grips of the Great Depression, Nogara's first move as the Vatican's financier was to take over principal interest in Banca di Roma, a firm that had many securities of *no call value*, that is, securities that would pay little, if anything, if sold on the stock market. He then managed to persuade Mussolini to include the bank in the creation of the Institute for Industrial Reconstruction (IIR). This was Italy's answer to the industrial devastation that ravaged the country. The function of the IIR was to capitalize industrial companies to stimulate economic growth. The companies agreed to provide one lira for every two raised from the private sector. All investments were secured by the government. Under this arrangement the worthless securities of Banca di Roma were restored to their original value and the Vatican, as the major shareholder, now boasted a fortune of US$632 million.
>
> (*The Vatican Exposed*, Dr. Paul L. Williams, Prometheus Books, New York, 2003, p. 36)

The Italian treasury subtly wrote-off the loss, which is another way of saying that ordinary hard-working tax-paying citizens picked up the bill for the Holy Mother Church. From the highly lucrative deal with the Banca di Roma, Nogara purchased stock on the open market in the Institute for Industrial Reconstruction so that by 1935, the Vatican became the largest shareholder of State-owned businesses in the country, and from holding these shares it would soon accrue millions of dollars in interest. No concern here about interest (usury) being forbidden in both divine and canon law; nor Gospel directions to lend money, even to their enemies, 'expecting nothing in return' (Luke 6: 34-35). In ancient times, usury carried extreme penalties including excommunication, and in 1179, the Third Lateran Council strictly forbade charges of interest because it was banned in the Bible.

Therefore, usury was considered a direct violation of scripture and, as such, a violation against God himself. However, in a religion populated with hypocrites, this 'serious crime ... condemned by all honest men' (*Catholic Encyclopedia*, Pecci Ed., ii, p. 488; also, *Catholic Encyclopedia*, Farley Ed., xv, p. 235) was conveniently overlooked by the Holy Mother Church.

CHAPTER 18

Church invests in War Industries

Nogara acquired for the Vatican outright ownership of a host of medium-sized and small rural banks in southern Italy, along with a controlling interest in the Banco di Roma (founded in 1808), the Bank of the Holy Spirit (founded in 1608), Banca Commerciale Italiana, Banca Cattolica del Veneto, Banca Unione, Credito Italiano, Banca Provinciola Lambarda, and the prestigious Banco Ambrosiano in Milan. This bank originally exuded religiosity, but in time to come it came under the control of the infamous Mafia figure, Roberto Calvi, 'God's Banker', whose influence will be addressed later (*Rich Church, Poor Church*, Martin Malachi, G. P. Putnam's Sons, 1984, p. 41; also, *The Vatican Exposed*, Dr. Paul L. Williams, Prometheus Books, New York, 2003, p. 39). Close links were forged with an array of other banks and when Nogara brought and sold stock on Wall Street he brokered his transactions through Chase Manhattan and the Continental Bank of Illinois, and others (*The Vatican Billions,* Baron Avro Manhattan, Paravision Books, London, 1972). The Continental Bank developed into a major conduit for all USA investment by the Vatican and that included its dealings in currency speculation. Through the Church's own banks Nogara could channel borrowings to finance the purchase of additional Vatican-owned companies and decline loan applications from competitors. For this reason the Holy Mother Church managed to prosper and thrive through the lean years of the 1930s.

The Papal States might have been lost forever but in their place was an extraordinary money-making machine. Nogara set out in earnest to devise schemes for the investment of the millions of dollars at the Vatican's disposal

© Rome Picture Library, photo by Luigi Buttazoni, 1934

This is old photo of one of the many branches of the Bank of the Holy Spirit of which the Church gained control after signing the Lateran Treaty. It is plastered with Communist posters and voting notices.

and did this by promptly investing a large proportion of the money in Italy itself. One company he purchased was Italgas, which by 1968, became the sole supplier of natural gas to 35 Italian cities, including Rome, Venice, Florence and Turin (*The American Pope; The Life and Times of Francis Cardinal Spellman*, John Cooney, Times Books, New York, 1984, p. 46). On behalf of the Vatican, he also purchased outright the giant telecommunications firm, Societa Finanziavia Telefonia, a major supplier of telephone and telegraph service with annual profits in excess of US$20 million (*Rich Church, Poor Church*, Martin Malachi, G. P. Putnam's Sons, 1984, p. 52; also, *The Vatican Exposed*, Dr. Paul L. Williams, Prometheus Books, New York, 2003, p. 84). Investments of Church funds in the *Société Anonyme* of Monte Carlo and interests in the Italian Catholic Action film productions were additional, and successful, income-producing ventures (*The Vatican*, Ann Carnahan, Odhams Press Limited, London, 1950; Published under the Imprimatur of E. Morrogh Bernard, Vicar General).

Untaxed profits

Buying, selling and banking matters passed over Nogara's desk and he and his team controlled and played with Church funds for decades, multiplying its millions a hundredfold. They adopted as their motto the earlier maxim of

Pope Benedict XV (1914-1922); 'Business is Business', and thus Catholic monies soon found their way into the sinews of Italian high finance, commerce, industry, and the like. This process was greatly facilitated by the Vatican's favorable political relations with the Fascist dictatorship, but if this was an important factor, it was by no means the only one. Others, no less important, contributed to the launching of the successful financial operation and they were of a varying nature, but their combined activities played no mean part in the venture. Some of the main ones can be summarized in the fact that the Holy See owned its own banks and had been exempted by Fascism from paying crushing taxation. Importantly though, the Vatican had an interest in the internal machineries of various other banking and financial interests which, while seeming remote from the Vatican, nevertheless cooperated closely with it. The Vatican's intelligence network, represented by the higher Church hierarchy as well as Catholic business people in key positions in the financial and industrial world, particularly in Italy, supplied Nogara's finance department with confidential information unavailable to other companies, thus making the Vatican privy to inside information in advance of official finances centers and the general public.

The rapid development of Vatican wealth

Throughout Italy, the Vatican empire developed into hundreds of companies, large and small, specializing in such matters as tourist and hotel developments, residential property developments, city property, children's toys, furs, shopping centres, salt production, electronics, clothing, and departmental stores. It purchased a controlling interest in Rizzoli, a massive publishing group, with interests stretching as far as Buenos Aires. Among its many books, magazines, periodicals and newspapers was *Corriere Della Sera*, Italy's most prestigious newspaper. This acquisition allowed for controlled release of disinformation to the public, or the suppression of information detrimental to Catholic portrayals. The 'Church for the poor' grew immeasurably richer. By this time, 'the Vatican acquired major interests in textiles, steel, mining, metallurgical products, fertilizer plants, farming products, timber, ceramics, railroads, timber mills, pasta products, and telephone and telecommunication companies' (*The Vatican Exposed*, Dr. Paul L. Williams, Prometheus Books, New York, 2003,

p. 38). Dr. Williams revealed that the list of 'such holdings filled over seventy pages of accounting ledgers, and several of the published companies produced items that were antithetical to Catholic teachings, including bombs, tanks, and even contraceptives' (ibid). The Vatican owned or controlled the Instituto Farmacologico Sereno and one of its big selling products was *Luteolas* (Ministry of Health Registration Number 20984), an oral contraceptive, packaged in a harmless-looking plain white box.

Nogara moved part of the cash at his disposal into gold bullion, and the resulting scandal is revealed in a later chapter. He also realized the inevitability of the Second World War and invested heavily in booming Italian munitions plants which Mussolini had set in motion in preparation for the forthcoming invasion of Abyssinia (1935-6). Italian military equipment was old and poor and mostly of World War I design. Armored vehicles were notoriously under-armored and machine guns, and anti-aircraft weapons, were obsolete. Thus, the armaments industry was actively involved in designing and building new and better equipment, and it was thriving. Nogara had invested and re-invested most of the money the Church received from the Lateran contract into these lucrative concerns via ingenious and elaborate financial devices, and his investments provided massive profits for the Holy Mother Church (*The Vatican Billions,* Baron Avro Manhattan, Paravision Books, London, 1972). It is not amiss to remind ourselves of the fact that in the 1930's the Catholic Church was intimately connected with the business of war, not only because of the basic policy of support for the anti-Communist front represented by Fascist Europe, but also because of the billions of lire it had invested in sundry factories within that beleaguered continent.

Vatican authorities kept a discreet silence about their participation in profitable armaments enterprises. Concerning the financial support, or rather partnership, which the Church gave Mussolini, Pope Pius XI (Pope from 1922-1939) was fully aware of the Vatican's financial investments in the war industry, but argued that Catholic finances were not in his hands (*The Vatican Billions,* Baron Avro Manhattan, Paravision Books, London, 1972). A group of monetary specialists had dealt, and were dealing with them as they thought fit and the ramifications and intricacies of their investments were probably beyond the pope's comprehension. However, he did not reprimand the Italian

CHURCH INVESTS IN WAR INDUSTRIES

Church for its part in the Abyssinian invasion in October 1935 (Ethiopia, as Haile Selassie and his people knew their country). He refrained from a detailed condemnation of the war although a pronouncement he made three months before the invasion (28th July, 1935) said that the Vatican 'must take into consideration the right to defense' was interpreted by many to mean that he gave it his blessing. However, the Vatican's millions had been dispersed in profitable ventures, among which were the chemical and war enterprises which were now supplying Mussolini's armies.

The tradition of the Holy See was one that supported wars, for in 1937, 'a Joint letter' to the 'Bishops of the Whole World' was signed by several Archbishops saying that 'the Church, though the daughter of the Prince of Peace, blesses the emblems of war, She has herself founded military Orders, and has organized Crusades against enemies of the Faith'. They were emphatic and drew upon the extraordinary words of Pope Gregory VII (1020-1085; pope from 1073-1085) who, as to bloodshed, wrote; 'Cursed is he that refraineth his sword from blood' (Ep., I, 9; a full analysis of Pope Gregory's letters can be found in *Crises in the History of the Papacy*, by Dr. Joseph McCabe, Chapter 8; see also a Catholic manual, *Public Church Law*). War industries have been renowned for the vast profits they generate and Nogara also invested in allied industries, steel plants, and the like. This he had done in so far as he judged this an excellent investment, since war industries, when serving a government in need of armaments and of ever more sophisticated weapons, had always been a huge yielder of profits. From Fascist Italy he extended his investments into semi-Fascist Yugoslavia, Albania, and above all Nazi Germany. Thus the Vatican, prior to the Second World War, had uncountable millions invested with a vast complex producing combat materials and when war broke out these plants became the main suppliers of the invading armies. The secretive financial transactions of Nogara saw to it that they became gold-mines for the Holy Mother Church and he also linked Vatican finances with certain large USA corporations also geared to war production (*The Vatican Billions*, Baron Avro Manhattan, Paravision Books, London, 1972).

The Vatican investment policy was a resounding success. For the next ten years, from the signing of the Lateran Treaty (1929) to the outbreak of the Second World War (1939), the papal millions had been so skillfully invested that they, like the wise servant with the talents in the Gospel parable, yielded vast profits in ready cash, and provided for an upward reassessment of its real estate investments, industrial concerns, and share portfolio. When eventually the USA was drawn into the conflict, the Vatican began to receive huge profits from the other side of the Atlantic. The true extent of the Church's financial involvement with the immense European and American war industries has never been fully disclosed, and probably never will be.

Mussolini, meanwhile, had embarked on his first large-scale foreign aggression. On October 3, 1935 newspaper headlines exclaimed: 'Mussolini's Fascist troops march into Abyssinia. At dawn yesterday Italian bombers roared overhead striking first at the border town of Adowa ... the first bombs struck a hospital bearing the Red Cross ... tonight the Italian force, under General Emilio de Bono and numbering 100,000 men, is advancing on a 40-mile front'. A substantial proportion of the armaments needed for the invasion and subsequent occupation came from a munitions plant that Nogara had purchased for the Holy See. Mussolini, in exchange for the support of the Church, had earlier agreed to exempt most of the Vatican's investments from taxation, thus indirectly adding more millions to those already received. The pope's European priests worked in the schools in co-operation with teachers who were corrupting the minds of children with the glorification of the sword, of conquest, of callousness to bloodshed. As their scriptural authority the priests quoted the Gospel narrative in which Jesus Christ ordered his followers to take up 'swords' (Matt. 10:34), and again we see the Holy Mother Church's official militant policy at work. In sights to shock the most cynical of unbelievers, the Catholic Church blessed the venture and priests and bishops sprinkled holy water on the departing troops, war planes, tanks and guns.

In addition to brazen support, the Church secretly helped Fascist Italy with money and loans from its banks, transacted through devious channels (*The Vatican Billions*, Baron Avro Manhattan, Paravision Books, London, 1972), thanks to the close links which existed between the Italian banks, industrial concerns, and the Government. It must be remembered that for some years most Italian industry had been geared to this war, and that was why Nogara

CHURCH INVESTS IN WAR INDUSTRIES

heavily subscribed to them. The Vatican, as an investor whose main concern was profit, acted as any lay corporation would, besides which, there was the allure of immense returns to come with the successful annexation of Ethiopia. Italy was flooded with picture-postcards, some of which showed the magnificent resources of gold, oil, wheat, etc., which were being acquired, while others showed Mussolini's tanks resplendent with plastic statues of Virgin Mary and St. Peter displayed for the benighted Ethiopians. Apart from bringing the whole Abyssinian Church into subjection to the pope, the Vatican had been impressed by the vista of great financial prospects and of profitable investments in land, real estate and commercial ventures in a vast new Empire in Africa. Mussolini had been generous with promises about the rewards for the Holy See as long as he was seen to be supported by the Catholic Church.

© Combat Picture-point Library

Italian-built CV35 tanks on maneuvers.

CHAPTER 19

Land speculations in Rome and elsewhere

In addition, the Vatican invested in sound, but slower, profit-yielding speculations. This it did by exploiting the rise in land values caused by the rapid growth and expansion of Rome itself. Within a few years, the Vatican became landlord of vast tracts of real estate within and around Rome and, after the Government, the pope, thanks to the success of his new administration, became the single largest landowner in Rome. The Holy Father owned large blocks of flats, offices and valuable stretches of sub-developmental land on the outskirts of the city. The latter yielded huge profits with the inevitable construction boom that developed. In this manner, thanks to its financial expertise, foresight and calculations, Government protection, and to its vast ecclesiastical and lay machinery, within the brief span of a decade the Vatican built up a large fortune within that very Italy which only 50 years before had deprived it of its Papal States. The Vatican did not pay taxes in Italy, as in so many other countries, so that it held a continuous advantage over its commercial, industrial and financial rivals, as much out to make profits as was the Catholic Church:

> Money poured into the Vatican from all corners of the country … so much cash that Nogara was faced with the problem of concealing the enormous holdings and vast earnings from public scrutiny. The money no longer flowed into the Special Administration for investment in private sector business or deposit in Vatican-controlled banks. The excess revenue was now diverted from the Church's corporations, which were tax-exempt and closed to audit, into Swiss bank accounts so that the money trail would lead to closed books and concealed records. The true wealth of the Roman Church would be

known to the pope and his trusted advisors. For everyone else the figure would remain a matter of conjecture.

(*The Vatican Exposed*, Dr. Paul L. Williams, Prometheus Books, New York, 2003, p. 39)

The coffers in St. Peter's were filled to overflowing and the faithful flock knew nothing of it. From its pious sermonizing, the Holy Mother Church constantly claims that all who aspire to follow her preaching must regard materialist possessions and riches as a problem. Nogara was untroubled by such spiritual dogma; his boss was the pope. Nogara retired in 1954 but remained on call as financial advisor to the Vatican until his death in 1958. Scant mention was made of his passing by the Press, as the majority of his investment activities had been, of necessity, cloaked in secrecy.

While engaged in building a financial *imperium* within Italy, the Vatican was by no means idle outside it and, indeed, its activities were no less varied and energetic abroad. Many of its Italian investments extended internationally and one example involves the Church's heavy involvement in the giant conglomerate, Societa Generale Immobiliare, one of Italy's oldest and largest construction companies (*Rich Church, Poor Church*, Martin Malachi, G. P. Putnam's Sons, 1984, p. 40). In time, Immobiliare would become an international conglomerate that would serve to topple governments, wreak financial havoc throughout the world, and embroil the Vatican in a host of sensational scandals (*The Vatican Exposed*, Dr. Paul L. Williams, Prometheus Books, New York, 2003, p. 37). Immobiliare also owned Paramount Studios in Hollywood, where the film, *The Godfather* was shot (*Power on Earth; Michele Sindona's Explosive Story*, Nick Tosches, Arbour House, New York, 1986, pp. 113-14). Through its shareholding in Immobiliare the Vatican came to own major hotels throughout Italy, including the Rome Hilton, Societa Italiani Alberghi Moderni and the Italo Americana Nuovi Alberghi (ibid). The Holy Mother Church's investment in the company enabled her to stretch her tentacles deep into the Western world:

> In France Immobiliare built blocks of offices and shops at 90 Avenue des Champs Elysees, at 61 Rue de Ponthieu, and at 6 Rue de Berry. In Canada, it owned the Stock Exchange Tower in Montreal, one of the world's tallest

skyscrapers; the Port Royal Tower; a 224-apartment block; and a large residential complex in Greensdale (outside Montreal). In Mexico it acquired an entire satellite city of Mexico City called Lomas Verdes. In the United States it came to own five large apartment complexes in Washington, D.C., including the Watergate Hotel; several hotels and office buildings in New York City; and a residential complex of 277 acres at Oyster Bay, New York.

(*The Vatican Exposed*, Dr. Paul L. Williams, Prometheus Books, New York, 2003, p. 85)

The Church's financial division also quietly amassed vast tracts of land in nominally Protestant countries like Holland and Germany, and continued its policy of acquisition, avoiding, whenever possible, any spectacular public moves, since silence and unobtrusiveness were the best methods for pursuing a policy of economic penetration in a potentially inimical community. In nations like Catholic Poland where its riches were secure and Church possessions had multiplied since the country's re-birth after the First World War, the Vatican seldom interfered with ecclesiastical pressure in domestic affairs of the country. The same was true of Hungary, Czechoslovakia, Austria, Belgium and other European countries where the economic affairs of the Church had certain stability and therefore a potentially bright future. Thanks to this, the real estate properties belonging to the Vatican in those countries continued to increase in value, while its financial transactions, mainly carried out by the national hierarchies enjoyed the favour of sundry governments.

CHAPTER 20

The fabulous wealth of the Church in Spain

Where, however, stability was lacking and Church riches were threatened, the Vatican intervened by means of religious, political and diplomatic pressure to defend its interests. Such problems were not always of a religious nature, since more often than not they had a solid, earthly character ... land, buildings, stocks and shares. Thus, when a semi-anarchical, Communist-inspired, political party called the Popular Front took the reigns of France in the mid-thirties, the Vatican, which had so strongly committed itself with Fascist Italy and Nazi Germany, started to worry. It seemed possible that the Popular Front could be the head of a Communist France and so far as the Church's interests were concerned, that could behave worse than the French Revolution or the atheistic French Republic of the beginning of the century. The Vatican, therefore, came out strongly against the Popular Front Government and Catholic right-wing organizations, modeled on Fascism, came to the fore, e.g. *Les Croix de Feu*.

There was talk of an impending civil war, and that was not mere scaremongering. Civil war had already broken out behind the Pyrenees in neighbouring Spain, where a similar government had abysmally failed. Economic crises, political chaos and assassinations had become the order of the day; Communism and anarchy loomed real, menacing and imminent. In the eyes of the Holy Mother Church, the continuation of such instability endangered her earthly riches; a large portion of these had already gone, for in 1931 the Spanish Republic did exactly what the French and Russians had already done during their revolutions ... dispossessed the Church of its property. Catholic land-estates had not been limited to small parcels that would enable the poor of Christ to plant green beans; nor were they designed solely to provide for destitute widows and orphans. The Vatican was the largest, richest landlord in the whole of Spain, even larger than the decadent aristocracy with which it had been so intimately linked that often it was difficult to distinguish one from the other. Referring to the Vatican's holdings in Spain at that commencement of the Spanish Civil War, a Catholic weekly paper made this comment about the Church; 'Its cardinal sin is that it is rich in a land of poverty'. However, the Spanish Republic impartially dispossessed both Church and Throne of their properties, with the result that it found itself in possession of 13,000 million acres of land, which, unlike the previous owners it parceled out free of charge in small-holdings to a million peasants.

In April, 1931, the transformation of Spain into a Republic was peacefully effected. Before the first month was out, however, rioting occurred in Madrid in which six churches and some religious houses (convents) were destroyed by fire. The torching of churches and convents then spread over Spain and the anti-clerical measures that the country had endorsed in the election were embodied in a new Constitution. Catholics were facing the total disestablishment of their Church, and this was not the worst blow. Full religious liberty was granted for the first time in the history of Spain. All religious orders which exacted a vow of obedience were to be dissolved and one of the Republic's first actions was to despoil the Spanish Catholic Church of everything it owned. This meant that its massive property holdings were to be nationalized and the proceeds used for 'educative and charitable purposes':

> The Spanish Catholic Church was, in proportion to the resources of the country, the richest in the world. Mgr. Jose Veleda de Gunjado, a priest-critic of the idle monks, estimated that the monks and nuns held two-thirds of what money there was in the country and one third of the landed property. The treasure accumulated in the older churches was enormous. One statue of the Virgin at Toledo had a crown worth £5000, bracelets worth £2000 each, and robes sewn with more than 150,000 pearls, diamonds and other jewels, while peasants worked the fields for 3 shillings a week.
>
> (*The Papacy in Politics Today,* Dr. Joseph McCabe, Rector of Buckingham College;

Watts and Co., London, 1937)

The situation worsened for the Church and thus developed a steady exodus of bishops, priests, nuns, and lay-folk from Spain to Italy. The Society of Jesus (Jesuits) was under sentence of expulsion from the country ... in summary, the Holy Father was losing Spain. The Spanish Republic then confiscated part of the Vatican's 'vast holdings' (ibid) and officially confirmed that they were worth 6000 million pesetas. Before the inflation that followed, this meant that the Catholic property in Spain at that time (circa 1932) was worth more than US$1000 million (quoted by John Gunther in *The Vatican Billions*, Baron Avro Manhattan, Paravision Books, London, 1972). This colossal sum, it must be remembered, was what remained after the Church's property had already been substantially reduced by legislators during the previous century, when Spain went through two bouts of anti-clericalism (1814 and 1822). In those days it had been estimated that the Vatican owned or controlled between 80 and 90 per cent of all accumulated wealth of the Iberian peninsular (*Unknown Facts about the Vatican Billions*, George Seldes, *The Independent*, New York, 1967), and by the start of the First World War (1914-18) this had been cut down to 60 per cent ... but it wasn't to stay that way.

No wonder, then, that in 1935, when Mussolini went to war in Africa and the Popular Front in France was threatening religion and Vatican property, the Catholic Church sided with a little-known general who in that same year revolted against the Spanish Government in Madrid. His name was General Francisco (Bahamonde) Franco (1892-1975), a wily and nimble Spanish military dictator. He issued his *urbi et orbi*, an elegant and dignified statement of his aims, which included a promise to the pope, saying that if the Church supported Franco's cause, he would 'pound up the flesh and blood of the Communists as mortar for the rebuilding of the churches' (*urbi et orbi*). Franco rose in arms on July 18th, 1936, and the Spanish Civil War begun. One incontrovertible fact is clear; the Vatican supported the rebellion to the hilt ... it actually sponsored it (*The Vatican Billions*, Baron Avro Manhattan, Paravision Books, London, 1972). Indeed, the Church was one of the most important agencies in hatching and promoting the revolt. The motive that prompted it to do this was not only the safeguarding of its spiritual monopoly, but also and above all the retention of its immense temporal wealth ... a veritable stranglehold on the economic and financial life of the nation.

Following almost four years of bloody civil slaughter (1936-1939) and the holocaust of nearly a million dead, the Nationalist forces finally won. General Franco then set out to revive his half-destroyed, war-torn land and, amidst his efforts, he restored the fortunes of the Church in Spain. On January 27th, 1940, he signed a decree formally reinstating the huge assets of the Society of Jesus, which had been confiscated by the Republic in 1932. The Holy Mother Church chanted *Te Deums* all over the Iberian peninsular as its billions of dollars of property holdings were restored to her Balance Sheet. At the same time General Franco also restored all lands which either the 1931 Republic or the loyalists had earlier taken from the Holy Father.

To the Vatican this was a great victory; additional wealth had returned to its coffers, but this created a problem. The Church needed to recover Share and Bond Certificates which had been lost during the Civil War and to do so it placed adverts in sundry newspapers, publishing registration numbers and other details necessary to identify missing share certificates. The efforts were crowned with success, but the triumph, however, was a mixed one. Devout Catholics, to their surprise, came to learn with exactitude how their Holy Mother Church, seemingly so concerned only with the riches of heaven, had been, and was still concerned with the riches it held on Earth. Earlier, during the conflict, the Church had publicly issued disclaimers saying that it had no temporal interests in Spain, but there in contrast, published in newspapers, was evidence that the Vatican had shares in banks, telephone companies, steamship companies; it owned orange groves in Andalusia, mines in the Basque Provinces, factories in Catalan, and other such unspiritual concerns, all procured before the commencement of the Civil War. The Holy Mother Church, a skilful master in international money games, had earlier ensured that Vatican investments were camouflaged behind the names of Companies, individual Catholic laymen or purely financial, banking, accountancy, or industrial concerns. Some of the holders of stocks listed in the newspapers were under the names of various Archbishops (those of Lerida and Madrid-Acala, for example), the Vice General of the

Congregation, the Metropolitan of Valencia, Rectors of Colleges, including the College of Maria the Immaculate, and, along with lesser-known Jesuits, sundry other Catholic congregations owned the remainder ... but all investments belonged ultimately to the hierarchy of the Roman Catholic Church.

Hitler and the Church tax
To believe, however, that the Church was amassing and multiplying its millions only in Spain before and during the war would be a mistake. The Vatican was equally active in other countries, for instance, Belgium, Holland, Poland and France, were it controlled the Franco-Italian Bank of South America and similar investments. At the same time the Church invested in the South and Central American Republics and, in some of these areas the Holy Father controlled a colossal fortune, represented by land, real estate, commercial enterprises, banking, building, stocks and bonds.

The Spanish War had no sooner ended than in September 1939, the Second World War broke out (1939-45). But what now that German dictator, Adolph Hitler (1889-1945), was challenging the whole of Europe ... and where did the Vatican stand as regards her political and economic power outside the Iberian peninsular? Hitler had ensured the stability of Vatican property within the Nazi Reich by a solemn treaty and a concordant that he had earlier signed with Pope Pius XI in June 1933, a few months after he became Chancellor of Germany. This happy state of affairs was due to the fundamental fact that the Roman Catholic Church and Nazism had agreed to support each other. For the Vatican, the major asset to emerge from the deal with Hitler was written verification of the *Kirschensteueu,* a Church Tax that was first inspired by the Weimar Corporation in 1919 and confirmed by Hitler in 1933. It was a levy on practicing Catholics in Germany, and the tax was passed to the Vatican ... a massive US$100 million income per year, with some researchers saying the figure was much more. This was a State tax which was (and maybe still is) deducted from wage-earners in Germany and the only way for Germans to nullify payment was to renounce one's religion. Therefore, in the pope's eyes, no matter how bad Hitler was going to be in the future, he would be useful, in so far as he was the opposite of the Soviet leader, Joseph Stalin (1879-1953), who sought to annihilate the Holy Mother Church and seize her property. 'Anything is better than Atheistic Communism', said Pope Pius XI in an Encyclical called *Mit Brennender Sorge*, written in German and not, as usual, in Latin. Hence, war or no war, Hitler became the most effective defender of the Catholic Church, and therefore its billions of dollars of assets. After signing the concordant, the Vatican ordered the German Centre party (Catholic party) to dissolve itself so as to remove political opposition to Hitler, which it did on July 5th, 1933.

While Hitler guaranteed the Church its property and sundry special privileges, the Holy Father, in return, agreed to some extraordinary conditions, such as that published in concordant Article 16; 'Before bishops take possession of their diocese, they are to take an oath of fealty to the Reich Representative'. In Article 30, the following arrangement was also agreed upon; 'On Sundays special prayers ... will be offered for the welfare of the Reich' (Nazi Germany). Prayers were said publicly for Nazi Germany and bishops made all Catholic priests swear that they would never oppose or harm the Nazi dictatorship. It was the same sort of formal marriage as that contracted with Fascist Italy four years earlier. When details of Catholic policy were first made public by Baron Avro Manhattan in his book, *The Vatican in World Politics* (Horizon Press, New York, 1952, 47 editions), the Holy Father immediately listed the best-seller on his *Index of Prohibited Books*, a device used for centuries by the Vatican to police literature available to the world by forbidding people to read authors who record historic facts.

CHAPTER 21

The failed attempt to bomb Vatican City

An extraordinary report that Baron Avro Manhattan brings us from the war years provides the most damning proof of the Vatican's deep involvement in war industries, and it came from an unexpected source, Yugoslavia's General Bora Mirkovich. When early in 1941 Yugoslavia signed a pact with Hitler, General Mirkovich (on March 27th, 1941), unseated the government, abrogated the pact, and brought Yugoslavia over to the side of the Allies. The importance of the move was tremendous and 'directly affected the course of the Second World War' (*Memoirs* (3 vols., 1960-65), Sir Anthony Eden (1897-1977), British Foreign Minister, later Lord Avon). General Mirkovich's victory totally upset Hitler's war plan, causing him to delay his attack against Russia by four weeks. The controlling interests in Yugoslav armament manufacture were closely linked with the Nazi war machine, and these were strongly associated with concerns directly manipulated by Vatican financial wizard Nogara, whose brother Bartolomeo once ran the Vatican museums. General Mirkovich had been given financial and diplomatic documents which revealed the true extent to which the Catholic Church had been involved in supplying war materials to Yugoslavia. According to General Mirkovich, the Vatican was so involved with the three partners, Yugoslavia, Italy and Germany, that he regarded it as a silent associate of this unholy trio. He called the Holy Mother Church 'a wolf in sheep's clothing' and the impact of the revelation concerning Vatican profiteering from war investments made such an impact on General Mirkovich that he made a decision that, had it been successful fulfilled, would have resulted in a tremendous calamity for world culture.

The General's bitterness was the greater since practically all the contraband weapons and armory which the Catholic Croats, the Ustashi (meaning, 'to rise up'), had assembled and which shortly afterwards was used ruthlessly against Yugoslavia itself, had been supplied from such quarters, so that the Ustashi, under the leadership of Ante Pavelic, had been directly financed, not by Mussolini, but by the Roman Catholic Church. General Mirkovich was so incensed that he issued instructions for squadrons of the Yugoslav Air Force to bomb Vatican City in a series of nighttime raids. He was unconcerned by the directions of Article 7 of 'The Lateran Treaty of 1929' which stated: 'In accordance with the provisions of International Law, it shall be forbidden for aircraft of any kind whatsoever to fly over Vatican territory'. The first fleet of military fighters was assembled and readied for an attack on the evening of April 5, 1941. Just before orders were given to take off, the weather turned inclement and the squadron was grounded. General Mirkovich postponed the first bombing run by forty-eight hours and the rescheduling saved Vatican City from obliteration. Twenty-four hours later (on April 6, 1941), the Yugoslav Air Force was crippled by low-flying Nazi bombers that swept over the airfield and destroyed most of Yugoslav's war planes on the tarmac. It was thus one of the paradoxes of the Second World War that the Catholic Church owed the salvation of its headquarters to none other than Adolph Hitler.

© Photograph by Luigi Petrona, circa 1950

This is an internal photograph looking upwards into the dome of St. Peter's Basilica. In silhouette below is part of the massive baldacchino designed and built by Gian Lorenzo Bernini (1598-1680), which stands above the papal altar. This massive building was only hours from being reduced to rubble.

The destruction of Vatican City, with its magnificent treasures of architecture, history and art, would have been unforgivable, a loss beyond reckoning for Western civilization. The Sistine Chapel with its ceiling by Michelangelo; the Basilica of St. Peter and its Square, the Vatican Library and Museum; the remnants of the ancient Leonine Wall; tapestries, statues, monuments and paintings; picture galleries and some building ruins dating back to the time of Constantine (c. 337). The loss of such treasures seems unimaginable, and with the planned nighttime air attacks it was possible that bombs missing their target could have devastated structures outside the environs of Vatican City, such as the Coliseum; the Arches of Titus and Constantine, Capitoline Museums and Palaces, the Pantheon, the Fora of Augustine, Nerva and Caesar and many of the magnificent churches in the city. However, the true extent of the Vatican's involvement in war industries will, in all probability, never be disclosed, although, no doubt, screened by the financial convolutions of certain huge industrial giants, it might one day be unearthed and brought to light.

Author's note:
In providing this extraordinary information the author is indebted to the works of Baron Avro Manhattan (1914-1991), a world-renowned authority on Roman Catholicism in political affairs. His book *The Vatican in World Politics* (1949) was one of the best selling books of all time, and in all, he wrote some sixty books, each well worthy of serious study. These particular publications by Baron Manhattan are highly recommended:

The Vatican in World Politics, Baron Avro Manhattan, first published in Great Britain by C. A. Watts and Co, London

Catholic Imperialism and World Freedom, Baron Avro Manhattan, Watts and Co. London, 1952

The Catholic Church Against the Twentieth Century, Baron Avro Manhattan, first published in Great Britain by C. A. Watts and Co, London, c. 1948

The Vatican Billions, Baron Avro Manhattan, Paravision Books, London, 1972

Murder in the Vatican; American, Russian and Papal Plots, Baron Avro Manhattan, Ozark Books, Springfield, Mo. 1985

Vatican Moscow Washington Alliance, Baron Avro Manhattan, Chick Publications, Chino, California, 1986

PART THREE

The dome of St. Peter's seen across the Vatican gardens ©Vaticana Photographica Collecta, Roma ... David Seymour, 1948

The Vatican's immense wealth includes gold bullion, prime real estate, stocks and bonds, a priceless art collection, secret Swiss bank accounts ... and international fraud investigators in the Vatican Bank.

CHAPTER 22

The Pope's new bank

Within the Holy Mother Church the progressive amassment of worldly riches continued unabated, indeed it gathered momentum. While there were still individual Christians who believed in poverty, the Church itself continued to seek secular wealth in leaps and bounds and that takes us right into the headquarters of the Roman Catholic Church in Vatican City. It was true that the Communists of France and, above all, of Italy were seriously threatening to take over the government in Paris and Rome. That danger was real and immediate and Pope Pius XII (1939-1958) deemed it necessary to politically intervene. He ordered the Italian Catholic electorate to vote against the Communists and even the Socialists, and anyone disobeying him was to be excommunicated. Besides this, the pope, while relying on Nazi armies to protect the Church's wealth from the Communists at home, nevertheless deemed it wise to protect the Vatican's mobile riches. The best policy was to help Providence by taking precautionary steps by transferring them to safer shores, and where better than within the distant borders of the USA? Thus, at the height of the Second World War, Pius XII founded the *Instituto per le Opere di Religione* (The Institute for Works of Religion), generally known as IOR. This division of Catholicism is today called the 'Vatican Bank' by all but the Vatican, and it operates from a stone tower in the heart of Vatican City. The building was originally constructed under the instructions of Pope Nicholas V (Tommaso Parentucelli, 1397-1445) who, during his pontificate, was forced to fortify Catholic headquarters against republican and local uprisings against the Church.

It was June 27th, 1942 when Pope Pius XII announced the formation of the new corporation, and he publicly stated that its basic objective was 'to keep and administer the capital intended for religious congregations'. At the time of the bank's inception, Hitler, after having successfully reached the outskirts of Moscow, was stuck there and, to His Holiness's chagrin, could not budge. Around the same time, Mussolini and his mistress, Claire Petacci were shot dead by Italian partisans and, amidst a ghastly retinue of corpses, were hung up by their heels from the façade of a petrol station in Milan's Piazza Loretto. This could only give the pope cause for worry for he was facing an impending debacle. A Communist Italy, France or Germany would mean one thing; the dispossession of all the wealth of the Catholic Church within that country. It was for this reason that Pius XII established the new bank, a clever move to safeguard the Vatican's financial interests. For the *Instituto*, while cleverly integrated within the ecclesiastical machinery of the Church, and to all appearances and purposes a purely religious institution, plausible and logical, in reality was a 'flexible instrument for arranging multiple financial activities' (*The Economist*, London, March 27th, 1965), and was later described by the Italian Minister of Foreign Trade, Rinaldo Ossola (1978) as 'to all effects, a non-residential banking institute' (*Commercial Bulletin*), in other words, foreign.

What did all this mean in the middle of the war? It meant, as an authoritative organ explained that; 'this bank allowed the Holy See to undertake transfers across closed frontiers, and it profited richly from the rare privilege of being able to transfer foreign exchange in a partitioned world' (*The Economist*, London, March 27th, 1965). And partitioned it was … by hundreds of thousands of armed men, by closed frontiers, barbed wire, bombers, war ships, tanks and submarines. Nobody could pass, and that applied to generals, politicians, diplomats and heads of state … but there was one exception … representatives of the Vatican. For them, there were no restrictions, for as envoys of a religion and the delegates of the officially neutral Vatican City State, they could travel at their pleasure from one belligerent country or continent to another. They were publicly seen as carriers of spiritual comfort, but dressed in clerical attire they were secretly the carriers of bank notes, stocks, share certificates, and bonds (*The Vatican Billions,* Baron Avro Manhattan, Paravision Books, London, 1972).

For that is precisely what the pope's new bank did. It enabled the transfer of increasingly large sums of Vatican money to the USA, Canada and Britain. The valuables were drawn, not only from the coffers of Rome, but from all over Italy, France, and from even inside Germany itself. The pope saw to it that certain trusted individuals within the national hierarchies, *uomini di fiducia*, as they were and still are called at the Vatican, were charged with this delicate task. Most transactions were camouflaged, as is the Vatican's custom, behind the screen of individuals, banks and corporations, who served as dummies to save the Church from potential embarrassment. The Vatican Bank, and its affiliate, the Catholic Bank, subsequently developed into one of the most mysterious institutions in the world and in the coming decades it was to cause the greatest possible discomfiture to the papacy.

It began to invest, not only in the USA, but also in South American countries, and this was publicly known at the time. But what came as a surprise after the Second World War was the extent of the Church's investment in the USA, and the degree of its participation in big business was revealed before hostilities ended when embarrassing documents fell into the hands of Italian Socialist leaders. Those records established that the Vatican had invested heavily throughout North America, but owing to the Church's policy of disguising its holdings behind a screen of Catholic and even non-Catholic lay concerns, the documents did not reveal the whole story. However, one Government valuation arrived at by means of reliable criteria placed the amount of the Vatican's stockholding in the USA at between US$80 and US$100 million dollars at 1947 values (*Commercial Bulletin*, January, 1948). This, it must be noted, excluded the value of Church real estate, which we shall scrutinize in more detail shortly.

The growth of Catholic investments did not stop with the cessation of hostilities, but gained momentum, with Nogara having at his disposal a massive yearly income. One of the Vatican's first postwar acquisitions was Finsader, a steel combine that counted among its subsidiaries Alfa Romeo, the automobile company; Finmeccanica, a holding company for thirty-five other Companies that specialized in every phase of engineering; Finmare, for example, that operated passenger shipping lines; the Terni Company that produced steel products; and Italsider that manufactured pig iron, steel ingots, and piping.

Another acquisition was Montedison that specialized in mining and metallurgical manufacturing, pharmaceuticals, electric power, and textiles. In 1968 Monedison displayed sales of US$854 million and a net profit of US$67 million. One of the Church's most lucrative new holdings was SNIA-Viscosa, a leading producer of textiles that by 1968 possessed capital of US$90 million and displayed an annual profit of US$15 million (*Rich Church, Poor Church*, Martin Malachi, G. P. Putnam's Sons, 1984, p. 52-53; also, *The Vatican Exposed*, Dr. Paul L. Williams, Prometheus Books, New York, 2003, p. 84). With mounting boldness, the Vatican also invested with industrial concerns in Britain, some of which were subsidiaries of the giant British Courtaulds (The Interfan and Novaceta). The Holy Mother Church continued to accumulate vast wealth, and to such an extent that by 1953, and still under the management of Nogara ...

> ... the Vatican controlled more than ninety of Italy's one hundred and eighty credit, banking and insurance institutions. One of the largest of these concerns was La Centrale, a company that provided medium and long term credit for projects in agriculture, hydro-electricity, mining and engineering ... by 1968 La Centrale possessed $107 million in capital and $277 million in assets ... Italcementi, another Vatican-controlled company, supplied over 30 percent of the cement in Italy and owned a financial house called Italmobiliare. Italmobiliare, in turn, owned eight banks with cumulative assets of $512 million and capital reserves of $22 million. In addition, the financial house held control of the Banca Provinciale Lombarda and the Credit Commerciale di Cremona whose combined deposits exceeded $1.2 billion.

(*The Vatican Exposed*, Dr. Paul L. Williams, Prometheus Books, New York, 2003, p. 83)

At the same time, the Vatican financiers were also increasing the Church's involvement in the USA, a country that prides itself on its separation of Church and State. It harbours over 300 prosperous and predominately Protestant denominations and numberless sects, one of which owns the real estate upon which Las Vegas sits. While the Roman Catholic Church is the USA's largest single religious unit, it is still a minority, with the Vatican estimating 40 million adherents (*L 'Osservatore Romano*, the Vatican's ecclesiastical newspaper, founded in 1861) from a population of around 290 million. However, during this time the Vatican's financial and legal headquarters were firmly established in New York City, one of the original thirteen United States of America.

CHAPTER 23

'Insider trading' in Vatican gold

At times, international financial deals were carried out above the heads of the American people by means of private and secret arrangements between high government officials and the Catholic hierarchy. We shall content ourselves by examining just one example, that concerning what the media termed the 'Strange Case of the Vatican Gold'. The first news of these celebrated gold transactions 'leaked' out through a story in the *United Nations World Magazine* of December 1952 and the whole affair had a number of unfortunate results for the Holy Mother Church. The investigative article asserted that the Vatican had brought and sold many millions of dollars worth of gold bullion from the United States gold supply in the previous few years. In Europe, rumour maintained that the Vatican was given preferential treatment in these transactions ... namely, that the pope was allowed to buy the precious metal at US$34 per ounce, US$1 less than market value. The *United Nations World Magazine* article also declared that the Vatican was 'heavy' with stock in leading American Industries, information that caused several American investigators to approach the US Treasury Department, as well as the Vatican representative in Washington, Mgr. Amleto Cicognani, for confirmation. Over the signature of A. N. Orarly, the Secretary of the Treasury, the US Government officially revealed that it had sold US$26.8 million in gold ingots to the Vatican in just one of many secret transactions. Bishop McShea, an American citizen and speaking on behalf of the Vatican, depreciated the value of the gold purchase to the degree of 'say, 17 or 18 million dollars' and denied any favoritism in price, adding that a large number of the papal ingots were held in the USA Federal Reserve Bank, while banks in England and Switzerland held the remainder (*United Nations World Magazine*). The bishop also revealed that the Vatican had, over a given period, 'sold back about US$5 millions, making a total net sale of US$21.8 millions'. After further enquires, denials, counter-denials and odd silences, finally, in a letter in the April 1953 issue of the *United Nations World Magazine*, there came a declaration from the very same Secretary of the Treasury, A. N. Orarly, declaring that there 'may be some truth in the suggestion that the gold had been sold to the Vatican at an advantage' (ibid).

The case was illuminating because it confirmed, as if there was any need of confirmation, that the Vatican was buying at one dollar per ounce below the market price, and selling for profit, millions of dollars worth of gold bullion in the USA. In financial jargon, the Roman Catholic Church, with a privileged buying structure, was trading in gold, and did so for years. It also appeared that sections of the US Government machine were influenced and controlled by certain American citizens; that is, by Catholics acting as agents of the Vatican, for example, Bishop McShea, who openly admitted, when asked how he was so well informed on the gold sales, that he had represented the Vatican at the time of the papal purchase (*Unknown Facts about the Vatican Billions*, George Seldes, in the *Independent*, New York, 1953). Around this time a plethora of Vatican financiers had taken over the responsibility of running Nogara's monolithic creation after his retirement in 1954. A few years later, the *Wall Street Journal* revealed that the Vatican's financial deals in the USA alone were so big that very often it sold or bought gold in lots of a million or more dollars every day (*Wall Street Journal*, September, 1960). At that time, the Vatican's treasure of physical gold bullion was estimated by the *United Nations World Magazine* to amount to several billion dollars. A decade or so later, reliable sources indicated that the Vatican had a gold reserve of US$11 billion, three times the gold reserve of Great Britain (*The Changing Vatican*, Alberto Cavallari, Doubleday, New York).

CHAPTER 24

Catholic Church investments in America

The news of the gold transactions revealed that it was Vatican practice to do business with the US Government to its own advantage. But Bishop McShea, denied that the Vatican had also invested in American industry and that these investments yielded heavily during the sales boom in the war years (*Let's Prey*, Madalyn Murray O 'Hair). He was proven to have lied because the Church was effective in a far wider and more comprehensive field of business, although great efforts were made to see that Vatican transactions remained as secret as possible. Furthermore, until news of the Vatican's gold trading was exposed, those dealings had never been made public knowledge. Here again, we see the Holy Mother Church accepting Gospel narratives as instructions and acting upon them; 'Be as wise as serpents and as innocent as doves' (Mt 10:16). These secret transactions were just some of many surreptitiously carried out and concealed behind endless legal devices; but the hold of the Vatican upon the financial life of the USA is not confined to gold trading and Share Market connections. Consider the following: In 1962, the US Treasury Department showed that churchgoers in America reported on their income tax returns that they had given US$2.9 billion to the churches. By 1966, The Protestant Churches were themselves reporting US$3 billion income annually, as shown in the *Yearbook of American Churches*. By 1967, annual giving was estimated by news services in America, drawn from unofficial governmental sources, as being about US$6 billion per year, or US$16 million per day (*Let's Prey*, Madalyn Murray O 'Hair).

For doubting Thomases, another proof that the Vatican's financial machinery had been geared to the American success formula was revealed in the trips of Pope Paul VI (born, 1897; pope from 1963-1978) to New York City. While there, he celebrated Mass at the famed Yankee Stadium and some TV viewers expressed surprise at his choice of location. 'What?' replied a USA Catholic bishop to the naïve remarks of some press correspondents who were also bewildered; 'Don't they know that the Stadium is ours too?' (*Rome and the White House*, Father L. B. Hyland, 'Notarial Review', Washington, 1979). That almost casual 'too' was more than significant; it was portentous in its implications, since to the bishop it had become as natural as the air he breathed to assume that, besides all the multitudinous ecclesiastical and semi-ecclesiastical concerns, the famous Stadium, celebrated for its sporting events, should also be the property of the Holy Mother Church (*The Vatican Billions*, Baron Avro Manhattan, Paravision Books, London, 1972). The cumulative result of this enormous collectivized energy is that the Catholic Church has truly attained the redoubtable status of a giant corporation. The boast of a Church prelate in 1966 who prided himself upon this reality was more than justified; 'We are already a lot bigger than Ford Motors, Shell Oil and Bethlehem Steel put together', he said (*Sunday Express*, London, 27th February, 1966). This was a terse summing up of one of the most striking facts of life in contemporary USA, but what the prelate didn't say, or didn't know, was that the Vatican was a major shareholder in those three companies. However, things don't always go the Church's way:

> For instance, in February 1973 when the American Stock Exchange stopped the trading in Vetco Industries because a Los Angeles investment adviser had gathered together nearly 27 per cent of Vetco's outstanding share and options (in violation of SEC regulations), it was learned that 20 per cent of the 27 per cent (454,000 shares worth about US$16.8 million) had been acquired by the Vatican through a Liechtenstein investment company in which Sindona had a substantial interest. In settling with the SEC by paying a fine of US$307,720, the Vatican sold all its Vetco shares at a profit ... but refused to make any public comment at this embarrassing time.
>
> *The Vatican Papers*, Nino Lo Bello, New English Library (a division of Hodder and Stoughton, Ltd.), Kent, 1982, pp. 230-1)

At this time, Sindona was the Vatican's main banking representative in the USA, and we will learn more about him in the next chapter. Around that time it was found in New York State banking records that the Roman Catholic Church showed investments in stocks and bonds with hundreds of corporations. Among others, were included Goodyear Tire & Rubber, Firestone, Colgate, Standard Oil, Atlantic City Convention Hall, Baltimore & Ohio R. R., Rock Island, General Foods, Savoy Plaza Hotel, Proctor & Gamble, Eire, Seaboard, Missouri, Pacific, Pere Marquette; Fisk, US Rubber; Bethlehem Steel, Press Steel Car, Unilever, Trumbull Steel, American Smelting; Commonwealth Edison, Brooklyn Edison, NY Edison, Pacific Gas & Electric, Montana Power Co., Indiana Electric, Oklahoma Gas and Electric, West Penn Power, American Commonwealth Power, Texas Electric, Louisiana Hotel Co., Squire Building, Lane Bryant, Fox Playhouses, Fox Theatre (St. Louis), Denver Joint Stock Land Bank, National Dairy, Thermoid, Washington Silk, Westinghouse, and Pillsbury Flour (*The Vatican Empire*, Nino Lo Bello, Trident Press, New York, 1968; *The Vatican Billions*, Baron Avro Manhattan, Paravision Books, London, 1972; *The Vatican Papers*, Nino Lo Bello, New English Library (a division of Hodder and Stoughton, Ltd.), Kent, 1982, pp. 229). At around the same time the Vatican became a major stockholder in US companies such as Gulf Oil, General Motors, and IBM. In 1971, Martin A. Larson and Stanley C. Lowell, in their book, *Praise the Lord for Tax Exemption,* conservatively estimated that the tax-exempt property value of the Roman Catholic Church in the USA at that time was US$110 billion. Furthermore, the Catholic Church, like the Protestants, conducts insurance business via Church-related companies. One of these is the Knights of Columbus, which, in 1972, held over US$1.5 billion of insurance 'for Catholics only'. The prestigious titles awarded to some of the Knights (Counts of the Papal Court, for example), their secret oaths, and the quality of their New York real estate would stun Catholics into disbelief.

Since then, the Vatican has managed to penetrate even more deeply within the financial and industrial framework of American society with its 19,000 parishes. The meaning of this becomes clear if we take a sample at random of, say, diocesan wealth, which is rarely disclosed. It is possible however, to provide an outline of this vast affluence by referencing a Bond Prospectus produced by the Boston archdiocese in 1967 that listed its assets at US$635,891,004, being 9.9 times its liabilities (Prospectus, May 1st, 1967). This leaves a net worth of US$571,704,953 (Figures given by M. A. Larson and C. S. Howell, *Praise the Lord for Tax Exemption* (Washington, Americans United), and many of the other 31 archdioceses and 174 dioceses (2007 figures) in the USA are even wealthier than Boston. For example, David Yallop revealed that the total assets of the Roman Catholic Church in Chicago 'were by 1970 in excess of one billion dollars' (*In God's Name, An Investigation Into the Murder of John Paul I,* David Yallop, Bantam Books, New York, 1984, p. 188). No wonder, then, that certain dioceses in the United States, thanks chiefly to their financial puissance, have been called, 'American Vaticans', and cardinals, 'American popes'. An authoritative document that came into the possession of this author in 2002 estimated the total worth of the Catholic Church's real estate in the United States alone to be in excess of US$200 billion. Because of its successful infiltration and astounding financial power, the Vatican, therefore, is *de facto* one of the most influential 'presences' in the economic activities of the USA and, as a result, of the economic well-being of the Western Hemisphere. The 'poor' Church of Christ in the USA is an economic giant, not so much because it has penetrated within the economic sinews of the major corporations, trusts and banks of America, but because it has accumulated lands, real estate, and controls institutions whose real, solid and material value in terms of money makes the Church an economic colossus in its own right, indeed, perhaps the greatest colossus of all.

CHAPTER 25

Scandal in the Pope's Bank

In recent years the Vatican Bank has become the source of sensational international scandals amidst dubious financial dealings involving billions of dollars and a considerable amount of bloodletting (*The Vatican Exposed*, Dr. Paul L. Williams, Prometheus Books, New York, 2003, p. 56). It remains the target of hundreds of lawsuits, several filed by Holocaust victims over the Vatican's alleged possession of Nazi gold, its laundering of ill-gotten gains, and its willingness to finance the Nazi 'ratlines'. Brilliant world expert on internal Vatican affairs, Baron Avro Manhattan (d. 1991), revealed that Karol Wojtyla, to become Pope John Paul II in 1978 (d. 2005) was once in the 'ratline' (*The Vatican Moscow Washington Alliance*, Baron Avro Manhattan, Chick Publications, California, 1986), an opinion supported by Wojtyla's personal friend, Polish Bishop Andre Deskur (*The Christ Scandal*, Tony Bushby, University Press, USA, 2008, pp. 319-320).

Around a decade after the exposure of its gold trading advantage, fraud investigators revealed that the Vatican Bank was in cohorts with both Italian and New York Mafia families. Importantly for this overview are two particular figures, Michele Sindona, a Sicilian merchant banker, and Roberto Calvi, who was engaged by Pope John Paul II to mastermind what came to be called the *Great Vatican Bank Scandal*. The Roman Catholic Church's relationship with Sindona and Calvi was an unmitigated disaster and the schemes these men devised were interlocked in joint operations with the Vatican Bank. Through their involvement with Chicago-born Bishop Paul Marcinkus, head of the Vatican Bank, a series of illegal transactions resulted in substantial gains for the Holy Mother Church:

For example, in 1980 the Vatican Bank sold 2 million shares in a Rome-based international construction company called Vianini. The shares were sold to a small Panamanian company called Laramie. It was the first stage of a deal in which it was planned that the Vatican would sell to Laramie 6 million shares in Vianini. The price of the shares was grossly inflated. The first two million cost Laramie 20 million dollars. Laramie is yet another of the companies owned by the Vatican. It might be considered a futile exercise to sell yourself your own shares at an inflated figure. It becomes less futile if you are using someone else's money, as Calvi has demonstrated over the years. The 20 million dollars to pay for the shares came from Roberto Calvi. And the Vatican Bank kept the shares it already owned and the 20 million dollars as well. Further, it did not and never has owned 6 million shares in Vianini. Its maximum stake in the company has never been more than 3 million shares. It was with schemes like this that Calvi paid off Marcinkus.

(*In God's Name*, David Yallop, Jonathan Cape, 1984, p. 301)

It was Bishop Marcinkus who made US$14 million profit for the Vatican in one day playing the New York Stock Exchange (*The Vatican Papers*, Nino Lo Bello, New English Library (a division of Hodder and Stoughton, Ltd.), Kent, 1982, pp. 223). The Vatican established Panamanian and other off-shore companies in various tax-havens, as was evidenced in a document issued on September 1st 1981 by Marcinkus and signed by bank executives, Luigi Mennini and Pelligrino De Strobel. This document was addressed to Banco Ambrosiano Andino in Lima, Peru, with a similar letter sent on the same day to the Ambrosiano Group Banco Commercial in Nicaragua. These letters were typed on official letter-heads of the '*Instituto per le Opere di Religione, Vatican City*', and in Curial circles they became known as 'the letters of comfort'. However, what they reveal offers very little comfort to pious Roman Catholics and provide no reassurance to any who believe in the falsely-portrayed moral integrity of the Vatican. The documents listed the names of some mysterious banking companies that Vatican Bank executives frankly admitted that the Roman Catholic Church 'directly or indirectly' controlled in Panama, Luxembourg, Switzerland, and Liechtenstein, and supported their claim with an inclusion of 'attached statement of accounts'. Most of the Church's billions are deposited in non-Italian banks; 'Some are in America and many are in Switzerland, where the Vatican maintains its funds in numbered accounts. Nobody knows how much money it has in Swiss vaults ... the Vatican also uses its Swiss accounts to maintain its anonymity when gaining control of foreign corporations' (*The Vatican Empire*, Nino Lo Bello, Trident Press, New York, 1968).

Vatican documentation on letterheads of the *Sacra Congregzione Dei Religiosi,* came into the possession of the FBI and revealed blatant acts of fraud, illicit transactions, and criminal conspiracy committed by the Holy See. One well-known example was that of the ill-fated billion-dollar counterfeit securities scheme instigated by the Vatican Bank in partnership with the New York Mafia. It was the brainchild of Cardinal Eugene Tisserant (d. 1972), and Bishop Paul Marcinkus (called the Gorilla because of his physical size) in their capacity as heads of the Vatican Bank and subsequently led to arrest warrants being issued for three Vatican bankers. Stories appeared in the press revealing that the Holy Mother Church had lost up to US$1 billion in illegal and clandestine dealings with the Mafia. The money disappeared and despite years of investigative court proceedings no one ever found out what happened to it. In February 1973, the *Traditionalist*, a Catholic weekly newspaper, published a detailed account of the Mafia transactions it called the 'Sindona Affair', and labeled Pope Paul VI 'a traitor to the Church'. As Italian Police investigations uncovered evidence of what they called 'the Vatican Connection' to the Mafia, the Church again became the subject of disdain and contempt. Over the decades, additional suspicious operations emanating from the bank's dealings have constantly attracted the attention of international fraud investigators and Dr. Paul L. Williams explains why the Church has escaped criminal conviction:

> Yet the Vatican Bank remains impervious to lawsuits and charges of criminal misconduct. It represents a fiscal (financial) agency of a sovereign state. As such, it cannot be compelled to redress wrongs ... not even the most egregious violations of international law. The only way it can be made vulnerable to litigation is by the designation of Vatican City as a 'rogue state' and the Vatican Bank as a 'rogue institution'. This requires that it be established that the Roman

Catholic Church is a corrupt organization and, as such, subject to prosecution under Racketeer and Corrupt Organization (RICO) statutes, which in recent history have been enacted against members of organized crime families.

(*The Vatican Exposed*, Dr. Paul L. Williams, Prometheus Books, New York, 2003)

The worth of the Vatican Bank today is unknown as its financial figures are strictly kept from public knowledge. However, in June, 1982, Roberto Calvi, 'God's Banker', had dealings with the *Instituto* and he estimated the patrimony of the Vatican Bank at that time to be 'far in excess of US$10 billion' (*Washing Money in the Holy See,* Richard Behar, Fortune, August 1999; also, *In God's Name, An Investigation Into the Murder of John Paul I,* David Yallop, Jonathon Cape, London, 1984, p. 295). Shortly after Calvi revealed his estimates, his body was found hanging by the neck under Blackfriar's Bridge in London, appropriately next to a sewer outlet. On the same day, Teresa Corrocher, Calvi's secretary and closest confidant, was found hanging in a locked closet in her apartment in Milan, also 'suicided' (*London Times*, 18 June 1982). Around the same time, Cardinal Vagnozzi commented that 'it would take a combination of the KGB, the CIA, and Interpol to obtain just an inkling of how much and where the monies are' (*In God's Name, An Investigation Into the Murder of John Paul I,* David Yallop, Bantam Books, New York, 1984, p. 105; quoted by Cardinal Vagnozzi). These are strange words from an official spokesman of the Holy Mother Church whose annual profit from just one of its other banks was US$120 million in 1978. It must be remembered that the Vatican Bank is just one of dozens of financial institutions owned by the Catholic Church and Calvi's conclusion on its worth is isolated from the value of its involvement in other banks. His estimate is revealing, since it did not include other major internal Church financial departments with highfaluting names operated by the Vatican, particularly 'The Administration of the Patrimony of the Holy See' (known as A.P.S.A), which had gross assets of US$1.2 billion in 1978 (Italian Senate figures). This organization, with its immense portfolio of investments, is recognized as a central bank by the World Bank, the International Monetary Fund and the Bank of International Settlement in Basle. A.P.S.A is a Vatican structure that has much to hide for one of its sections was specifically structured to administer a great deal of the real estate holdings owned by the Church, which in Rome alone, amounts to over 5,000 rented apartments (ibid). Other financial departments of the Vatican are 'The Congregation for the Evangelization of Peoples', 'The Fabric of St. Peter's', 'The Pontifical Society for St. Peter Apostle', and 'Propaganda Fide', all revealed by the Italian Senate as major players of the Italian Stock Market. Nor did Calvi's estimate take into account the large Vatican investment in State Bonds and Debentures released to the public in March 1967 by the then Italian Finance Minister, Luigi Preti.

CHAPTER 26

Cardinals into stockbrokers

The Vatican, once all its assets have been gathered together, is the most formidable stockbroker in the world. In Italy, it is possible to estimate the extent of the Vatican's share portfolio around 20 years after the Second World War (say 1965). It is difficult to accurately establish a precise figure, since the Vatican is the only State which has consistently refused to disclose its real budget or let 'outsiders' know the true value of its assets. But unofficial estimates by Italian governments at various times, based on information they were able to glean, seemed to coincide with nebulous hints dropped by insiders at the Vatican itself. According to these estimates, the Holy See owned between 15 and 20 per cent of the total stocks quoted on the Italian Stock Exchange. In December 1964 the total value of these shares, it was said, was 5,500 billion lire, which put the capital invested by the Vatican in Italian stocks alone at about US$500 million. In 1967 the Italian Press, specifically the left-wing Press, attacked the Vatican, wanting to know why the Church had not paid tax on its share trading. They also wanted to know how many shares the Vatican held in their country and extraordinary figures relating to the value of those shares began to fly. They ranged from estimates that put the worth of the Vatican investment on the Italian Stock Exchange between US$600 million and US$850 million. By 1972 this figure was estimated by conservative financiers to be in excess of US$1000 million (*The Vatican Billions*, Baron Avro Manhattan, Paravision Books, London, 1972), but conceded that that figure could possibly be doubled or tripled. Around that same time, a financial writer for the *New York Times,* Robert. C. Doty put the value of the Vatican's Italian stocks and shares at '5 billion to 10 billion dollars'. That is in Italy only and the approximations are of only Vatican Stock Exchange investments.

The economic weight of the Church's wealth and hold on Italian finance, industry and commerce had now become one of the main factors in the prosperity of the Italian peninsular. The authoritative *Economist* of London, at this period, did not hesitate to say; 'The Vatican could theoretically throw the Italian economy into confusion if it decided to unload all its shares suddenly and dump them on the market'. Yet Church investments in Italy represented at that time, according to reliable Vatican sources who spoke to Baron Avro Manhattan, between only one-tenth and one-twelfth of the whole of its world Stock Market investments. This gives the total worldwide figure of funds astronomically totaling US$10,000 million (US$100 billion), at a conservative estimate, and 30 years later that figure was estimated to have more than tripled to US$30,000 million (*Fortune*).

But this is just a small portion of the riches of the Catholic Church, which in 1971 was in the USA alone greater than the five wealthiest giant corporations of the country (*Praise the Lord for Tax Exemption*, Martin A. Larson and Stanley C. Lowell, 1971). When to the stocks and bonds is added real estate holdings, and other investments, then the staggering accumulation of the Catholic Church's fortune becomes so formidable as to defy any rational assessment. The Holy See has large involvements with the Rothschilds of Britain, France and America and besides being a shareholder in the Hambros Bank, the Credit Suisse in London and Zurich, the Morgan Bank of New York, the Bankers Trust Company and major holdings in the Bank of America, had invested additional millions with sundry corporations ... to quote only two; the American Anaconda Copper Company and the Sinclair Oil Company ... and this was believed to be to the tune of about US$100 million (*The Vatican Billions*, Baron Avro Manhattan, Paravision Books, London, 1972). The Vatican unashamedly invested money in Riviera casinos, such as the San Remo, in beverages as alien to holy water as that of Perrier in France; in advertising agencies; it has ownership of denominational cemeteries; in liquor manufacturing; garbage dumps, and in building concerns with, at one stage, the heads of Fiat and Italcementi Cement group as directors (ibid). Confronted with the developing public exposure of the evils of a wealthy

Roman Catholic Church, Pope Paul VI in conjunction with Cardinal Guerri, Head of the Special Administration of A.P.S.A., decided to unload from the Italian portfolio most of the Vatican's 36,000,000 shares in Societa Generale Immobiliare and re-invest the proceeds in other areas. With assets in excess of half a billion dollars scattered around the world, Immobiliare was highly visible earthly wealth and the pope was concerned by negative media comments about the Church's heavy financial involvement in the company. He also thought the moment seemed propitious to jettison a few other embarrassing investments and various Vatican departments unloaded a variety of companies on Sindona (who was later also 'suicided'), and later, on Roberto Calvi. Included were Ceramiche Pozzi and Condotte d'Acqua and then, in 1970, the Vatican sold Sindona the Instituto Farmacologico Sereno, the pharmaceutical company which featured an oral contraceptive pill among its more successful lines.

In 1972, it was alleged that the Vatican owned 98 publishing houses for books and over 517 Catholic periodicals with a monthly circulation exceeding 40 million. Later, in May 1995, the Holy Mother Church offered her *Encyclopedia Britannica* for sale at around US$450 million after suffering three consecutive years of losses and dwindling sales. The Vatican had purchased the publication some 100 years earlier, and in due course (1943) assigned it to the Roman Catholic University in Chicago (*Encyclopedias: Their History Throughout the Ages*, 1966, two editions. The 2nd Edition pays particular attention to *Encyclopedia Britannica*). Catholic scholars rewrote sections detrimental to Church projections and in subsequent decades Christian missionaries went door to door the world over selling the sanitized *Encyclopedia Britannica* into millions of unsuspecting households (*The Criminal History of the Papacy*, Tony Bushby, in *Nexus New Times*, vol., 14, No. 2, February-March, 2007, p. 43).

Up until this stage in the story of the Holy Mother Church's accumulation of material assets, there has been no mention of her immense possessions in Australia, which, like other countries, is impossible to calculate. The present writer knows of an entire city block owned by the Catholic Church in the Central Business District of Melbourne, complete with its high-rise buildings and multi-level car-parks. Similar investments are held in Adelaide, the 'City of Churches', Sydney and Brisbane. The Vatican also owns a vast tract of sub-dividable waterfront property in one of Queensland's top tourist locations that has been in the possession of the Church for more than a generation. There is also an undeveloped parcel of land on Mt. Tamborine that in 1995 was valued by a local estate agent at Aust$12.7 million if subdivided. In the Australian outback it owns, and then sub-leases, a prestigious cattle station that literally covers hundreds of thousands of square kilometres. There is something else that is little known about Vatican affairs Down-under. An authoritive source close to this author revealed that the Vatican owes both the Maori tribes of New Zealand and Polynesian Pacific Islanders 'billions of dollars' that originated from 100-years of collection of taxes and shipping levies by Church missionaries and supposedly held by them in trust. It seems that the Vatican later loaned the money to the US, and the natives have yet to receive repayment.

Economic factors behind the mysterious death of Pope John Paul I?
In the first few days of his 33-day papacy, Pope John Paul I (Albino Luciani, d. 1978), commenting on the ethics of the Curia, said: 'I have noticed two things that appear to be in very short supply in the Vatican ... honesty and a good cup of coffee'. Earlier, the pope's secretary, Jack Champney called the Curia, 'a group of mentally-deranged theologians' (*Murder in the Vatican*, Lucien Gregoire, 2005, p. 150), and Luciani maintained the same thoughts. This pope was a man of immovable integrity and with him the Roman Catholic Church had a major opportunity to at last turn respectable. He had never been a fan of the pomp and splendour of the Church, and regularly quoted this Gospel narrative: 'lay not treasure up on this earth where moth and rust doth corrupt but lay up treasure in heaven'. The new pope didn't believe in the existence of Jesus Christ but he believed in what he called 'the principle of the Gospel message' (*Messaggero Mestre*, Albino Luciani in Venice, April 19, 1973), and adopted the view that a Church with its appurtenances of worldly grandeur should be replaced by a Church which represented underprivileged concepts. He issued instructions to his Secretary of State, Cardinal Jean Villot for a complete review of Church finances, including a tally of its worldwide liquid assets. He personally participated in an internal audit of the Vatican

Bank and invited a number of art dealers to Rome to appraise some of the Church's art treasures.

> He reduced in half the substantial bonus that Vatican cardinals receive upon the election of a new pope. This seemed a forewarning to his eventually reducing the salaries of Vatican cardinals, which at that time was the equivalent of what is a hundred and ten thousand pre-tax dollars today; spending money for the cardinals as all of their living expenses were paid for by the Church, most of them living in the lap of luxury ... there was considerable apprehension among the cardinals that they might end up sharing their sprawling mansions and palaces with the homeless and poor ... and worst of all there was an underlying dread among all the cardinals and bishops of the Church that they might be soon taking a vow of poverty.

(*Murder in the Vatican*, Lucien Gregoire, USA, 2005, pp. 86-7)

To the Christian priesthood, the principle of such a vow would be a fate worse than death. Bishop Agostino Casaroli, Vatican Foreign Minister under Pope Paul VI, was reported in an Italian newspaper to have said this about Pope John Paul I: 'It is as if Martin Luther has come back from the dead to take his revenge on all of us: first to take from us our bonuses; and soon our salaries; and then our rank; and possibly even our palaces; and perhaps eventually end in our excommunication'. Earlier, in 1958 when the new pope was the Bishop of Vittorio Veneto, he revealed his thoughts about Christian preachers, calling them 'the enemy ... whose make-believe credibility preys on the ignorance and weakness of the minds of men' (*Murder in the Vatican,* Lucien Gregoire, 2005, p. 192). Here was the most influential man in the western world preaching a redistribution of the massive Church wealth by selling the Vatican treasures, and the possible dismissal of many of the priesthood. However, the precedent of maintaining worldly riches set by Pope St. Peter provided for the provocation of particular people to the most prompt and drastic coercion to silence anyone likely to divest the churchmen of their riches. John Paul I died suddenly under suspicious circumstances, and there were many people with an ecclesiastical motive, and the opportunity to assassinate him:

Then there are those who might have been bothered by the threat this pope posed to the regency of Rome: that the Vatican Museum, the Sistine Chapel and the Castel Gandolofo and other royal assets of the Church, including the Vatican itself, might be liquidated to help the poor.

(*Murder in the Vatican,* Lucien Gregoire, 2005, p. 245)

The Vatican was caught in a series of lies concerning the mysterious circumstances surrounding the pope's death, and those conflicts are confirmed in an absorbing book called, *Murder in the Vatican* written by Lucien Gregoire (2005; vatican@att.net; www.murderinthevatican.com). Additional information is also found in David Yallop's powerful book, *In God's Name; An Investigation into the Murder of John Paul I* (Bantam Books, New York, 1984). Yallop's revelations detail a miasma of criminal activities operating within the sprawling network of the Vatican's institutions which have lead to bribery, blackmail and on more than one occasion, to murder.

The Palace swimming pool

Luciani's successor was Polish cardinal, Karol Wojtyla, and the methods he used to achieve the position of pope are to be revealed in an upcoming book by this author. Accepting the advice of his consultants, Wojtyla assumed the title of John Paul II, mainly to capitalize on the massive international popularity of the previous down-to-earth nature of the earlier pope John Paul I. Wojtyla was the most widely-traveled churchmen in the history of the Catholic Church, visiting over 80 countries as cardinal, and over 100 countries as pope. Always traveling First-Class, this man had an overwhelming desire to stay in expensive Alpine resorts and 5-star international hotels. Shortly after he inherited the Chair of Pope St. Peter, John Paul II embarked on an unprecedented papal spending spree that stunned 'Vatican watchers' in the world media. He built a magnificent state-of-the art kitchen in the Papal Palace and then employed a world renowned chef to prepare his gourmet meals. He added a professional photographer to his staff to present to the public a false illusion that the new pope was a simple, pious man living in humble circumstances, and then employed a designer-label fashion house to create his chic purple and crimson silk, satin and velvet gowns. He moved quickly to reward the cardinals of the conclave that elected him, and the *World Press* confirmed the centuries-old tradition of cardinals buying papal-winning votes in exchange for financial rewards: 'John Paul raised the Vatican cardinal salaries so quickly after his election that anyone other than a moron would see it as a part of the deal' (*World Press*, 1-5 November, 1979). In fact, he raised their salaries by approximately twenty-percent to a level of what amounts today to around US$135,000 per year, and that excludes adding to their incomes by discreetly selling their influence to Italians needing a favour from a Vatican official. In 1979, Cardinal Leon Joseph Suenens, Archbishop of Brussels, criticized the pope for having used monies deposited by Mother Teresa in the Vatican Bank to build for himself a luxurious $2 million dollar swimming pool and gazebo at his majestic papal mansion at the Castel Gandolfo, the vast and opulent Vatican-owned estate consisting of five stately palaces overlooking the Lake of Albano, near the Mediterranean Sea.

© University Press.

This is the Popes' summer residence, a 17th century mansion designed by Carlo Maderno for Pope Urban VIII (d. 1644). The papal palace, and the adjoining Villa Barberini that was added to the complex by Pius XI (1922-1939), have enjoyed extraterritorial rights since the 1929 treaty with Mussolini, the little piazza directly in front was renamed Piazza della Libertà in the first flush of Italian unity after 1870. The papal palace remained unused from 1870 until 1929. Popes Pius XII (1958) and Paul VI (1978) died at Castel Gandolfo.

The pope's original ambition, in fact, had been not to be a religious man, but an actor, something which Wojtyla himself openly confessed when a cardinal; 'I trained for the stage as a young man' he admitted to J. Michener of the PBS series in 1977: 'Yes, I wanted to be an actor'. He got his wish. His personal vanity, to be always the principal actor, never left him since his early days. 'One can tell that Wojtyla studied for the stage', commented a cardinal after the election; 'He does not miss a trick'. The Propaganda division of the Church was traveling at 'full speed ahead', and the pope's performances were carefully stage-managed for public consumption. This public relations department of the Church is vibrantly active today just as it was when Pope Gregory XV (d. 1623), on 22nd June, 1622, issued a papal bull called *Inscrutabila Divine* and established for the Church the new promotional division he called the Sacred Congregation of Propaganda. Pope John Paul commissioned more than fifty biographies to be written about his life, each full of disinformation and pious sermonizing that were, under his direction, paid for, published in large numbers, and promoted by his Church. Not one of Pope John Paul's biographies mention his wife or the years he spent with the I. G. Faben Chemical Company selling cyanide gas, Zyklon B and Malathion to the Nazis for extermination of groups of people in Auschwitz (*Behold a Pale Horse,* William Cooper, U.S.A. Naval Intelligence Officer, Light Technology Publishing 1991, p. 89). After the war, he 'hid' (*The Vatican Moscow Washington Alliance*, Avro Manhattan, Chick Publications, California, 1986, p., 40) in the palace of Cardinal Sapieha to avoid War Crime charges pending against him, and there in the 'Ratline' studied theology to fill in the days (ibid). Seminaries, conventional studies, diplomatic training, had been conspicuously alien to Wojtyla from his early youth.

Baron Avro Manhattan revealed that Pope John Paul II publicly berated Nicaraguan priests for their involvement in politics and simultaneously gave his blessing for large quantities of Vatican dollars to be made available, secretly and illegally, to Lech Walesa's Solidarity movement in Poland (*Murder in the Vatican; American, Russian and Papal Plots*, Baron Avro Manhattan, Ozark Books, Springfield, Mo. 1985). Interestingly, immediately after becoming pope he personally took over direct management of the Vatican Bank (*Il Messaggero*, October 19, 1978), maybe to allow him to covertly divert those Vatican funds to the Solidarity movement in his native Poland. In 1981, John Paul II appointed a commission of 15 cardinals to study the finances of the Roman Catholic Church, its specific function being to recommend improvements to various Church departments that would increase Vatican revenue (*In God's Name,* David Yallop, Jonathon Cape, London, 1984, pp. 288-9). The commission pleaded poverty, and announced that the State of Vatican City would suffer a deficit of $25,000,000 by years end if a closer 'collaboration on the part of churches' was not established. This proposed deficit was not a deficit as such for the Vatican itself, since Vatican City is just a small part of the operations of the Holy Mother Church and separate from the Vatican. This message, true or false, was primarily intended for the faithful in the United States and intimated that Catholic Americans should increase their contributions to the Vatican. Later, Pope John allocated US$20,000,000 of Church funds to build the ultra-luxurious 150-room Palace of Santa Marta in Vatican City, a sumptuous establishment where visiting cardinals can stay in ultimate opulence. The pope was probably making good on his campaign promises:

> The new palace rivals the finest ultra-luxury hotels in the world. It was the availability of vacant rooms in this palace at the time a dozen or so American cardinals together with their aids flew first class to meet with the pope concerning the pedophilia problem that prompted Maureen Dowd of the New York Times to criticize some of them for staying at a five-hundred-dollar-a-night hotel near the Roman Forum.

> (*Murder in the Vatican*, Lucien Gregoire, 2005, p. 364)

John Paul's attitude and expressions towards wealth and a sumptuous existence are in keeping with a history of lavish papal lifestyles that has been a characteristic part of the Roman Catholic Church since its inception.

CHAPTER 27

Imponderable sources of income

There are other streams of gold for the Church that should be mentioned, one being the rich spring of private contributions and legacies left to the Vatican by devout Catholics. This tradition originally developed in the 14th Century when it was not only regulated, but also legalized. It was imposed by Archbishop Winchelsey about 1305, confirmed by Langham in 1367, and then documented in the *Pupilla Oculi*, a Church manual for priests. It became a set custom, acknowledged by both spiritual and temporal authorities in practically every country of Christendom. In this manner the Church, with its blood-hounds, the Inquisitors, were let loose to appropriate one-third of a dead man's personal estate, and the rapacity of the clergy in collecting the assets and revenue reached unprecedented lengths. Today, however, the Mortuary, as it was once called, is no longer an ecclesiastical requirement but it is perhaps worth relating, how, in many countries but particularly the United States, the practice of legacies collection has become a concrete system yielding vast sums.

In the USA the Catholic Church, in common with other churches, has tax-exempt foundations whose business it is to systematically solicit for large donations and bequests. Catholic groups actively solicit wills … they send letters to lawyers reminding them that a good Catholic is expected to put his in his will, for at least 10% of the corpus, and money collected from legacies in the USA alone runs into hundreds of millions of dollars. Believers are apt to remember the Holy Mother Church in their wills, so that very often monasteries, convents or other Catholic institutions become the beneficiaries of small and large legacies, sometimes in real estate, bonds, shares or cash. This constant income is far more rewarding than is generally believed, as any bishop or primate could testify. Giovanni Montini, prior to becoming Pope Paul VI in 1963, was a specialist in legacies, and in that capacity he handled the legalities of the millions of dollars left to the Church by the faithful. The habit has become so widespread that even in the USA more than one diocese has come to rely upon Divine Providence in balancing maladjusted budgets or for dispensing further bounties to outdo the bishop next door. The affluence accumulated by such means is remarkable and one example should suffice to show the extent of bequests. Around 25 years ago, an Associated Press dispatch reported that Mrs. R. T. Wallace of Saratoga Springs, New York, bequeathed US$2.5 million 'to the Pope' and an additional US$2.5 million to the Redemptorist Fathers of New York. In this manner the Holy Mother Church netted US$5 million tax free from one single estate on one day, from just one death. The Vatican has never disclosed how much it receives from legacies, wills and bequests, but the sum is huge, for a Curial source revealed that a special international dicastery, the Vatican term for an office of the Vatican Curia, is engaged in collecting the monies received by such channels. The practice is widespread, with the result that legacies are continually putting money into Vatican coffers, year in and year out.

Another and obvious source of income is Sunday offerings. This form of monetary tribute is not to be dismissed as unworthy of mention because it is a steady and regular habit of the believer and of the happy recipient, the Holy Mother Church. Conservatively assuming that 20 million Catholics attend mass weekly and each gives 50 cents, the total income would therefore be 100 million cents each Sunday (US$10 million weekly), fifty-two times a year. But an even more profitable and regular source of revenue for the Vatican is the wafer, and Catholic priests, friars and monks are obliged to say mass at least once a day. The mass is a sacrifice, and a Catholic may have this sacrifice, that is the mass, offered for personal benefit, or for a dead relative, for the liberation of a soul from purgatory, or a thanksgiving, and such. The Church fixes a minimum tariff for any believer who wishes a mass to be celebrated for his or her intention. In the USA many priests now charge five or ten dollars or even more per private mass and with thousands of priests saying mass daily, the yield is enormous. This form of income has been conservatively calculated by the US media at about US$50 million a year. Add the Central and South American republics, the European lands and all Catholic communities the world over and the annual revenue to the Church from masses alone runs into maybe US$100 million per year.

A pope sells Ireland to England

Last but not least, a strong steady source of regular income is Peter's Pence (the tax on Catholic dioceses) which originated during the pilgrimages to Rome at the height of the cult of St. Peter. Those ancient events have been paralleled in more modern times with the pilgrimages to Lourdes and Fatima. Early West Saxon King Ina or Ine (Seventh Century) enforced a tax of one penny on every family in the Kingdom of Essex who went to Rome to do homage to St. Peter. The tax, later called Peter's Pence, was originally called the Romscot, which meant the 'scot' (a tax) to be paid to Rome. 'Rome's scot' was ratified by the King of Mercia, Offa II (d. 796), overlord of all England, and later, by others. The Holy Roman Emperor Charlemagne (747-814) made Peter's Pence compulsory to owners of houses and lands throughout his empire and King Canute (Knut) the Great (d. 1035) did the same in Denmark, as did the Normans in Sicily (1059) to indicate the end of the Arab occupation. It was introduced in Spain in 1073, in Croatia and Dalmatia in 1076, and in Portugal in 1144. It was imposed also in the Ukraine, Poland and other countries (*The Vatican Billions,* Baron Avro Manhattan, Paravision Books, London, 1972). Shortly after Englishman, Nicholas Breakspeare, became Pope Hadrian IV in 1154, he sold the hereditary lordship of Ireland to King Henry II (1133-89) and part of the sale conditions stipulated that each and 'every subject is to pay an annual tribute of one penny to the Holy See, commonly called Peter's Pence' (*Bull Laudabiliter*).

Peter's Pence subsequently developed into a mixture of spontaneous offering and tax. In England it was terminated by Henry VIII in 1534, re-established by Queen Mary, and finally abolished by Queen Elizabeth 1 in 1558. It either continued or was suppressed in sundry countries according to the political vicissitudes of the times. As a contribution to the papal coffers, it almost dwindled away in the 18th and 19th Centuries but that changed when, on November 15, 1849, an angry mob killed Count Perigrino Rossi, a lay government minister of the Papal States. The next day, republican revolutionaries stormed and sacked the Quirinal summer palace of Pope Pius IX (1792-1878), and he was forced to flee from Rome to Gaeta in disguise (*Lives of the Popes,* Pope Pius IX, Richard P. McBrien, Harper, San Francisco, p. 345). Catholics came to his help and in December 1849 a committee was formed in Paris to collect the *Denier de Saint-Pierre,* the French name for Peter's Pence. Bishops asked for money to help Pope Pius IX and Ireland became the most enthusiastic collector. From that time on, Peter's Pence was revived all over Europe and the funds became so impressive that in 1860 the Vatican established a special body to administer the revenue (*The Papal States*, Professor Patrick J. J. Ryan, Professor of Church History, Ireland, 1903). When in 1870 the popes lost their temporal domains, Peter's Pence became the cash saviour, and in Germany, and particularly Ireland, parish priests turned into zealous collectors of money for the papal treasury. It was widely reported in the media (Euobserver, 1980) that the influence of Pope John Paul II upon the pastors of the rich parishes of the world caused Peter's Pence to increase to US$75,000,000 per year.

Whether that support is still current today is debatable for the recent international explosion of priesthood sex-abuse scandals threw the Church into convulsions unseen in the modern history of Christianity. Commenting on the public global outrage in 2002, Father Richard McBrien, Professor of Theology at Notre Dame, a leading US Catholic university, said, 'One of the remarkable aspects of the tragic crisis confronting the Catholic Church today is the widespread collapse of support for the hierarchy on the part of the traditionally loyal and dutiful laity'. The Church admitted that in the USA alone, US$1660 million in compensation has been paid out to victims of priesthood sex-attacks and that amount is set to grow (*REUTERS*, July, 2007; *Time Magazine*, April, 2002; *Church Sex Crimes,* Awareness Quest, Tristan Rankine, Australia; *New York Times; Chicago Tribune,* etc). Keeping the skirts of priests and monks down, and trying to still the unnatural ardor that runs deep in the sexual psychology of the priesthood, has been a fundamental aspect of Christianity since its commencement.

CHAPTER 28

Intangible billions

The Holy Mother Church firmly believes that the right to acquire property was given to them by Pope St. Peter who, in anger, struck 'down dead' Ananius and his wife Sapphira for giving only half the proceeds of the sale of their property to his Church (Acts of the Apostles, 5:1-11, Sinai Bible). Following his example, the Vatican became the largest owner of historic, architectural and artistic buildings in the world. Some of its buildings go back to the ancient cultures or the early centuries of Christianity. Besides their 'historicity', the sites upon which they are erected, as a rule within the precincts of ancient cities, are immensely valuable. The accumulation of riches was an enduring feature of the Roman Catholic Church and this was reflected in the multiplying erection of prestigious churches, the opulent choice of vestments for Church prelates, the construction of magnificent gold-coated carriages, luxurious banquets, and development of the splendor of their liturgy.

For example, what value would an automobile museum put on the beautiful carriages and motor vehicles in the Vatican garage? There to be found are 14 highly-wrought hand-built coaches of regal splendor and an immaculate 1930 Mercedes Benz once owned by Pope Pius XI (d. 1939). And how would anybody value the Vatican's Numismatic Library with its extensive collection of stamps, coins and medals; preserved in this establishment are almost 100,000 fine examples, including many coins supposedly struck by the Papal Mint in the 14th Century.

In addition, the artistic, religious and national patrimony attached to them is incalculable, not easily defined and consequently not easily assessed in terms of contemporary currencies. Thus, for instance, to confine ourselves

© Rome Picture Library; photograph by David Seymour, circa 1948

This old photo of the interior of the Vatican garage shows one of fourteen elaborate coaches (left), and, on the right, a 1930 Mercedes-Benz, once owned by Pope Pius XI.

to Italy alone, what would the Florence Cathedral, the Pisa Cathedral in the Piazza dei Miracoli, the Basilica of St. Mark's in Venice, or the four main Roman basilicas of the Holy See, i.e. St. Paul's Outside the Walls, St. Mary Major, St. John Lateran and St. Peter's itself, although built on quicksand, bring if they were put up for sale? Considering that the Catholic Church owns hundreds, indeed thousands, of such historic buildings throughout Europe alone, it can be imagined that the wealth they represent in monetary terms is, to say the least, beyond ordinary calculation. Their actual intangible value, however, is not all, for very often they house ecclesiastical objects which, because they have been accumulated over the centuries, acquired a considerable antique value in addition to their intrinsic worth. Thus a gold chalice, because of its historicity, in addition to its actual gold, is worth ten, one hundred or one thousand times more than the value of the precious metal itself. Speaking of chalices, how would one value approximately 1000 golden chalices that exist within the walls of Vatican City, many of them 'studded with diamonds, rubies, emeralds and pearls'? (*Murder in the Vatican,* Lucien Gregoire, 2005, p. 223) Additionally, the value of the Sèvres vases, the gold-crested china, the candlesticks by Gentile da Fabriano, the Belvedere Apollo and Torso, Bernini's sculptures, jeweled crowns and gifts presented to popes by royalty over the centuries, such as the priceless Farnese clock given to Pope Leo XIII (d. 1903), are difficult to calculate.

The treasures of famous cathedrals, basilicas and churches throughout the Western world are true treasures in the most prosaic, and business parlance. Anyone who has seen those of the Cathedral of Valencia, of St. James of Compostella in Spain, of St. Anthony's of Padua, St Mark's in Venice, St. Peter's and similar others, will have no doubt that the Church that owns them is a multi-millionaire in its own right. Add the numberless statues of angels, saints and martyrs, which adorn most Catholic churches everywhere, some beautified with crowns of solid gold, silver and precious stones, rare pearls, diamonds and other valuables. The prices which such items would achieve at any contemporary antique auction would run into 100s of millions of dollars, at the lowest possible estimate.

A billion dollar art collection

But that is not all. Then there are readily-saleable Church assets that would probably be best termed as non-productive riches, unlike its income-producing assets. The Catholic Church is the oldest, largest and most impressive art collector in the history of the world. The most celebrated painters, sculptors and artists of the Western world, from the early centuries of the Christian era down to our times, have worked for the Vatican or have contributed to the beautification of its edifices. Titian, Fra Angelico, Botticelli, Benozzo Gozzoli, Giovanni Bellini, Mantegna, Piero della Francesca, and the Leonardo-Michelangelo-Raphael triumvirate, to mention only a few, some of them bequeathing their masterpieces to the Church. In November 1969, the Press reported that three 'small and medium-sized' paintings had been stolen from the private Vatican apartments of Pope Paul VI while the pontiff was at his summer residence at Castel Gandolfo outside Rome. The paintings were works by Perugino, Weyden and Mino da Fiesole, and were conservatively valued at more than US$2 million (*The Times*, London, November 5th, 1969).

Consider the additional works of art the Church owns throughout Europe. Baron Avro Manhattan calculated that Renaissance masterpieces worth at least a million dollars each exist in over 600 churches, cathedrals, monasteries, convents, basilicas, and the like, in Italy alone. If we add France, Germany and above all, Portugal and Spain, at least another 400 masterpieces

THE PAPAL BILLIONS

© Frederico Arborio Mella; Rome Picture Library, 1959

This painting is by Giovanni Paolo Panini (1692-1765) and he reproduces an exotic picture gallery reeking of wealth in Vatican City at his time. The opulence of this magnificent building is more apparent when viewed in the original coloured version. On the walls hang original works of great Renaissance painters, one example being the portrait by Raphael of Pope Leo X and two of his cousins, one of who later became Pope Clement VII. It hangs to the right of the right-hand column, around two-thirds distance up. The value of this collection of artworks is beyond calculation.

worth one million dollars each also exist in those countries. The monetary value of these paintings is startling, being in excess of US$1,000 million. The mere fact that these paintings exist renders the Catholic Church a billionaire in its own right and since the value of these masterpieces increase each year, the Church becomes *ipso facto* the greatest art collector in the world. Consider the collection housed at the Vatican itself, or those in the churches of Florence and Venice. If one single small work by Leonardo da Vinci is valued at US$3 million, what would the combined masterpieces by Michelangelo and Raphael, and other great artists be worth if presented for sale in an art auction? Author of *Murder in the Vatican*, Lucien Gregoire was personally shown through the Papal Palace and he made this comment about one painting that is not publicly displayed;

> There is one work of art that has stood the test of time and it is a fixture in the Pope's private library, a magnificent painting of Michelangelo's Ascension, housed in a solid gold frame that by itself could easily feed a thousand children for a year, and the carpet on the floor could feed a thousand more. And the painting? Well, easily ten to twenty thousand more.
>
> (*Murder in the Vatican*, Lucien Gregoire, 2005, p. 227)

He commented about 'Persian carpets of superlative elegance in the Papal Palace which houses the corporate boardroom of the Roman Catholic Church' (ibid, p. 226), and added this comment; 'the Raphael bathroom … with its marble statuary worth millions and golden fixtures and artwork worth millions more, perhaps, more than anything else in Vatican City emphasized to me the contrast of immense wealth of the Church as compared to many people in third world countries who don't have a pot to piss in. Thinking back to that time I can understand today where John Paul I was coming from when he ordered that appraisals be made of the vast treasures of the Vatican Empire' (*Murder in the Vatican*, Lucien Gregoire, 2005, p. 232).

Can any art dealer, museum or Real Estate agent value the vaulted and frescoed Sistine Chapel … or the Dominican convent of Santa Maria delle Grazie in Milan that houses Leonardo's 'Last Supper' on a refectory wall? And what value is to be put on some rarely seen works:

> Italy's Renaissance period produced an impressive lineup of great masters who were to produce their share of works that have remained for the most part unseen by the public. One of the best of these is a collection of frescoes that the great painter Raphael and his most gifted pupils did for Cardinal Bernardo Bibbiena's bathroom on the third floor of the Vatican in 1516. Although access to the Bibbiena bathroom is officially discouraged, the great Bernard Berenson [1865-1959], the respected art historian who lived most of his life in Florence, once saw the prohibited Raphael's and described them as true masterpieces of Renaissance art.
>
> (*The Vatican Papers*, Nino Lo Bello, New English Library (a division of Hodder and Stoughton, Ltd.), Kent, 1982, pp. 182-3)

At a modest estimate, these buildings in an open market would fetch hundreds of millions of dollars each, and the income they could generate from entry fee charges would make them a gilt-edge investment for the purchaser. And what about the Roman and Greek sculptures of the Vatican galleries; Michelangelo's Pieta is priceless and the great obelisk in the Piazza, brought from Egypt by Roman Emperor Caligula (d. 41) and said to hold the ashes of Julius Caesar in the gold ball on its apex, has a value that is simply indeterminable. These magnificent stone carvings are only a few of thousands owned by the Church, each of inestimable financial worth, and far from devaluing.

The value of suppressed artworks

And what about the US$40 million (1966 estimate) collection of suppressed artworks kept under lock and key in permanent storage by order of the Italian Government acting on a Vatican directive? After heavy rains on November 4th in 1966, the Arno River flowing through Florence burst its banks and flooded the Uffizi Palace, the most exotic Renaissance museum in Europe that also houses the State Archives. This elegant manneristic building was originally built for Cosimo (the Elder) de' Medici (1389-1464) to house his administrative and judicial offices. Before the floodwaters peaked, Florentine Mayor Bargellini received an emergency phone call from the Vatican (*The Vatican Papers*, Nino Lo Bello, New English Library (a division of Hodder and Stoughton, Ltd.), Kent, 1982, p. 181) expressing alarm about protection of a specific collection of secret art treasures of major importance to the pope and Vatican officialdom held in the basement of the Uffizi Palace. It seems from the information available that there was concern that this collection could be swept away and later recovered and photographed by media representatives after subsidence of the floodwaters. Because these artworks are generally of a pornographic nature, they have been classified by the Vatican, and, at Vatican command, legally certified by the Italian government as 'unfit for human observation' (ibid), in spite of the fact that many of them were created by Italian artists Leonardo da Vinci (1452-1519), Michelangelo Buonarroti (1474-1564), and Raphael Sanzio (1483-1529). However, the Vatican's concerns that the public were not to see these masterpieces were ill-founded, for Dr. Maria Becherucci, the chief conservator of the Uffizi had perceived the imminent danger of flooding, and she and her small staff had earlier moved the collection to a higher level, and thus it was saved.

Although art directories and Italian guide books never officially list which painters and sculptors created these works, it is generally known that the banned masterpieces depict scenes of a sexual nature, and invariably involve certain of Christendom's most revered heroes and heroines … Jesus Christ, Virgin Mary, and Mary Magdalene. These paintings have been in seclusion in the Uffizi Palace for centuries and various staff members have, at times, provided descriptions of these works, and they reveal why they are so sensitive to the Vatican. There is not the slightest chance that these masterpieces will be seen openly or put up for sale, not publicly anyway, for one painting by Raphael shows an ecstatic and naked Jesus Christ having passionate sex with an equally naked and voluptuous Mary Magdalene. For the growing body of international authors who believe that Jesus was married to Mary Magdalene, this image would provide a graphic cover photo for a book, and, for that reason it is highly improbable that the Vatican will ever allow it to photographed or reproduced. Of a similar vein, another masterpiece the Church would

© Film Library of Renaissance Art, Italy; also Becocci, Italy

View of the Uffizi Palace and the Palazzo Vecchio in Florence, taken shortly before the flood of 1966. The basement of this building contains a multi-million dollar art collection yet be shown to the world.

rather the world not see is called 'The Conception of Jesus Christ', and it depicts Virgin Mary nude and in sexual rapture with a bearded, long-haired old man also in heavenly bliss ... God, who, according to the Gospels, 'came upon her'.

But there is something of more importance in this hidden collection and it has far-reaching implications for the Holy Mother Church. It is a recorded fact that the Leonardo-Michelangelo-Raphael triumvirate was in receipt of a papal secret that had been confided to them by three particular popes ... Alexander VI (1431-1503), Julius II (1443-1513), and Leo X (1475-1521). It was these three popes who commissioned the creation of a considerable number of artworks and sculptures by the three masters who all, at some period in their lives, lived in luxurious quarters at the Palazzo del Belvedere (British Museum, 279, v), a villa on the Vatican Hill. They dined regularly with the popes, and it is generally believed that Leonardo was involved in a homosexual relationship with one or more of the popes. It was with a series of documented papal confessions that strengthened the suspicion that these three masters were in receipt of forbidden knowledge about Christian origins, and surreptitiously secreted that information into their sculptures and paintings. A number of the suppressed paintings and statues show Jesus naked on the cross, and as can be seen, not one of these works is visible anywhere in Italy because of the Vatican's intervention and control of these ancient works. Any artwork that depicts a naked crucified Jesus is anathema to the Church ... especially if the figure is not that of a man, but of a woman. There are at least 50 such works in this collection, and in the opinion of this author, the depictions of a female Jesus Christ, a Goddess, is the reason why these masterpieces are being kept under wraps. The cover-up of the 'female principle' in Christianity is revealed in an upcoming new book by this author called, *The Secret Gospel Ciphers* and it unlocks the great secret of the popes, the Cathars, the Knights Templar, and the priest at Rennes-le-Château, in the South of France.

The value of rare Bibles

Spectacular old Bibles and manuscripts are held in the Vatican Library and the monetary value of these treasures is impossible to calculate. Probably the most valuable, and of extreme importance for Catholics, is the original version of St. Jerome's Vulgate, believed lost in the Fifth Century. It was never 'lost' but exists today in the Church's Secret Archives and is 'called the Amiatino Gospel' (*The Lost Scrolls of the Essene Brotherhood*, Professor E. B. Szekely, International Biogenic Society, 1989 Edition). The Vatican also houses the priceless 1500-year old *Codex Vaticanus*, believed to be the third oldest Bible in the World. Its value can be estimated by a comparison with a similar Bible, the *Codex Sinaiticus* now on display in the British Library in London. In 1972, the Trustees of the British Museum turned down an offer of US$25 million for its purchase by American millionaire Howard Hughes (British Museum lecture attended by this author). In the same year, Hans Kraus, a New York bookseller, sold the Shuckburgh Gutenberg Bible for almost US$3 million. Based on these figures, the sale of the Vatican's Bible collection would bring into Church's coffers an unknown amount of tens of millions of dollars. Ten years ago the British Museum paid £1,000,000 for an original first-printing of the English-language version of the 1611 King James Bible. Likewise, some years earlier the same Establishment paid more than £500,000 for one ancient manuscript and the Vatican owns thousands of such Bibles and manuscripts, most of them unique.

© Rome Picture Library, 1946

This Gutenberg Bible, the first printed book in the world, is one of the treasures in the Vatican Library.

Also held in the Vatican archives is a collection of ancient writings from the library of the monastery of Monte Cassino. In 1943, German war officials warned the Abbot that within days the monastery would be at the battle's centre and advised him to evacuate the premises. Under the Abbot's direction, the monks improvised with wooden crates and hurriedly packed together the invaluable collection of rare manuscripts, scrolls, and codices housed for centuries in the monastery's catacombs. They included the works of Cicero, Senaca, Josephus, Tacitus, Jerome, Augustine, Philo of Alexandria and more than 40,000 additional parchments, all of which found refuge in the Secret Archives of the Vatican (*Discovery of the Essene Gospel of Peace,* Edmond Bordeaux Szekely, 1989 Edition). According to the records of Vatican archivist, Edmond Bordeaux Szekely, 'unexpurgated editions' of ancient Gospels carrying the titles of Mark, Matthew, John, Barnabas, James, Peter and Thomas are also stored in the miles of the Vatican bookshelves, along with a series of other writings used by presbyters in the Fourth and Fifth Centuries. In addition, Professor Szekely confirmed the existence of such rare writings as the Gospel of Julius Caesar, the Book of the Obstetrician, the Book of Jasher, the Canto of Krst and the Physiologist, supposedly written by 'Essene heretics' and later attributed to Ambrose, Bishop of Milan (339-397). He spoke of a bundle of pamphlets written by Bishop Quintus Tertullian (c. 160-220), the author of works entitled *Apology* and *Prescriptions*, and some manuscripts supposedly written by Simon the Magician of New Testament fame. The wealth of these old documents could only be assessed if they were put up for sale. Some of the Vatican scrolls are thought to have originally been part of an antiquated collection assigned to the Church in 1810 by the Bolognetti-Cenci family and contain documents of great antiquity. Another collection of rare manuscripts once belonging to the House of Barberini were consigned to the Vatican during the papacy of Pope Leo XIII in 1902. Cardinal Carpegna's renowned 'library of manuscripts' is also preserved in Church archives and 'consists of 229 volumes in folio … an extensive mass of ecclesiastical lore … including treatises of the fathers of the Asiatic and African churches … which in themselves, form a library' (Professor Edmond S. Bordeaux).

In the more modern sense, it is believed that the Vatican also holds thousands of priceless letters in its archives, some being, a letter from the nephew of Genghis Khan (d. c. 1227); the 'D'Arcis Memorandum', written by Bishop Henri (c. 1357) declaring the Shroud of Turin a fraud; a exotically-produced parchment from the court of King Henry VIII of England to Pope Clement VII seeking a divorce (there were two popes who called themselves Clement VII). This petition was sealed with 75 coloured ribbons and 75 red wax seals; decrees of the Council of Constance proclaiming John (Jan) Hus (1415) and Jerome of Prague (1416) heretics, and the records of their sentencing to death by burning at the stake; correspondence relating to the first printed version of the Latin-language Bible from Johann Gutenberg, inventor of the movable-type printing press in the 1450's; a letter from Pope Paul III to Michelangelo granting him free trips on the ferry across the Po River for life; letters written by Donna Lucrezia Borgia; the original diaries and records of Cardinals Pietro Bembo and Jovius (c. 1514) who were witness to Pope Leo X's celebratory confession declaring Christ a 'fable' (*Confessions of a Vatican Archivist*); correspondence from Queen Victoria and Pius IX; letters from Martin Luther (d. 1546) from Wittenberg in 1520; the letter of Mary I (Mary Tudor) and her husband Philip II (1527-98) of Spain who was declared King of England in 1554 (pictured); the court proceedings against Galileo (d. 1642); the abdication document of Queen Christina of Sweden in 1654, and various letters and notes from Copernicus, Voltaire, Erasmus and Napoleon.

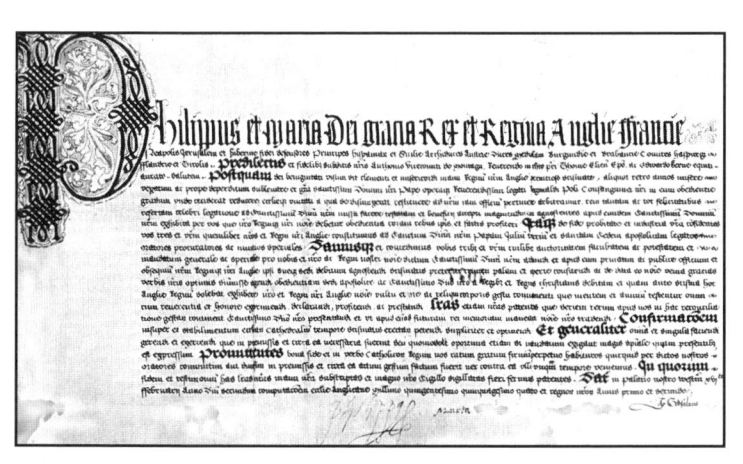

© Rome Picture Library, c. 1939

This is the letter of Mary Tudor and her husband Philip II. He was the only son of the Emperor Charles V and became King of England in 1554. In this correspondence he announces that he appointed three ambassadors to the court of

Pope Paul III in February, 1554. His marriage to Mary I was extremely unpopular in England, and he spent only 14 months in that country.

The intangible wealth which the Church possesses in these matters, therefore, makes it an elusive and yet potentially concrete multi-billionaire, since the artistic treasures at present in its possession are capital assets which are not only increasing in value with the passing of time, but which could yield far more profits than any investment in the contemporary stocks and shares of the most prosperous trusts and corporations of the world. But if the intangibility of the Vatican's historic and artistic patrimony is a real asset, the most profitable investment in her multi-billion dollar portfolio is the imponderability of her religious attributes. This is a most valuable asset since most Catholics are ready to acknowledge the Church as their spiritual mistress, mother and dispenser, and as a result are eager to part with their money, valuables and earthly riches to gain her favour, or to gain through her intercession, the favour of Heaven. In this element the Vatican has a type of wealth which, although it cannot be reckoned with what could be termed as business assets, is nevertheless as real, concrete and as valuable as any gold ingots or parcels of real estate. These are the intangible, invisible and spiritual riches at the Church's disposal. Some of these grow daily in value just by reason of their existence. Others are exploited through religious emotion and the hopes and fears of believers.

Thanks to these circumstances, therefore, the Roman Catholic Church is the most redoubtable financial power, wealth accumulator and property owner in existence. She is a greater possessor of material riches than any other single institution, corporation, bank, giant trust, government or State of the whole globe. The pope, as the visible ruler of this immense fortune, is consequently the richest individual of the 21st Century and no one can realistically evaluate how much he is worth in terms of billions of dollars. In the past, the Vatican never openly released financial figures and never disclosed its monetary affairs, and has never been required to give account of its income, expenses and growing funds to anyone. Not so long ago, the pope, under American influence, set up a new department, the Prefecture of Economic Affairs to administer the funds of the Vatican. It was said that the task of this new body was to work out a yearly 'budget' for the pope's approval, but the reality of the matter was that the wealth of the Church had reached such colossal proportions that the co-ordination of its immense global assets and activities had become not only useful but a dire necessity. For, verily, no one in the Vatican hierarchy knew how much the Church was now worth in terms of dollars and other currencies, even His Holiness. That this is the true situation was borne out by a Vatican official, who, when asked to make a guess at the value of the Church's fortune today, replied, very tellingly, 'Only God knows'. The accumulation of Vatican riches derives solely from it being a Church and that leads to the intriguing question; 'What value can one put on spiritual belief', whether it be true or false?

CHAPTER 29

What is the Roman Catholic Church worth today?

Before he retired to the USA in 1990, Archbishop Paul Marcinkus, President of the Vatican Bank, and President of the Sovereign State of the Vatican, said: 'you can't run the Church on Hail Marys'. It is not doubted that the Vatican needs income to operate but it is impossible to gauge the amount of those expenses as the Vatican makes a fetish of secrecy about its budgets and receipts and they are not made available to the public. It seems that the pontifical payroll could be about US$30 million per year, with many employees, like the flashy Swiss Guards, constantly complaining of being underpaid. However, the US$2.5 million per year annual profit from the sale of Vatican stamps, guide books, and postcards to tourists, and the revenue from Peter's Pence (US$75,000,000 per year; see Chapter 27), should more than cover its outgoings. All said and done, the concrete, substantial and fantastic yields of voluntary contributions given out of religious zeal by the faithful the world over are given specifically for the maintenance of the Holy See. The Church's Balance Sheet is also made black rather than red by means of entry fees received from public access to various Church displays, not only in Vatican City State, but in other areas of Catholicism.

Nino Lo Bello, a liberal Catholic author and European correspondent of the *New York Herald-Tribune* who specialized in European economic affairs, wrote a book called *The Vatican Empire* which revealed the extent of the Holy Mother Church's involvement in, and control of, secular business. After its publication by Simon and Schuster in New York in 1968, Nino Lo Bello was approached by a cardinal after a press conference who offered him this gratifying comment:

It is good this book was written, for we know of these things, but we who are with the Church are not able to speak out so frankly and tell our people what they should know. It is good that you, a layman, and a Roman Catholic, are able to do so.

(*The Vatican Papers*, Nino Lo Bello, New English Library (a division of Hodder and Stoughton, Ltd.), Kent, 1982, p. 154)

Nino Lo Bello learnt from his sources behind the Leonine Walls that *The Vatican Empire* had created quite a stir there and that Pope John XXIII had personally read it (ibid). In July 1970, about 18 months after *The Vatican Empire* appeared, *L'Osservatore Romano* did something it had never done before ... it published 1800 words of caustic refutation, accusing Lo Bello's book as a 'fantastic exaggeration'. *The New York Times*, commenting on the unusual denial made by the Vatican which was reported in nearly every newspaper in the Western world, said that *L'Osservatore Romano* had raised more questions than it had answered, and concluded its editorial comment by saying that no matter how rich or poor the Vatican was, 'there is plenty of evidence that its canny businessmen are doing their best to make it richer'.

After years of research into the Vatican's riches, Lo Bello admitted that 'so widespread and complex are the Vatican's money making enterprises that it is almost impossible to get a clear picture of all of them' (*The Vatican Empire*, Nino Lo Bello, Trident Press, New York, 1968). Around five decades ago, pious author Ann Carnahan, in her book, *The Vatican*, made this comment: 'It is true that there are not a half-dozen men in the world who know how much money the Vatican has, or where it goes' (*The Vatican*, Ann Carnahan, Odham's Press Limited, London, 1950; Published under the Imprimatur of E. Morrogh Bernard, Vicar General). Nothing has changed to this day, and requests put by investigators to the Vatican Press Office concerning the finances of the Holy See have been met with the icy answer; 'The Holy Father does not publish a budget' (*Commercial Bulletin*).

As in Italy, the USA and other countries, most of the Church's property, shares, bonds, currency transactions, and investments are camouflaged behind the names of Companies, Dow Jones corporations, individual Catholic laymen, agents, or financial, accountancy, banking and industrial concerns.

Then there are the 'men of trust' who …

> … come from families that are either directly related to high-ranking Vatican officials in the past … often with a pope himself … or from families that have had a long and intimate association with the Vatican. Most of these families have members who hold titles that have been issued to them by the Vatican, such as prince, duke, count or baron, but have no real royal connection with Italy's past kings or queens. There are some 25 so-called Vatican families whose names are fairly well known.
>
> (*The Vatican Papers*, Nino Lo Bello, New English Library (a division of Hodder and Stoughton, Ltd.), Kent, 1982, p. 158)

This stratagem of guile cover-up is in place to prevent the world from coming to the knowledge of the truth, and because of papal obfuscations, this book of necessity can only provide estimates gleaned from international published press reports, and the work of other investigators. It is fair then to say then that under the Roman law of '*Novella*', this book is best termed a '*Historicus Novus*' for it is not possible to know what the Vatican has purchased or sold in modern times, or how it reinvested the incoming funds.

The wealth of the Catholic Church has come a long way since Benito Mussolini gave it its modern impetus in 1929 and this was shown in an article published in a Swiss newspaper in the mid-1970s. It declared 'the productive capital of the Vatican can be reckoned at between 50 and 55 billion Swiss francs', estimated at that time as being around US$13 billion. *L'Osservatore Romano*, the Vatican's eccentric newspaper, denied the estimate, and said no more. However, the US$13 billion estimate is that only of 'productive capital' and excludes all other areas of vast Church riches. Lately, several financial experts have figured that the value of the Vatican's holdings has tripled or quadrupled during the boom years of the 1990s, making the Swiss estimate as high as maybe US$52 billion. There are no paper trials leading to and from the Vatican Bank, and the secrecy surrounding the Church's financial affairs has inevitably given rise to one of the world's greatest unsolved questions … what is the worth of the Roman Catholic Church towards the end of the first decade of the 21st Century?

Devoutness a false front

A hypothetical reconstruction of what is known assumes that the successors of Pope St. Peter are owners of one-third of all the wealth of Europe and America. This is a case where the absence of records is more eloquent than their presence, but a recently released estimate by a Church of England source revealed the total world-wide value of the Catholic fortune at US$3500 billion. As this estimate was put forth by opponents of Catholicism, it is difficult to regard it seriously, and is only given here for the sake of completeness. It is possible, however, that if the pope was turned upside down and shaken, maybe US$2500 billion (US$2,500,000,000,000) or so would tingle from his pockets. That figure excludes the wealth of Protestant Christianity which, in international real estate holdings, has a similar value to the Roman Catholic Church. The point must not be overlooked that there is just as much wealth in Protestant Churches, and be reminded that TV evangelist Jim Bakker defrauded his followers of more than US$155 million, and nobody missed it.

The combined fortune of Christian Churches, it should be remembered, evolved without an historical Jesus Christ, and writings today official to Christianity are Fourth Century fabrications. The Church admits that it cannot prove the existence of Jesus Christ (*Catholic Encyclopedia*, Pecci Ed., ii, pp. 391-393), and that disclosure should cause alarm for believers. In 1514, one of many of Christianity's disbelieving popes, Leo X, called Christ a 'fable' (*Cardinal Bembo, His Letters and Comments on Pope Leo X*, Reprint 1842; also, *De Vita Leonis X*, originally published in 1551), and later Pope Paul III (1534-1549) expressed similar sentiments, saying that there 'was no valid document to demonstrate the existence of Christ' (Papal pronouncements submitted at Luigi Cascioli's 2002 lawsuit against the Catholic Church for deceptive representation of facts; Court of Justice, Viterbo, Italy; no. 45/b). Paul III added that Jesus 'never existed', confessing that he 'was no other than the sun, adored in its Mithraic sect' (ibid), and here we see the hollow nature of the papal Church. From those and similar papal pronouncements, it is apparent that the Holy Mother Church views the faith of its followers only as a novel kind of folly and thus Christianity should be treated as an insolent novelty. The abstraction in the New Testament called Jesus Christ expressed Mithraic concepts when he was made to say, 'blessed are the poor', and compared the difficulty of a rich man entering the Kingdom of Heaven with that of a camel attempting to pass through the eye of a needle. The 'theory of evangelical poverty' (Pope John XXII, d. 1334) was never adopted by the Vatican hierarchy, and this book stands in the public forum as the sentinel of supportable evidence to that effect.

Like Pope St. Peter, the Christian priesthood began its life motivated in accumulating monies, not the abandonment of pleasures for the seclusion of the cloister. One would think that if St. Peter returned to Earth today and saw the vast assets his Church has developed, he would be delighted. He could wander through the hallowed halls of his Vatican Bank and then peruse the offices of 'The Administration of the Patrimony of the Holy See' (A.P.S.A). There he would see computers set up in specific rooms and watch clerical stock analysts following the minute-by-minute fluctuations of Vatican shares, securities and investments that his Church owns throughout the world. He would be pleased with the fact that his successor today is the richest man on Earth, and that the Catholic magnates dress in designer-label suits, wear Rolex watches, and are chauffeured to and from the Holy City in stretched limousines. He could watch with awe the spectacular ceremonies and theatrical performances of grown men wearing lady's dresses constructed of fine lace and satin that probably reflects the sexual preferences of St. Jerome, a self-confessed transvestite (*De Viris Illustribus*, 135, D. Vallarsi trans., Verona, 1734-42). These ceremonies, with popes, cardinals, bishops and priests as the actors, hide the Church's true original principle, that being the accumulation of riches under a religious pretext. It was with John Paul II that the world watched the best-imaged pope in its history, and his performances of contrived holiness were supported by a slick Vatican multi-million dollar public relations campaign. Whatever may be its guises, promises, or honey-ed words, the Holy Mother Church has but one object in mind, and that is her own financial elevation. Divisions of the Vatican Curia, with a staff nearing 3000 people, oversee the Church's international business operations, and silently sustain her financial character, sometimes with a finger in the pie.

Is a financial crisis looming for the Church?

In 2007, an article written by Mr. Tim Padgett called PILFERING PRIESTS was published in *Time* magazine (*Time*, February 26, 2007, South-east Asian Edition, pp. 48-9). He introduced startling new evidence revealing a looming catastrophe for the Church ... the extent of priesthood theft of offertory monies given by believers, and the figures Padgett provides are stunning: 'In a recent study co-authored by Zech and Villanova accountancy professor, Robert West, 85% of the 78 U.S. Catholic dioceses responding to their survey (out of a total of 174 queried) reported embezzlement cases ... and 11% had scandals of $500,000 or more' (*Time*, Tim Padgett, February 26, 2007, p. 49). Padgett's revelations continue:

> Last month [January, 2007] a Virginia priest was indicted for allegedly embezzling $600,000 from two Catholic churches ... in part to help support the woman and three children he had been secretly living with. Last year [2006] a Connecticut priest was accused of pilfering up to $1.4 million to pay for his Audi cars, luxury-hotel stays, jewelry for his boyfriend and a Fort Lauderdale condo. And last June [2006] another priest was sentenced to five years in prison after the misappropriation of $2 million from the Church of the Holy Cross in Rumson, New Jersey.
>
> (*Time* Magazine, February 26, 2007, Tim Padgett, p. 49)

From the level of theft that diocesan administrators are uncovering, this is just the thin edge of the wedge, for many churchmen are on the monetary band-wagon (ibid). For example, in September 2006, the community in Delray Beach was shocked to learn of the arrest of two trusted pastors at St. Vincent Ferrer Catholic Church for the alleged misappropriation of a massive US$8.6 million.

Pope verifies the claims in this book

History will pass a severe verdict upon the opulent wealth of the Catholic Church, and the question which believers should ask themselves with mounting urgency is a pertinent one ... if Jesus Christ today became an earthly entity, what would he do with such a colossal accumulation of

Christian riches? Upon their answer hangs, not only the right or wrong interpretation of the Gospels, but equally the future of organized Christianity itself. Who then shall testify on behalf of the Holy Mother Church, since the words of her own Gospels impeach her? 'If thou will be perfect, go and sell what thou hast, and give to the poor, and thou shalt have treasure in heaven' (Matt. 19:21). The record shows that the Church has no intentions of doing that, and its fortune grows and lives on in perpetuity. The religious aspect of the Christian Church is an obscuration, a corrupt and false pretence, and when Pope Leo X (d. 1521) called Christianity a 'profitable superstition', he spoke the truth. Catholic author, Nino Lo Bello made this comment:

> Contrary to what the millions of Roman Catholics throughout the world might believe about Christ and the Vatican, the subject of Christ inside the Vatican is not a popular one. There is even an inept joke about Christ inside Vatican City to the effect that if he ever came back to Earth and paid a call on the Vatican, he would be thrown out.
>
> (*The Vatican Papers*, Nino Lo Bello, New English Library (a division of Hodder and Stoughton, Ltd.), Kent, 1982, p. 186)

The reader should not forget that the Catholic priesthood is obliged to swear an oath of allegiance to 'our lord the Pope', not Jesus Christ. Thus, the Roman Catholic Church, an established and unashamed accumulator of temporal riches, is in reality, a soulless and spiritual-less corporate organization clothed in false theological garb and feigning religious orthodoxy. That makes every pope, cardinal, archbishop, bishop, priest, and parson a spiritual criminal and a moral bankrupt.

The end, thanks be to God!

BIBLIOGRAPHY

Works of Reference

Included now is a list of additional principal authorities consulted, referenced, or quoted in the preceding work. The Author wishes to express his grateful acknowledgment to the help he has received from the following books and manuscripts, and thanks the authors, translators and publishers for making those works publicly available. However, due to mergers, closure or relocation of some publishing houses, efforts to trace some copyright owners proved difficult, and many letters were returned marked, 'unknown at this address'. If such works are referenced in this book, copyright is hereby acknowledged and grateful appreciation is extended to those persons whose thoughts and talents assisted in the development of this book. Any omissions, errors or oversights should be brought to the attention of the Author for correction and appropriate acknowledgment in future reprints.

Abbe Francois Berenger Sauniere's Diary (handwritten)
About Ancient Britain, J. L. Stuart, Historical Publishers & Co, Edinburgh, 1949
About Jerome, Bishop Jewell's works, London Folio, 1611
About the 'Books of Hystaspes' (Quoted by Justin Martyr), Chicago Public Library
Acta Archelai, The Dialogue Between Manes and Archelaus (issued by Hegemonius), trans. 1806
A Compendious History of the Council of Trent, B. W. Matthias, M.A., Dublin, 1832
Acta Concilii Niceni, Colon 1618
Acts of Justin (Martyr)
Acta of Pilate (sometimes called the *Gospel of Nicodemus*)
Adverse Javianum, Jerome, N&PNF
Against Heresies (Adv. Haer.), Irenaeus (was originally called *The Detection and Overthrow of False Gnosis* and was re-titled at the Council of Trent)
Against the Claims of the Monks of Bangor

Age of Reason, The, Thomas Paine, 1793-5

A Gospel of Shame, Elinor Burkett and Frank Bruni, Viking 1993

A History of the Council of Trent, Thomas Nelson and Sons, 2 Vols, Hubert Jedin (Trans. D. E. Graf), 1949

A History of the Jewish People in the Time of Jesus Christ, E. Schürer, 5 vols., Edinburgh, 1886-1890

A History of the Papacy from the Great Schism to the Sack of Rome, M. Creighton, London, 1903-5

A History of the Popes, Dr. Joseph McCabe, Rector of Buckingham College, C. A. Watts and Co, London

Alford's Regio Fides, Griffiths, the Society of Jesuits

A Life of Constantine (7th Ed.), Dean Dudley, Attorney at Law, 1925, Ill. USA

Against Marcion (Adv. Marc.), Tertullian, MS. 1727

Against the Ebronites (Contra Ebronites), St. Epiphanius

Against the Gentiles (Adv. Gentiles), Tertullian

Albion, A Guide To Legendary Britain, Jennifer Westwood, Granada, 1985

Anacalypis, Godfrey Higgins

Analects of Confucious, The

Analytical Concordance of the Bible, Robert Young, LL.D. (Eighth Ed.), 1939

Anatomy of a Phenomenon, Jacques Vallee, Neville Spearman, London, 1966

Ancient Christian Writers, Trans. J. H. Crehan, the Newman Press, c. 1900

Ancient Rome, Rodolfo Lanciani, Boston, 1889

Ancient Secret, The, Flavia Anderson, Victor Gollancz Ltd, London, 1953

A New History of Great Britain, R. B. Mowat, Oxford University Press, 1923

Angilicae Histories Libra, Polydore Vergil (1470-1555)

Anglo-Saxon Chronicle, The

Annales Ecclesiastici (12 Vols.), Cardinal Caesar Baronius, Vatican librarian and church historian, 1538-1607

Annals of the Four Masters, c. 806, Dublin reprint, 1854

Ante Nicene Library, The, (ANL) A collection of writings of early churchmen prior to the Council of Nicaea, Edited by the Rev. Professor Roberts, D.D., and Principal James Donaldson, L.L.D, St. Andrews. 24 Vols. (Includes additional volumes of recently discovered manuscripts), circa 1900; also, American Reprint, eight volumes, The Christian Literature Publishing Co., Buffalo, NY, 1885. Also, *The Nicene and Post-Nicene Fathers,* cited as N&PNF; First and Second Series; many volumes; same publishers.

Antioch, the Mithraic City, Rev. L. B. Ralston, Berkeley Square, London, 1921

A Patriotic Greek Lexion, Ed. G. Lampe, Oxford, 1961

Apology of Bishop Jewell, London Folio xxii, 1595

A Preliminary Dissertation about the Authors of the Bible, Bishop Louis Dupin, Catholic historian, Third Edition, London, 1696

Arcane Schools, The, William Tate, 1909

Archaic Roman Religion (2 Vols), Georges Dumézil, University of Chicago Press, Chicago, Ill. 1970

Archbishop Ussher's Works, 8 Vols, London 1613

Arthur and the Lost Kingdoms, Alistair Moffat, Weidenfeld & Nicolson, Great Britain, 1999

BIBLIOGRAPHY

Authentic and Acknowledged Standards of the Church of Rome, The, J. Hannah D.D., 1844

Bad Popes, The, E. R. Chamberlin, Dial Press, NY, 1969
Bea-Methodius, supposed writings of St. Methodius of Olympus (d. 311)
Bede's Ecclesiastical History
Behold a Pale Horse, William Cooper, Light Technology Publishing, 1991
Beveridge's Pandecta Canonum, includes 60 Canons of the Synod of Laodicea still extant in original Greek
Bible and its Painters, The, Bruce Bernard, Orbis Publishing, 1988
Bible Criticism (2 Vols.), Professor Samuel Davidson D.D. LC.D, Contributor to *Encyclopedia Britannica*
Bible Fraud, The, Tony Bushby, Joshua Books, Australia (Website; www.joshuabooks.com), 2001
Bible in History, The, How Writers Create a Past, Professor Thomas L. Thompson, Pimlico, London, 2000
Bible Myths and Their Parallels in Other Religions, Reverend T.W. Doane, 1882
Bible Unearthed, The: Archaeology's New Vision of Ancient Israel and the Origin of its Sacred Texts, Free Press, NY, 2001
Bibliotheca Veterum Patrum, 28 Vols., Patristic writings of the Latin Church, 1765
Biblitheca sanctorum, Rome 1965, V1, 1132-7
Bishop Jewell's History of the Church, Reeves, London, 1611
Blake's Jerusalem
Book of Cornwall, The
Book of Enoch, The, Oxford Clarendon, U.K. 1912, Dr. Richard Lawrence's translation
Book of Taliesin
Book of the Church, The, Bishop R. Southerly, Fourth Ed., London, 1837, *etiam,* 1841
Book of the Entrance to Eternal Life, The, Ani, Royal Scribe, Alexandrian Library, Egypt
Book of the Roman Catholic Church, Charles Butler, 8 Vols., 1825
Books of Alexander, The, Questions he asked the Brahmans; first published circa 1490, Alexandrian Library, Alexandria, Egypt
Boudica, Dr. Graham Webster, Book Club Associates, London, 1978
British Church, The, Major J. Samuels, V. D., R. G. A, undated
British Ecclesiastical Antiques, Bishop Ussher
British Parliament Records, Hansard
British Place Names, M. J. Stewart, Edinburgh, 1928
Bryant's Analysis of Ancient Mythology
Bull of Pope Pius, VII, To the Primate of Poland, Section 2, 3
Butler's Lives of the Saints, Rev. Alban Butler, 1926

Can A History of Israel Be Written? L. L. Grabbe, European Seminar on Historical Methodology 1 (Sheffield Sap, 1997)
Cannibalism: The Religious Significance, Eaton University Press, USA, 1943

Cannibals and Kings, Marvin Harris, Fontana/Collins, 1977
Cardinal Bembo, His Letters and Comments on Pope Leo X, 1842 Reprint
Catalogue of the Greek and Latin Papyri in the John Ryland's Library, by C. H. Roberts, c. 1934
Catholic History, Dom Arnold Wion, Benedictine historian, 1596
Catholic Imperialism and World Freedom, Avro Manhattan, Watts and Co., London, 1952
Cave's Primitive Christianity, William Cave, D.D. 1682, reprint by Akerbar, 1790
Celt, Druid and Culdee, I. L. Elder, Covenant Publishing Co. Ltd, London, 1994
Censoring of Diderot's Encyclopedia and the Re-established Text, The, D. H. Gordon and N. L. Torrey, NY, 1947
Christ in Art, Mrs. Jameson, British Library
Christian Forgeries, Major Joseph Wheless, Judge Advocate, Idaho, 1930
Christna Et Le Christ, Translated from the Hari-Purana, by Jacolliot
Chronicles of:
Holinshed
William of Malmesbury
Geoffrey of Monmouth
Matthew of Paris
Jon Hardynge
Chronicles of the Popes, (1305-1394) edited by Baluze in 1693
Church History of Britain
Church of the Cymry, Rev. W. Hughes, undated
Church Sex Crimes, Tristan Rankine, Awareness Quest, Australia, 1995
Church of Rome, The, Rev. Charles Elliott, D.D, 1844
Church History, Socrates Scholasticus (the Scholar), Jenning's Trans., 1911
Ciceronians es, non Christianus
City of God, Augustine, 1609 trans., (a plagiarization of *The City of Zeus*)
City of Saints, The, Miscellaneous Tracts, Thomas Hawkings, c. 1890
Civilization of Rome, The, Donald R. Dudley, A Mentor Book, 1962
Claudia and Pudens, Archdeacon Williams, 1927
Classical References: The works of;
Herodotus
Virgil
Martial
Juvenal
Caesar
Clement of Alexandria, Fragment from Cassiodorus, ANL
Codex of Hillel, 600 manuscripts, first published in England in 1780
Codex Sinaiticus, 8th Ed., Prof. C. Tischendorf, The Letterworth Press, UK
Coelbren, The
Colloquies, Desiderius Erasmus, London, reprint 1878
Commentaries of Julius Caesar, The
Commentary and Notes on the Apostolic Epistles, James Macknight, London, 1821

BIBLIOGRAPHY

Confessions of Augustine, A Library of the Fathers, Oxford Movement, 1838
Confessions of a French Catholic Priest, New York, Mathers, 1837
Confessions of a Vatican Archivist; Inside information from suppressed Church scrolls; written by a Catholic priest and released after his death to Tony Bushby; proposed publication date, late 2008
Confessions of Tertullian, Tertullian, The Ante Nicene Library, circa 1900
Constantine's Letter (in regard to having the first 50 copies of the New Testament written and bound)
Constantinople: Byzantium-Istanbul, D. Talbot Rice, London, 1965
Constitutions of Constantine
Constitutions of Egbright, Archbishop of York, c. 740
Constitutions of the Church, Vatican Council 1
Contra Celsum (Against Celsus)
Contradictions in the Bible, Prof. Eugene McArthur, Edinburgh, 1936
Contradictions in the Catholic Encyclopedias, A Record of Conflictions in Accredited Church Expositions, by Major Joseph Wheless, Judge Advocate, USA, 1930
Controversy with Breckenridge, John A. Breckenridge, 1836
Corruptions of Councils, Dr. Philip Morney, 1889 reprint of 1612 edition
Cosmic Top Secret, Jon King, Hodder and Stoughton, London, 1998
Council of Nicaea, The History of, Dean Dudley, first printed 1886, reprinted in 1965 by Health Research, California
Court of the Gentiles, The, Oxford, 1671
Court Chronicles, Froissart
Creators of the Renaissance, The, Lionello Venturi, Geneva, 1950
Creed of Nicene, The, Formulary (first printing 1807)
Crime and Immorality in the Catholic Church, Emmett McLaughlin, Catholic priest, undated
Criminal History of Christianity, The, Free-thinking Press, Conn., USA, 1969
Criminal History of the Papacy, The, Tony Bushby, *Nexus New Times*, vol. 14, Nos., 1, 2, and 3; proof-read by Julie Halligan; edited by Ruth Parnell, 2007
Crucifixion of Truth, The, Tony Bushby, Joshua Books, Australia (Website; www.joshuabooks.com), 2005
Cyprian, Epist. 74, ed. Pamel. 1589

Damascus Document
Dark Side of Christianity, The, Helen Ellerbe, Morningstar Books, USA, 1995
D'Aubigné, History of the Great Reformation, 3 Vols; J. H. Merle, London, 1840
Dead Sea Scroll Deception, The, Michael Baigent, Richard Leigh, Corgi Books, 1992
De Antiqua Ecclesiae Disciplina, Bishop Lewis Du Pin, Catholic historian, (Folio, Paris, 1686), English translation by J. H. C. Hopkins, D.D
Decay of the Church of Rome, The, Joseph McCabe
Decisions of the Council of Trent, Edmund Gibson, Bishop of London, 1738
De Civitate Dei, Augustine, Bishop of Hippo
De Excidio Britanniae, Gildas (c. 493-570)

De Fide, long attributed to Augustine, but now known to be the work of Bishop St. Fulgentius (*Catholic Encyclopedia,* vi, 317)
Delineation of Roman Catholicism, Rev. Charles Elliott, D.D., 1844
Descent of Manuscripts, The, Albert C. Clarke, University of Oxford, 1918
De Statu Mortuorum, Dr. Burnet, English author, c. 1840
Detection and Overthrow of False Gnosis, Irenaeus
Development of the Catholic Church, Ernest Renan of the French Academy, 1880
De Viris Illustribus, 135, D. Vallarsi trans., Verona, 1734-42
Did Our Lord Visit Britain? Destiny Publishers, 1944
Diegesis, The, Reverend Robert Taylor, Boston, 1873
Difficulties of Romanism, The, George Stanley Faber, London, 1826
Discovery of the Essene Gospel of Peace, 1989 Edition, Edmond Bordeaux Szekely
Divine Carnage; Atrocities of the Roman Emperors, Stephen Barber, Jeremy Reed, Creation Books, 2000
Doctrine of Justification, The, James Buchanan DD. LL.D (Reprinted 1977 from the 1867 version by T. T. Clarke, Edinburgh), Baker Book House, Grand Rapids, Michigan
Domesday Book, The
Drama of the Lost Disciples, The, George F. Jowett, Covenant Publishing Co. Ltd, London, 1975
Druids, The, Stuart Piggott, Penguin Books, 1968
Dungeons, Fire and Sword; The Knights Templar in the Crusades, John Robinson, Michael O'mara, London, 1994
Du Pin's Ecclesiastical History, Oxford, 1725

Early Christian England, Professor Jonathon Ferguson, London, 1872
Early Christian Classics, 2 Vols. J. A. Robinson, 1916
Early History of the Ancient Israelites, The, Professor Thomas L. Thompson, E. J. Brill, Leiden, The Netherlands, 1992
Early Theological Writings, G.W.F. Hegal
Ecce Homo, Joseph Jobe, Macmillan, 1962
Ecclesiastical History, John L. Mosheim, 6 Vols. W. Baynes, London, 1803
Ecclesiastical History, Eusebius of Caesarea
Ecclesiastical History, Sozomen
Ecclesiastical Policy of the New Testament, The, Professor Samuel Davidson D.D. L.C.D
Eclectric Review, Melancthon, 1497–1560
Edgar's Variations of Popery, Second Edition, 1838
Edict of Callistus I, bishop of Rome, 217-222
Edict of Callistus I, Commentaries, J. Cosin, Bishop of Durham, 1594-1672
Edicts of Justinian (Dictionaire de Theologie, 1920)
Eleusinian and Bacchic Mysteries, The, Thomas Taylor, 1875
Elliott's Delineation of Romanism, 1844
End of Controversy, The, Dr. Milner, c. 1840
Epistolae, Hugo Grotius (1583-1645)
Epitome of the General Councils of the Church, from the Council of Nicaea, to the Conclusion of the Roman

BIBLIOGRAPHY

Council of Trent in the Year 1563, The, Reverend Richard Grier, D.D., 1828
Erasmus, Desid, in Nov. Test. Annotations, Fol. Basil, 1542
Erasmus of Rotterdam, J. Huizinga, Phaidon Press Ltd, London, 1952
Essene Origins of Christianity, The, E. B. Szekely, International Biogenic Society, 1989
Essenes and the Vatican, E. B. Szekely, International Biogenic Society, 1989 Edition
Eusebius of Caesarea, J. B. Lightfoot, World Publ. Co. 1962, NY (in, *A Dictionary of Christian Biograph, Literature, Sects and Doctrines,* London 1880)
Evargrius, A History of the Church from AD 431 to AD 594, E. Walford, Bonn's Ecclesiastical Library, London, 1851
Excavations of a Tumulus at Lexdon, Colchester, in 'Archaeology'
Extermination of the Cathars, The, Simonde de Sismondi, 1826
Exhortation to the Heathen (Exhort), Clement of Alexandria

Fabiola, Cardinal Wiseman, undated
Fake Apostolic Letters, Rev. Charles Elliott, D.D., Wesleyan Conference Office, London, 1844
False Decretals, The, E. H. Davenport, Oxford, 1916
Far Hence Unto the Gentiles, Major Samuels, 1964
Fathers of the Church (6 Vols.), Translated by Thomas B. Falls, Publ. Christian Heritage, Penns, 1938
Fathers of the Greek Church, The, Hans von Campenhausen, trans. Stanley Godman
Fides Regia Britannica, Cardinal Alford
Fifty Years in the Church of Rome, Chas. Chiniquy, First Printed 1885
First Gay Pope, The, Lyn Fletcher, Alyson Publications, 1992
First Apology and the Second Apology, The, Justin Martyr (Oxford University Trans.)
First Seven Ecumenical Councils, The, L. D. Davis, 1987
Five Centuries of Religion, G. G. Coulton, Cambridge University Press, 1923
Five Gospels, The, The Jesus Seminar, Macmillan Publishing Company, N.Y., 1993
Florence and Venice, H.A. Taine, New York, 1869
Forgery in the New Testament, Professor S. Patrick, Shaftsbury Ave. Bloomsbury, London, 1952
Fourth Century Rumors About Christ, P. M. Cozzia-Leone, Archives de Louvre, 1857
Foxe's Book of Martyrs
Free Enquiry, Thomas Middleton (1570-1627)
Frenzy to Create a God, The, Development of New Testament texts, Rev. F.G. Miller (revised by Dr. A. Frenlon in 1907), UK, 1895

Genesis of Christianity, Plummer, Edinburgh, 1876
Genuineness and Authenticity of the Gospels, B. A. Hinsdale (MA)
Georges Clemenceau, Joseph McCabe, Watts and Co., Fleet Street, London, 1919
Glascock, Dr. Henry, (notes) McLaughlin Foundation, Los Angeles, 1996
Glimpses of Life Beyond Death, Tony Bushby, Joshua Books, Australia, 2004 (Website address; www.joshuabooks.com)
Glories of Mary, Mother of God, The, Alphons de Ligorio, Dublin Ed, 1835
God and Greater Britain, Rev. R. Douglas

God's Book of Eskra
Gods of the Egyptians, Sir E. A. Wallis Budge, Dover Publications, NY, 1969
Golden Legend, The, Jacobus de Voragine, Longmans, Green and Co, New York, 1941
Good News of the Kingdoms, The, Mr. Norman Segal, Australia 1995
Gospel of the Kailedy, The, The Hope Trust, New Zealand, 1998
Great Invasion, The, Leonard Cottrell, Evan Brothers Limited, London, 1958
Gregory the Great, W. F. H. Dudden (2 vols.) 1905
Gutenberg Revolution, The, John Man, Headline Book Publishing, London, 2003

Handbook of Christian Archaeology, Kaufmann, Paderborn, 1905
Harlequin M.S.S. British Museum
Harlyn Bay Discoveries, R. A. Bullen, BA, undated
Hearings of the Scholars, Calder, undated
Heresies (Epip., Haer), Epiphanius
Heresies (Hippo, Haer), Hippolytus
Heretic Popes, Rev. Elliott, D.D, Wesleyan Conference Office, London, 1844
Herods, The, Dean Farrar, undated
History in the Encyclopedia, D. H. Gordon and N. L. Torrey (NY. 1947)
History of European Morals, William Lecky (1838-1903)
History of Rationalism, William Lecky (1838-1903)
History of the Bible, Bronson C. Keeler, C. P. Farrell, Publ 1881, Reprint 1965 by Health Research
History of the Anglo-Saxon Church, 1845
History of the Culdees, Jamieson
History of the Franks, William Lecky (1838-1903)
History of the Holy Eastern Church, Neale, London, 1847
History of the Kings of Britain, The, Geoffrey of Monmouth, Penguin Classics
History of Literature, The, Freculphus apud Godwin
History of the Papacy During the Reformation, Mandell Creighton, London, 1882
History of Popery, The, 2 Vols. London, 1735
History of Purple as a Status Symbol in Antiquity, M. Reinhold, Brussels, 1970
History of the Christian Church, Philip Schaff, D.D., Ms. No. 283, Chicago Public Library
History of the Christian Church, H. H. Milman, D.D. 1871
History of the Christian Religion (to the year 200), Judge C. B. Waite, 6th Ed. 1908
History of the Culdees, Jamieson
History of Dominic, Castiglio, Venice 1529
History of England, Hulme
History of the English-Speaking Peoples, The, Winston S. Churchill, Cassell and Company Ltd, London, 1957
History of the Knights Templar, The, Charles G. Addison, First Publ. 1842, Republished by Adventures Unlimited, 1997
History of the Popes, B. Maclean (Ferrier), 1907
History of the Popes, Leopold von Ranke, London, 1878

BIBLIOGRAPHY

History of the Popes from the Foundation of the See of Rome to the Present Time, The, Archbishop Bower, 3rd Edition, London, 1750
History of the Vulgate, Paolo Sarpi, Translated by Brent, London, 1676
Holy Blood and the Holy Grail, The, Michael Baigent, Richard Leigh and Henry Lincoln, Corgi Books, 1990
Holy Kingdom, The, Adrian Gilbert, Alan Wilson and Baram Blackett, Corgi Books, 1999
Holy Place, The, Henry Lincoln, Jonathon Cape, London, 1991
Homosexuality in the Church, Confidential Diocesan Report to the Bishops (UK) 1994
Howard's State Trials, 1798-99
How the Great Pan Died, Edmond S. Bordeaux, Mille Meditations, 1968
Hyptatia, Pagan Origins of Christianity, Dean, 1792

Illustrissimi, Albino Luciani, Little Brown, New York, 1978
Index Librorum Prohibitorum, Antwerp, 1571
Indian Review, The, Del Mar, 1903
Indulgences, Their Origin, Nature and Development, Quaracchi, 1897
In God's Name, An Investigation into the Murder of Pope John Paul I, David Yallop, Corgi Books, London 1984
Inquisition, The, Michael Baigent and Richard Leigh, Penguin Books, 2000
Inquisition and Liberty, G. G. Coulton, London, 1938
Institutes of Christian History, Johann Mosheim, 1755
Introduction to New Testament Times, Ventnor Publications, Ventnor, NJ, 1958
Introduction to the New Testament, Professor Davidson (MS 104)
Index of Prohibited Books, 'By Command of the Present Pope Gregory XVI', London, 1840
Index of Prohibited Books; the last Index list in 508 pages came out in 1948, with a short supplement added in 1964 that included 14 new names
Index Expurgatorius Vaticanus, Edited by R. Gibbings, B.A., Dublin, 1837
Intellectual Development, Dr. James McCabe, Bloomsbury, 1927
Irenaeus, A. Stieren, Leipzig, 2 Vols., 1848
Irenaeus of Lyons, trans. John Keble, London 1872
Irenaeus, writings in the ante-Nicene Fathers, N.Y. 1926
Isis Unveiled, H. P. Blavatsky, 2 Vols. Theosophical University Press, California, 1976
Isle of Avalon, The, Gazette
Isle of Avalon, The, Prof. Smithson, Glastonbury, 1944
Itinerary, Pausanius

James the Brother of Jesus, Professor Robert Eisenman, Faber and Faber Limited, 1997
Jasher (Yasher), 1751, oldest known version is called *The Essene Book of Genesis* and held in the Vatican Archives (E. B. Szekely)
Jebamoth, The
Jerome, A Summary of his Three Writings, Prof. Isaac Muir, 1889
John Marco Allegro, The Maverick of the Dead Sea Scrolls (Judith Brown, Wm. B. Eedmanns Publishing

Company, 2005).
Joseph of Arimathea at Glastonbury, Rev. L. S. Lewis, A. Mobray, London, 1927
Justin Martyr, writings contained in the *Ante-Nicene Fathers,* N.Y. 1926
Justinian and Theodora, Robert Browning, Thames and Hudson, London, 1987

Key for Catholics, Richard Baxter, London 1839
King Jesus, Robert Graves, Cassell and Company, London, 1946
Knights Templar, The, Stephen Howarth, Collins, London, 1982
Kolbrin, The, The Hope Trust, New Zealand, 1994
Koran, The Holy, trans. by A. Yusuf Ali, Amana Corp., Maryland, USA
Koran, The, trans. by George Sale, Frederick Warne and Co., London, 1734
Krata Repoa (or, Initiation into the Ancient Mysteries of the Priests of Egypt), C. F. Koppen and J. W. B. Von Hymmen, Berlin, 1782

La Demononie, ou traite des Sorciers, Bodin, Paris, 1587
Lead Us Not Into Temptation, Jason Berry, Doubleday, NY, 1992
Lectures on the Council of Trent, J. A. Froude, New York, 1896
Lectures on the Doctrine of the Catholic Church, Wiseman, 2 Vols, London, 1836
Leonardo da Vinci, Sigmund Freud, New York, 1947
Letter to Heliodorus, originally written in 374 by Jerome
Letter to the Bishops of Egypt and Libya
Letters of St. Bernard of Clairvaux, translated by Bruno Scott James, Sutton Publishing Limited, Gloucestershire, 1998
Letters of Jerome, The (Library of the Fathers)
Liber Pontificalis, Duchesne, undated, but c. 1900
Liberian Catalogue
Liberty, Bishop Jeremy Taylor, 15 Vols. Heber's Ed., 1822
Library of the Bulls, The
Library of the Fathers, The, 'Damasus', Oxford, 1833-45
Life and Pontificate of Leo X, 2 Vols, William Roscoe, London, 1853
Life and Times of Herod the Great, The, Stewart Perowne, Hodder and Stoughton, London, 1956
Life of Constantine, Bishop Eusebius Pamphilius of Caesarea, c. 335)
Life of Lardner, by Dr. Kippis
Life of Michelangelo Buonarroti, J. A. Symonds, Modern Library, c. 1883
Life of Petrarch, Ernest Hatch Wilkins, The University of Chicago Press, 1961
Life of St. Francis, Demonoligia
Life of Vespasian, Suetonius, Second Century Roman historian
Light in the Sanctuary, Sandra Hodson, The Theosophical Publishers, Inc. Manila, Philippines, 1988
Literary Policy of the Church of Rome, The, Rev. Mr. Mendham, Second Ed., 1840
Literary Source Book of the Italian Renaissance, M. Whitcomb, Philadelphia, 1900
Lives of the Most Eminent Painters, Sculptors, and Architects, Giorgio Vasari, 1907
Lives of the Popes, Mgr. H. A. Mann, c. 1905

Lives of the Popes in the Early Middle Ages, Mgr. H. A. Mann (18 vols.), 1902
Lives of the Roman Pontiffs, The, Bartolomeo Platina (1421-81), Vatican librarian
Lives of the Saints, The, Reverend S. Baring Gould, 16 Vols. 1872
London Beneath the Pavement, Michael Harrison, (Peter) Davies, London, 1961
London Quarterly Review, John W. Burgon, Dean of Chichester, 1883
Lost and Hostile Gospels, Reverend S. Baring Gould, circa 1872
Lost Gods, John Allegro, Publ. by Michael Joseph Ltd, London, 1977
Lost Gods of England, The, Brian Branston, London, 1957
Lost Scrolls of the Essene Brotherhood, The, E. B. Szekely, International Biogenic Society, 1989 Edition
Lucrezia Borgia, Ferdinand Gregorovius, London, 1901

Mabinogion (Gwyn and Thomas Jones, trans), Everyman's Library, J. M. Dent and Sons, London, 1970
Magical Mystical Sites, Elizabeth Pepper and John Wilcock, Sphere Books Ltd, London, 1976; Harper & Row, New York, 1977
Mahabharata, The Hindu Epic, trans., Minisus, London, 1910
Maiden Castle, Sir Mortimer Wheeler, Ministry of Work's pamphlet, HM Stationery, Office, 1951
Man and his Gods, Homer Smith, Little, Brown and Co., Boston, 1952
Manual of General Church History, Cardinal Hergenrother, 1880
Manuscripts in the Glastonbury Library, Prof. S. L. MacGuire, Salisbury, 1922
Marian Conspiracy, The, Graham Phillips, Sidgwick and Jackson, London, 2000
Martin Luther and the Reformation, Chas Beard, London, 1896
Mary Magdalene; Christianity's Hidden Goddess, Lynn Picknett, Robinson, London, 2003
Medici, The, G. F. Young, Modern Library, undated
Medicine Chest, St. Epiphanius
Medieval Papacy, The, G. Barraclough, London, 1968
Meditations, Marcus Aurelius
Mentality of the Clergy, The, Psychologist Quarterly, Professor R. L. Hugo, Calif. 1969
Messiah Myth, The, Professor Thomas L. Thompson, Basic Books (a member of the Perseus Group), New York, 2005
Michelangelo and the Pope's Ceiling, Ross King, Random House, London, 2002
Michelangelo's Message … The Women Who Wrote the Bible, Julie Halligan, pre-publication manuscript, 2007
Mission of St. Augustine, The, Mason
Monks of the West, Montalembert, Edited by Rev. Peter Douglas, 1917
Monumental Christianity, J. P. Lundy, 1876
Mothers, The, Robert Briffault, Macmillan, NY, 1927
Murder in the Vatican, Lucien Gregoire, 2005
Mysteries of Britain, The, Lewis Spence, The Aquarian Press Limited, Rider and Company, Great Britain, 1928
Mysteries of Catholicism, The, G. H. Pember, MA, Oliphants Ltd, London, 1942
Mysteries of the Bible, Reader's Digest Association, New York, 1988

Name of the Furies, The, Eumenides
National Message, The, Kathleen Brown, 1947
Nazareth, the City, Dr. Stanton, Gemma, London, circa 1905
Nexus New Times, Nexus Magazine Pty Ltd, Australia, ed. Duncan M. Roads

Of the Five Plagues of the Church, Count Antonio Rosmini, priest, 1848
Old Christian Literature, Van Manen of Leyden (contributor to *Encyclopedia Biblica,* circa 1895)
Old Christian Texts, A Collection, M. Collins, London, 1890
Old Church Records, Thomas Harding, Antwerp (Bibliotheca Alexandrina), 1565
Oldest Manuscripts in New Zealand, The, David M. Taylor, 1955
On God's Government (De Gubernationale) Salvanius of Marseilles, circa 450, Trans. by E.V. Sanford; found in the 'Records of Civilization, Sources and Studies', published by Columbia University
On the Errors of the Trinity, Michael Servetus
On the Government of the Ancient Church, William Cave, D. D. London, 1683
On the Roman Forgeries in Councils, Thomas Comber, D. D. London, 1689
On the Veiling of Virgins, Tertullian
On the Work of Monks, St. Augustine, circa 420
Optatus of Minevis, Early Fourth Century
Oracles of Callistus I, translated by Victor Germaine, 1822
Origen Against Celsus, translated by James Bellamy, London, 1660
Origen, De. Princip., Commentary on Rome
Origin of Religion Belief, Draper
Orosius, Paulus, Fourth Century church historian who records extracts from Josephus's writings that are not present in the modern text of Josephus
Orpheus, Salomon Reinarch, Horace Liveright, Inc, NY, 1930
Orthodox Corruption of Scripture, The, Prof. Bart D. Ehrman

Panegyric on the Emperor Trajan, Pliny the Younger, Roman Senator, c. 112
Papal Monarchy, The
Paraphrase and Commentary on the New Testament, 2 Vols. London, 1703
Pastoral Theology, Professor J. Beck, 1910
Peter the Sinner, Angelo Mercati (1870-1955), Prefect of the Vatican Archives
Petrus Cluniacensis, Peter, Abbot of Cluny, c. 1310
Piers the Ploughman, William Langlande, 1362
Pilgrimage to Rome, Rev. Seymour, 1832
Poedagogus (or Instructor), Clement of Alexandria
Popes and Social Problems, The, J. W. Poynter, Watts and Co, London, 1949
Popes and Their Church, The, Dr. Joseph McCabe, Watts and Co., London, 1933
Prehistoric London, E. O. Gordon, Covenant Publishing Co. Ltd, London
Prescriptions of Tertullian
Primitive Christianity, Professor Rudolf Bultman, The Fontana Library, 1956
Princess Diana ... The Hidden Evidence, Jon King and John Beveridge, S. P. I. Books, NY, 2002

BIBLIOGRAPHY

Printer's Marks, W. Roberts, G. W. Bell and Sons, London, 1892

Queen Mabel, Percy Bysshe Shelley, 1813

Rape Crisis Centre Report on the Church, Victoria, Australia, 1994
Raphael, Eugene Muntz, London, 1882
Ratzinger Report, The, Joseph Ratzinger, San Francisco Ignatius Press, 1985
Records of Events, Marcellinus Ammianus, in the Loeb Classical Library
Rectification of Names, The, E. S. Burt, Mentor Books, New York, 1949
Reformation, The, Dr. Will Durant, Simon and Schuster, New York, 1957
Regio Fides, Griffiths (one of the most learned Roman Catholic historians)
Religion of Ancient Britain, The, 1898
Religion of the Romans, New York ed., Adams, 1826
Religious Life of Ancient Rome, The, J. B. Carter, Cooper Square, NY, 1972
Renaissance Painting, Barron's
Repellers of Wolves, Professor John Telfer, Pre-publication manuscript, 2007
Revelationum, Lib, 1, cap. X, Rome, St. Bridget of Sweden, reprint 1628
Rise of Benedict XVI, The, John L. Allen, Jr., Penguin Books, 2005
Roman Emperors, The, Michael Grant, George Weidenfeld and Nicholson Limited, 1985
Roman Martyrology, British Library, London
Roman Myths, Jane F. Gardner, British Museum, 1993
Roman State and Christian Church, (A collection of legal documents, 3 Vols; Vol. 3 contains translations of all Emperor Justinian's religious legislation, with full discussions), London, 1966
Romer's Egypt, Book Club Associates, Michael Joseph Ltd and the Rainbird Publishing Group Ltd, 1982
Rousseau and Revolution, Dr. Will and Ariel Durant, Simon and Schuster, New York, 1967

Sacred Geography, British Library, London, author unknown, c. 1704
Sayings of the Christian Priests, Rev. J. Desmond, W. D (War Damaged), Russell Square, London, 1946
Scorpiace, Tertullian
Scribes and Correctors of the Codex Sinaiticus, H. J. M. Milne and T. C. Skeat, British Museum, London, 1938
Scrolls of Nebeseni, The, Priest of Memphis, Alexandrian Library, Egypt
Second Marriage a Species of Adultery, Tertullian
Secret Gospel, The, Professor Morton Smith, The Aquarian Press, Northamptonshire, 1985
Secret in the Bible, The, Tony Bushby, Joshua Books, Australia, 2003; Reprinted in 2005 (Website; www.joshuabooks.com)
Secrets of Rennes-Le-Chateau, Lionel and Patricia Fanthope, Samuel Weiser, Inc. USA, 1992
Secrets of the Christian Fathers, Bishop J. W. Sergerus, 1685, reprint 1897
Secret Gospel of Mark, The, Professor Morton Smith, 1974
Secret History of the Court of Justinian, Procopius, publ. by the Athenian Society, 1896
Secreta Monica, The (The Secret Instruction), English reprint, 1857

Secret Teachings of All Ages, Manly P. Hall, Philosophical Research, The Society Inc., L.A., Calif. 1901
Servetus and Calvin, R. Willis M.D., London, 1877
Short History of the English People, Green, undated
Sibylline Oracles, Extant are Nos. 1, 2, 3, 4, 5, 6, 7, 8, 11, 12, 13, 14
Sibyllini Libra
Soliloquies of Augustine, R. E. Cleveland, London, Williams and Norgate, 1910
Source Book of Medieval History, Frederic Ogg, New York, 1907
Spies in the Vatican, David Alvarez, Univerity Press of Kansas, 2002
Stolen Identity; Why the Vatican denied the existence of an archival nun (Upcoming title by Tony Bushby)
St. Paul & Britain, Edwin Wilmshurst, T. G. Willis & Co, Chichester, 1910
St. Paul in Britain, R. W. Morgan, 1860
Stromata (or *Miscellanies*), Clement of Alexandria, held in the Florence MS.
Summa Theology, St. Thomas Aquinas
Sungods in Mythology, Dr. J. L. C. Lugo, Vienna, c. 1870
Supremacy of the Pope, Samuel Edgar, 2nd Edition, London, 1838
Sussex Archeological Collections, vol. XXII, 1871

Tacitus on Britain and Germany, A new translation of the '*Agricola*' and the 'Germania' by H. Mattingly, Penguin Books, 1951
Talmud in History, The, G. R. S. Mead, B.A., London and Benares, 1903
Telling Lies for God, Professor Ian Plimer, Random House, 1994
Templars and Assassins, James Wasserman, Inner Traditions, Rochester, VT, 2001
Templar Gold, Patrick Byrne, Symposium Publishing, an imprint of Blue Dolphin Publishing, Inc, Nevada City, CA, 2001
Templar Revelation, The, Lynn Picknett and Clive Prince, Corgi Books, London, 1998
Templar Treasure at Gisors, The, Jean Markale, Inner Traditions, Rochester, VT, 2003
Temples, Tombs and Hieroglyphs, Barbara Mertz, Victor Gollancz Limited, London, 1964
Testament of Christian Civilization, The, Joseph McCabe, Watts and Co. London, 1946
Theological Tracts, 'On Councils', 6 Vols, London, 1791
Theological Works, Isaac Barrow, Oxford, 1830
Theophilus to Autolycus, Theophilus of Antioch
Testament of Solomon, The, Ed. C. McCown, Leipzig, 1922
The American Popes, Bishop S. L. Hughes, University Press, 1999
The Avignon Papacy, 1305-1403, Professor Yves Renouard, trans. by Denis Bethell, Faber and Faber, London, 1970
The Bible Fraud, Tony Bushby, Joshua Books, Australia, 2001
The Constantine Constitutions
The Council of Nicaea, Dr. H. C. Castle, Perth, Scotland, c. 1901
The Creed and Oath of Pope Pius IV, bearing the date November 1564
The Day They Wrote the Bible, Dr. James J. Wordsworth, USA, 1932
The Early Church, Prof. James Orr, D.D., Hodder and Stoughton, London, 1901
The Forgotten Monarchy of Scotland, HRH Prince Michael of Albany, Element Books Limited, 1998

BIBLIOGRAPHY

The Lady was a Bishop, Joan Morris, Macmillan, New York, 1973

The Mission of St. Augustine, Mason

The Moment After Death, Tony Bushby, due for publication in late 2008-9

The Mystery of Easter Island, Katherine Routledge, 1919

The Popes; A Concise Biographical History, Burns and Oates, Publishers to the Holy See, London, 1964

The Popes and Their Church, A Candid Account, by Joseph McCabe, Watts and Co, London, 1918

The Roman Invasion of Britain, Prof. Wilfred Owen, Whitehorse, London, 1948

The Royal House of Britain, Rev. W. M. H. Milner, M.A., F.R.G.S., 1902

The Records of Rome, 1868, British Library

The Selling of Jesus, Arthur Frederick Ide, Liberal Arts Press, 1985

The Twelve Caesars, trans. by Robert Graves, Penguin Classics, UK, 1958

The Twilight of Christianity, Dr. H. Elmer Barnes, c. 1930

The Twin Deception, Tony Bushby, Joshua Books, Australia, 2007 (Website: www.joshuabooks.com)

The Vatican Empire, Nino Lo Bello, Trident Press (Simon and Schuster) New York, 1968

The Vatican Papers, Nino Lo Bello, New English Library (a division of Hodder and Stoughton, Ltd.), Kent, 1982

Three Early Doctrinal Modifications of the Text of the Gospels, The Hibbert Journal, London, 1902

To His Wife, Tertullian, circa 210

Traces of the Elder Faiths in Britain, Schleimann, London, 1898

Treasure of Montségur, The, Walter Birks and R. A. Gilbert, The Aquarian Press, London, 1990

Triads of the Isle of Britain

Trias Thaumaturga, John Colgan

True Story of the Popes, The, Prof. Robert H. Benson, London, 1922

Twelve Years in the Secret Vatican Archives

Uncertain History of Christian Beginnings, The, Jack G. Patterson, B. A., B. Arch., Auckland, N.Z, 1996

Underside of History, The, Elise Boulding, Boulder, Colo, Waterview Press, 1976

Unknown Books of the Essenes, The, E. B. Szekely, International Biogenic Society, 1989

Unpublished records of Josephus, The (Freiburg), held by Tony Bushby

Unzipped, the popes bare all, Arthur Frederick Ide, Liberal Arts Press, 1987

Valleus' Notes (Valleus Paterculus), (*Acta Pilati*)

Vatican Billions, The, Avro Manhattan, Paravision Books, London, 1972

Vatican Exposed, The, Dr. Paul L. Williams, Prometheus Books, New York, 2003, highly recommended

Vatican Moscow Washington Alliance, The, Avro Manhattan, Chick, Publications, California, 1986

Venetian Painters, F. J. Matther, New York, 1936

Venus in Sackcloth, Marjorie Malvern, Carbondale, Ill, A. S. Barnes and Co., Inc; 1964

Vicars of Christ, Peter de Rosa, Crown Publishers, New York, 1988

Victims of the Marmertine, The, Rev. A. J. O'Reilly, D. D., undated but pre-1929

Vindicae Ecclesia Anglicanne, Robert Southey, London, 1826

Volume Archko, archaeological writings of the Sanhedrin and Talmud

Vows of Silence, Jason Berry and Gerald Renner, Free Press, NY, 2004

Vulgar Verses, Rev. Joseph Burke, London, 1840

When Women Where Priests, Karen Jo Torjesen, HarperSanFrancisco, 1995
When Women Ruled the World, Julie Halligan, pre-publication manuscript, 2007
Whores in History, Nicky Roberts, Grafton, 1993
Why Councils Differed, George Campbell, McDougal Press, Aberdeen, 1816
Wisdom of the Ancients, The, Sir Francis Bacon, 1619, reprint by Berington, 1894
Woman as a Force in History, M. R. Beard, Collier-Macmillan, London, 1946
Works of Nathaniel Lardner, D.D. 10 Vols. Bloomsbury, London, 1824
World's Sixteen Crucified Saviours, The, K. Graves, Banner of Light Publishing Co., 1900
Writings of Michelangelo, The, Pietra de Monic, France, 1878
Writings of Saint John of Damascus, The, F. H. Chase, publ. By 'Fathers of the Church'
Writings of Saint Justin Martyr, The, trans. T.B. Falls, publ. Christian Heritage

The Library of the Fathers
This is a series of English translations of early Church writings, the first being, *The Confessions of Augustine* (Published by the Oxford Movement, 1833-45). Included is a later document called, *Sayings of the Fathers.*

The writings of Dr. Constantin Von Tischendorf
(Available in the British Library, London)
Alterations to the Sinai Bible ... Are Our Gospels Genuine or Not? ... Codex Sinaiticus ... The Authenticity of Our Gospels ... The Origin of the Four Gospels ... The Various Versions of the Bible ... When Were Our Gospels Written?

Encyclopedias and dictionaries consulted
A Basic Jewish Encyclopedia, Rabbi Harry A. Cohen, Ph. D, Wyndham and Stacey Ltd, London, 1965
A Dictionary of Biblical Tradition, David Lyle Jeffrey, William B. Eerdman's Publishing Co., Grand Rapids, Michigan

A Dictionary of Universal Knowledge for the People, Lippincott and Co. 1877
Ancient Egyptian Dictionary, R. Johnson and E. Rumbel (in Cairo Library)
An Encyclopedia of Occultism, Lewis Spence, 1920
An Illustrated Encyclopedia of Mysticism and The Mystery Religions, J. Ferguson, Thames and Hudson, London, 1976
Annales Ecclesiastici (12 Vols.), Cardinal Caesar Baronius, Vatican librarian and church historian (1538-1607), published in 1592-7
Annales Ecclesiastici, J. D. Mansi and D. Georgius, 38 Vols. Lucca, 1738-59
An Expository Dictionary of Biblical Words, W. E. Vine, M.A., Merrill F. Unger and William White Jnr., Thomas Nelson Publ. 1984

BIBLIOGRAPHY

Bingham's Antiquities of the Christian Church, Straker's Ed. 1840, London
Blair's Chronological Tables

Catholic Dictionary, The, Addis and Arnold, 1917
Catholic Encyclopedia, The, 3 volumes, Ed. Cardinal Cardozia, published under the Imprimatur of 'De Romano Pontiff' (Pecci), 1897 (very rare)
Catholic Encyclopedia, The, 15 volumes, plus index, 1907-1914 published under the Imprimatur of Archbishop Farley; American Edition, New York, Robert Appleton Co., 1907-9
Catholic Encyclopedia, The, Published under the Imprimatur of John Farley
Catholic Encyclopedia, Modern, The, The Liturgical Press, 1994
Catholic Encyclopedia, New (N.C.E.), 1976
Catholic Encyclopedia, The, Robert C. Broderick, Thomas Nelson Publ. 1976
Catholic History; From Christ to Today, Christian Publishing Press, 1903
Chambers Biographical Dictionary, Ed. Magnus Magnusson, Edinburgh, 1992
Classical Dictionary, William Smith, Harper and Brothers, New York, 1877
Code of Canon Law, The, The Canon Law Society of America, 1985
Companion Encyclopedia of Theology, Routledge, 1995
Concise Oxford Dictionary of English Place-Names, The, Editor, F. Eckwall, Oxford Universal Press, London, 1960

Decrees of the Ecumenical Councils (2 Vols.), Sheed and Ward
Devil's Dictionary, The, Ambrose Bierce, circa 1900
Dictionaire de Theologie, 1920
Dictionary of Beliefs and Religions, Wordsworth Reference, Publ. by Wordsworth Editions Ltd, England, 1995
Dictionary of the Bible, Grant and Rowley; 2nd Ed., 1963
Dictionary of Christ and the Gospels, Hastings
Dictionary of Christian Antiquities, ed. Smith and Cheetham, London, 1875

Dictionary of Christian Biography, Smith and Wace, c. 1879
Dictionary of Classical Mythology, Religion, Literature and Art, Oskar Seyffert, Random House, 1995
Dictionary of Firazabadi (14th Century)
Dictionary of Greek and Roman Antiquities
Dictionary of Islam, London, 1895
Dictionary of National Biography, Daniel, Hervey, Deane, Skevington, Bulkeley
Dictionary of Proper Names and Places in the Bible, O. Odelain and R. Seguinean, 1981
Dictionary of Rare Words, Isaac Burrows, Cambridge, 1830
Dictionary of Sects, Blunt
Dictionary of the Bible, original edition by James Hastings D.D., revised by F. C. Grant and H. H. Rowley, 1963
Diderot's Encyclopedia, a tome that Pope Clement XIII ordered destroyed immediately after its publication in 1759

Encyclopedia Biblica, four volumes; Adam & Charles Black, London, 1899; also, American Reprint, The Macmillan Co., New York, 1914
Encyclopedia Britannica (Old and rare Editions):
First Edition ... 3 Volumes, 1768-1771
Second Edition ... 10 Volumes, 1777-1784
Third Edition ... 18 Volumes, 1788-1797 (Edinburgh Edition): Also, James Moore's Dublin Edition, 1790-97
Fourth Edition ... 20 Volumes, 1801-1810
Fifth Edition ... 20 Volumes, 1815-1817
Sixth Edition ... 20 Volumes, 1823-1824
Seventh Edition ... 21 Volumes, 1830-1842
Eighth Edition ... 22 Volumes, 1853-1860
Ninth Edition ... 25 Volumes, 1875-1889
Tenth Edition ... ninth and eleven supplementary volumes, 1902-1903
Eleventh Edition ... 29 Volumes, 1910-1911
Encyclopedia Britannica: also Twelfth to Fifteenth Editions
Encyclopedia Britannica, New, 1987
Encyclopedia Dictionary of the Bible, McGraw, New York 1963
Encyclopedia Ecclesiastica, Prompta Biblioth, Lucii F. Ferraris, Francof, 1781
Encyclopedia Judaica (16 vols.), Ed. Cecil Roth, Jerusalem, 1974
Encyclopedia Judaica Jerusalem, 1971
Encyclopedia of Catholic Doctrine, 1997
Encyclopedia of Catholicism, 1989
Encyclopedia of Early Christianity, Everett Ferguson (Ed.), St. James Press, Chicago and London, 1974
Encyclopedia of Freemasonry, Albert Mackey, MD, McClure Publishing, 1917
Encyclopedia of Religion and Ethics, Edited by James Hastings, T. & T. Clark, Edinburgh, 1914
Encyclopedia of the Early Church, English Trans. 1992
Encyclopedia of the Roman Empire, Matthew Bunson, Facts on File, NY, 1994
Encyclopedias, Their History throughout the Ages, 1966

Funk and Wagnell's New Encyclopedia, 1988
Funk and Wagnell's New Standard Dictionary, 1913
Funk and Wagnell's New International Dictionary, 1972
Harper's Bible Dictionary, Paul J. Achtemeier, Harper and Row, 1985
Historical Dictionary of the Orthodox Church, Prokurat, Golitizin, Peterson, Scarecrow Press Inc. 1996

Jewish Encyclopedia, N.Y. 1903

Lakeland Bible Dictionary, Zondervan Publ. House, 1966
Larousse Encyclopedia of Mythology, Hamlyn Publishing Group Ltd, London, 1968
London Encyclopedia

New American Cyclopedia, The, circa 1890
New Bible Dictionary, Inter-Varsity, Leicester, England, 1986
New Dictionary of Theology, Inter-Varsity, Leicester, England, 1988
New Jewish Encyclopedia, The
New Larousse Encyclopedia of Mythology, 1984

Our Sunday Visitor's Catholic Encyclopedia, 1986 Edition
Oxford Classical Dictionary, The, 1949
Oxford Dictionary of Popes, The, Oxford University Press
Oxford Dictionary of the Christian Church, Cross 1974, 1997
Oxford Icelandic Dictionary

Papal Pronouncements (2 Vols.), The Pierian Press, 1990
Pope Encyclopedia, The, Matthew Brunson, Crown Trade Paperbacks, New York, 1995
Popular and Critical Bible Encyclopedia, Samuel Fallows, Chicago, 1919

Smaller Classical Dictionary, 1910
Steinberg's Dictionary of British History, Book Club Associates, London, Edward Arnold (Publishers) Ltd, 1973

Tanner's Notitia Monastica, 1744
Theology Dictionary of the New Testament, W. M. B. Eerdman's Publ. Co., U.S.A. 1981
The Universal Jewish Encyclopedia, New York
Topographical Dictionary of Wales, Lewis

Vines Expository Dictionary of New Testament Words, W. E. Vine, M.A. 1996

Wade's British Chronology
Webster's Unabridged Dictionary
Woman's Encyclopedia of Myths and Secrets, The, Barbara G. Walker, Pandora, 1995

Zondervan Pictorial Encyclopedia of the Bible, Merrill C. Tenney, 5 Vols, 1975

Bibles used as comparative references
Alexandrian Bible, translation by Tischendorf
American Standard Version by the American Revision Committee, 1901
Anonymous Bible, The, 1762. In this Bible an attempt was made to correct the text of the King James Version (Extract from Preface, by F. S. Paris)
Bear Bible, The,
Bezae Bible, The
Bible of St. John, The, 1690
Bible of the Church, 1765

Bible in Verse, The, 4 Vols, 1778
Bishop's Bible, The, 1608 Edition
Chaloner-Douay Version of the Catholic Vulgate
Christian's Divine Bible, Corrected by Henry Southwell, London, 1773
Constantine Bible, The
Ethiopian Bible
First Catholic Bible in the English Language, The, 1563
Fool Bible, The, printed during the reign of Charles 1, the text of Psalm 14:1 read, 'The fool has said in his heart there is a god'. The printer was fined ?3000 and all copies withdrawn
Forgotten Sins Bible, See Luke 7:47 (1638)
Good News Bible, The, Today's Version (English), 1976
Gospel of Thomas the Twin
Interlinear Translation of the Greek Scriptures, The, 1969
Jefferson Bible, The
Jerusalem Bible, The, 1966
Judas Bible, The, Jesus is called Judas at Matthew 26:36
King James Bible (K.J.B.), 1611, revised 1881-1885; 1901; 1946-1952; 1971
Latin Vulgate, Trans. R. Challoner, 1609; 1749; 1750; 1752; 1764; 1772
Matthew Bible, The
Mount Sinai Manuscript of the Bible, (British Museum, addit. MS. 43725), 1934
New American Bible, The, St. Joseph Edition, 1970
New English Bible, The (three variations)
New International Version, The, 1973
New Testament According to the Eastern Text, George M. Lamsa
Poor Man's Bible, The, 1806
Priest's Bible, The
Printers' Bible, 1702
Profit Bible, Oxford edition (1711)
Revised Standard Version, Catholic Edition, 1966
Roman Bible, The
St. Augustine's Bible
Syrian Bible, The
The Common Translation Corrected, Oxford, 1718-1724
Universal Bible, 1766
Variorum Teacher's Edition, The, Eyre & Spottiswoode
Vatican Bible, The

From the publisher

As publishers Joshua Books believe in freedom of speech and your right to have access to all points of view. The controversy created by Tony Bushby will continue as more and more people seek the Truth.

Joshua Books is also the publisher for the acclaimed author Ian Ross Vayro.

If you have enjoyed reading *'The Papal Billions'* then please take time to look at these other titles featured over the following pages.

We also invite you to log on to www.joshuabooks.com and subscribe to our **free newsletter**. That way you will be kept right up to date with all that is happening at Joshua Books.

Joshua Books
JoshuaBooks.com

ALSO BY TONY BUSHBY

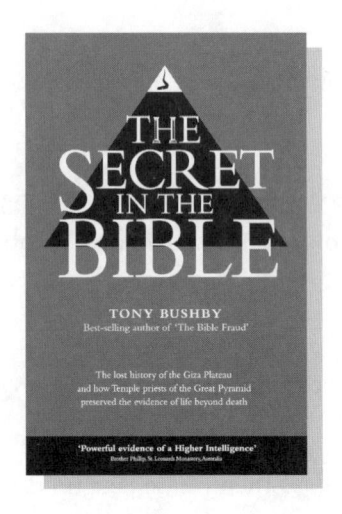

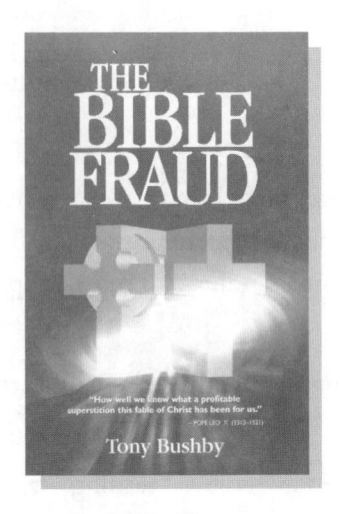

What others have said about Tony Bushby's books...

*I thoroughly enjoyed Tony Bushby's **The Bible Fraud**. Its tale ended my own research into the origins and source material of the Bible (not for a book! Just my own curious hunger to know!). This author has done in a careful and extremely well researched book, far better than most in this genre. The attention to detail, which I have confirmed myself over the past twenty years from various sources, is validated and more accurate than many academic papers found in our universities.*

It is undoubtedly the most important book on Christianity and the Roman legacy ever written, and most likely will have the least impact because it explodes the mythology and power basis for a religion which will be impossible for most to swallow. A truth that will choke rather than enlighten. I look forward to his next book and I do hope that it opens eyes to the true wonders and we finally put away the destructive toy of over simplified pacification tripe that exists in political, commercial establishment religions.

MAE, Isle of Sanday, Orkney, Scotland

The Bible Fraud*. The ramifications of this evidence are impossible to calculate.*

Rev. Herbert O'Brien, Ordained Minister of the Reformed Baptist Church, Melbourne, Australia

*I have just finished reading **The Secret in the Bible**. For some reason it doesn't take long to read any of Tony Bushby's work. Perhaps it's the fact that I couldn't put it down once I started reading it! Reading is a passion for me and I must say rarely do I get so much in a book as what Tony Bushby offers to his readers. I eagerly await the publication of his third book. I cannot thank the author Tony Bushby, or Joshua Books for making his books available, enough. Of course the service from Joshua Books was impeccable.*

Edward Sloan, International

*Thank you for devoting so many years to finding out what **The Secret in the Bible** is and for sharing it with others. I'm still in awe over the revelation.*

Charis, International

*I have purchased and read **The Bible Fraud** and **The Secret in the Bible**. I find the information in them tremendously exciting. They supply missing pieces to the historical puzzle, and lead in a much more realistic direction than traditional explanations. Truth is always better than fantasy, because it is real.*

Whitney Prescott, Stone Mountain, GA, USA

***The Bible Fraud** is a real eye opener. It is well documented and easy to understand. Everyone should read this book to understand how we have been deceived. Especially all Christians who think they know the truth. You will never think the same once you have read this book.*

JS, Jacksonville, Florida, USA

TONY BUSHBY'S PREVIOUS BOOK

To purchase visit www.joshuabooks.com

THE TWIN DECEPTION
The Hidden Messiah

Recently discovered biblical texts reveal that Jesus Christ had a twin brother who was one of his trusted disciples.

YOU HAVE READ THE FICTION, NOW READ THE FACTS!

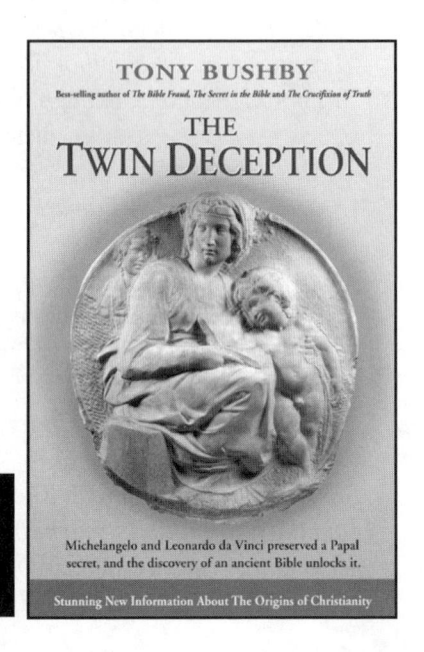

Tony Bushby has already fuelled worldwide controversy with his books and, in shattering old myths, he provokes a fresh debate on the most controversial figure in history, Jesus Christ.

Reading like a suspense novel, *The Twin Deception* unlocks the concealed evidence of Jesus' twin brother and reveals how the church contrived for centuries to hide the information from the public.

ALSO AVAILABLE NOW

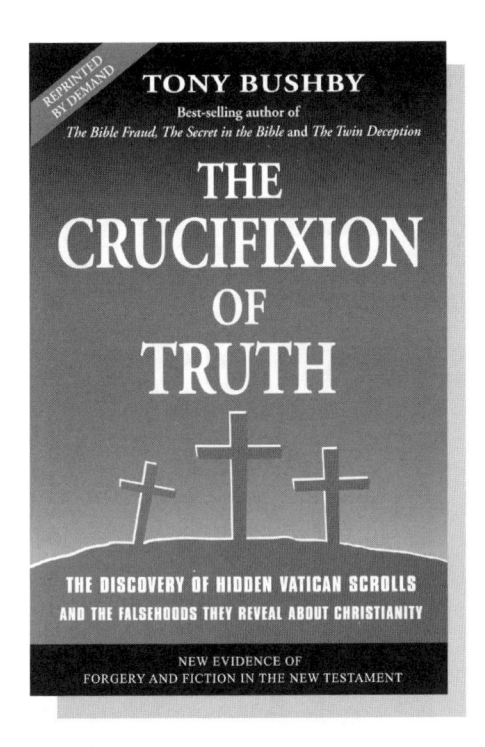

TONY BUSHBY
Best-selling author of
The Bible Fraud, *The Secret in the Bible* and *The Twin Deception*

THE CRUCIFIXION OF TRUTH

THE DISCOVERY OF HIDDEN VATICAN SCROLLS AND THE FALSEHOODS THEY REVEAL ABOUT CHRISTIANITY

NEW EVIDENCE OF FORGERY AND FICTION IN THE NEW TESTAMENT

'A knock-out blow for Christian Fundamentalism'
Michelle Daniels, Independent

'A mesmerizing account of deceit and dishonesty that is impossible for the church to deny'
Mr. John Telfer, Director, Stanford Books

Joshua Books
JoshuaBooks.com

ALSO AVAILABLE NOW

WHAT HAPPENS WHEN WE DIE?

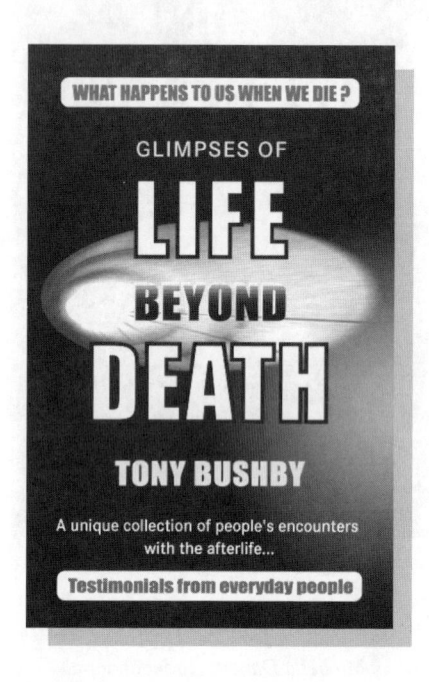

A classic collection of stories drawn from research carried out over 30 years by the author Tony Bushby.

Joshua Books
JoshuaBooks.com

OUTSTANDING TITLES FROM IAN ROSS VAYRO

To purchase visit www.joshuabooks.com

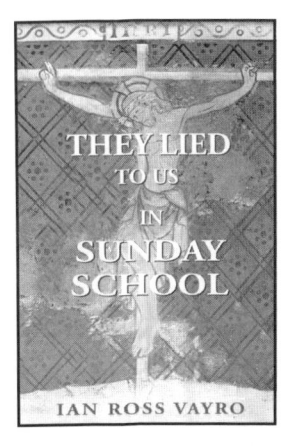

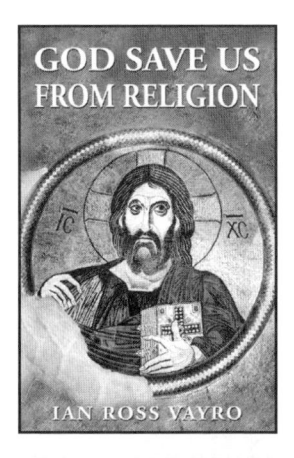

THEY LIED TO US IN SUNDAY SCHOOL

In this book Ian Ross Vayro has given us the facts in a way that is impossible to dispute. This book provides proof of the tampering that has altered the Word of God into the deception that we have today. Ian is trained in Archaeology and Ancient History and has spent a lifetime studying Theology.

GOD SAVE US FROM RELIGION

Read about the deception, tampering and conspiracy within the Roman Church. No stone is left unturned as Ian Ross Vayro walks us through various versions of the Bible, Sumerian tablets and early Egyptian papyrus records in a vigilant search for the truth.

TEARS IN HEAVEN

In the past, the Church has been the arbitrator and authority on theology and learning, but the facade is now falling apart as an absolute multitude of lies and deceptions are being exposed almost daily. Despite a mandate of helping the people of this planet, the cleverly veneered assurances of the Church under a guise of 'goodness', have served only to create distrust, disharmony and religious wars.